CHARLES AT FIFTY

CHARLES

─── AT FIFTY ───

ANTHONY HOLDEN

RANDOM HOUSE

NEW YORK

In affectionate and respectful memory of
JOE FOX
1926–1995

CONTENTS

LIST OF ILLUSTRATIONS

PROLOGUE AND ACKNOWLEDGEMENTS

THIS IS MY THIRD BIOGRAPHY OF THE PRINCE OF WALES IN AS MANY decades, a bizarre and relentless punctuation to both our lives.

Written to mark his thirtieth, fortieth and fiftieth birthdays, hard on the heels of my own, this dogged trilogy now consists of three different books about three completely different men. The first was a lonely, confused bachelor, still living at home with his parents as he entered his thirties; the second was a driven but still troubled husband, the father of two sons, claustrophobically trapped in an unhappy marriage. The third is a divorced widower, looking older than his years, and facing a stark choice between his children, the love of his life and the throne – or, by trying to have all three, playing a dangerous long-term game that could threaten the future of the very institution which gives his tortured life any meaning.

Neither of us could have imagined that it would all come to this when I first met the Prince of Wales in the cocktail bar of a Canadian hotel, the Four Seasons in Calgary, Alberta, in July 1977. It was an amiable encounter, the first of many all over the world before I ventured to voice a note of dissent. 'What on earth are *you* doing here?' were the first words he ever addressed to me, as indeed they were the last, rather less kindly meant, in a Melbourne park during Australia's bicentennial celebrations eleven years later.

Between those two landmarks, and indeed since, we have both been on a long and fascinating, if at times bumpy, journey. I was married before he was, had children before he did, got divorced before him, and am now very happily remarried. At each stage, until he stopped speaking to me, he plied me with questions about married life. 'Fun, is it?' – one of the remarks quoted in these pages – was an early, endearingly direct example. Had we remained on speaking terms – we were never, as is still alleged, often in print, friends – I might have been able to offer him the same comfort and advice as other male friends our age who have been down the same road, desperately trying to ensure that their children do not suffer from their own mistakes.

The first prince I chronicled, at the time of both our thirtieth birthdays, was a young man full of idealistic promise, whom I admired but did not envy. The second, ten years later, was a prematurely middle-aged man, whose admirable public aspirations belied his less than admirable private conduct. No doubt the same could be said of me; but I harboured no ambitions to become the nation's moral figurehead, let alone titular head of its established Church. I was, frankly, disappointed in the promising prince I had once known, and intimated as much in a book that spelt out his public work in uniquely positive detail, while also suggesting – four years before Andrew Morton – the parlous state of his marriage. As it happened, I did not share his taste in architecture, nor think it an appropriate use of his unelected office to put British architects out of business; so I said so. But it was the marital chapter that did it. Through his aide and friend Tom Shebbeare, director of the Prince's Trust, the prince denounced my book as 'fiction from beginning to end', protesting that it had 'ruined' his birthday.

I was none too happy to turn forty, either. But I was naïvely unprepared for the invasion of my own privacy that followed, as the tabloids declared open season on a fellow journalist who happened to be living with someone who was not then his wife (but who now, I am happy to say, is). Today, towards the end of this dire decade for the Windsors, it seems hard to imagine that, just ten years ago, these were still the days of devout deference, when any mention of the royal family still suspended all critical faculties, and a hint of royal disapproval was enough to unleash the dogs of tabloid war.

Indignantly I consulted lawyers, who told me I had a prima facie case for defamation against the Prince of Wales, but advised me not to proceed, as no jury in the land would take my side against the heir to the throne. Knowing they were right, I had no option but to learn to live with his economy with the truth.

It was, perhaps, a salutary lesson in giving me a glimpse of life

as the kind of public figure I had never sought to be. Clearly, however, I did not succeed in summoning quite the degree of
insouciance to which I aspired. Accusations of 'sour grapes' have
pursued me ever since, as my public pronouncements about the
Prince of Wales have grown increasingly harsh. I am aware of this,
and unabashed by it – as unabashed as one of my literary heroes,
the poet and journalist Leigh Hunt, who was imprisoned in 1813
for describing the fifty-year-old Prince of Wales, recently appointed
Prince Regent, as 'a violator of his word . . . a despiser of domestic
ties . . . a man who has just closed half a century without one single
claim on the gratitude of his country or the respect of posterity.'

Nearly two centuries later, more loyal commentators have
occasionally suggested my own incarceration in the Tower. I recall
the 1988 episode here only to reassert my credentials as a writer who
has studied the prince for twenty years, who has made many lasting
friends among those around him, and who shares their disappointment in the way that he appears to have betrayed his early promise.
If the present volume is dominated by analysis of his private life, at
the expense of his well-meaning, if often misjudged, public work, it
is really his fault, not mine. I regret it as much as he must.

Ten years on from that quasi-marital spat between prince and
biographer, the injustice was finally righted. At, of all places, a
Spice Girls concert in Johannesburg, South Africa – graced by the
presence of HRH the Prince of Wales and his son Harry – the
instrument of his revenge, Tom Shebbeare, came over to me and,
to his credit, in front of my colleagues in the press corps,
apologized. 'I owe you an apology,' said the man who had
denounced me in the prince's name in 1988. 'You were right and I
was wrong.' I thanked him, I hoped, with all the grace he himself
had displayed. An honourable man, devoted to his master, he
nevertheless had the decency to acknowledge that a wrong had
been done, and to attempt to put it right. There are, I am sorry to
say, few others around the prince of whom this is true. If Shebbeare
loses his job within months, even years of this book's publication,
because I have made that moment public, I trust the entire nation
will join me in suing for wrongful dismissal.

Shebbeare and I subsequently enjoyed, at my suggestion, a
private, off-the-record lunch – not a word of which appears in
these pages – at which we candidly discussed the man who had
haunted both our lives for many years. Our conversation that day

has since proved very helpful to me in the writing of this book. If he of all people can accept as genuine my informed disillusion with the prince to whom I once warmed, I devoutly hope that the reader of this book, if not others around Charles, let alone the man himself, can be as fair-minded. Three-quarters of this third book post-dates my second study of the prince, not least because, as last time around, the most recent ten years of his life have been the most eventful, and by far the most significant. I have attempted to tell the tale as objectively as possible, from the respective points of view of its three main players: Charles, Diana and Camilla. As a professional biographer, if intermittent royal-watcher, I know that the reader would expect no less.

As my previous two studies of the prince have become standard works of reference, whose early pages are summarized in this third volume, it seems appropriate to reassert their credentials here. The section on Charles's days at Hill House and Cheam schools were checked for accuracy by their respective headmasters during his schooldays, Colonel Henry Townend and Peter Beck; the section on Gordonstoun read and approved by the teacher closest to the prince, Robert Waddell, and discussed with a subsequent headmaster, Michael Mavor; the section on his university years by the late Lord Butler, master of Trinity College, Cambridge; Dr Dennis Marrian, senior tutor; Dr Anil Seal; and by his tutor at the University College of Wales, Aberystwyth, Edward Millward. The entire text of the first volume was read by the prince himself, whose fascinating marginal annotations I still treasure – and have never made public – and other members of the royal family, as well as senior members of his then staff.

Others whose help with the earlier volumes are reflected in this one include: Edward Adeane, private secretary to the Prince of Wales, 1979–85; Ronald Allison, press secretary to the Queen, 1973–8; the late Stephen Barry, valet to the Prince of Wales, 1970–82; Melvyn Bragg; David Campbell; Canon Sebastian Charles, former secretary, Inner City Aid; Sir David Checketts, private secretary to the Prince of Wales, 1970–9; Lt.-Col. David Cox, former director, the Prince of Wales's Committee; Sir David Frost; the late Sir Martin Gilliat, private secretary to Queen Elizabeth the Queen Mother; General Sir Ian Gourlay, director-general, United World Colleges, 1975–90; Rod Hackney, president of the Royal Institute of British Architects, 1987–9; Sir Harold Haywood, director of the Prince's Trust, 1977–88; Sir William Heseltine, private secretary to the Queen, 1986–90; Maxwell Hutchinson, president of the Royal Institute of British Architects, 1989–91; Hywel Jones, Cambridge friend of the prince; Charles Knevitt, founder-director, Inner City Aid; Sir Tom McCaffrey, press secretary of the Prime Minister, 1976–9; John Maclean, royal protection officer; Sir Philip Magnus, official biographer of King Edward VII; Michael Manser, president of the Royal Institute of British Architects, 1983–5; the late Sir Iain Moncrieffe of that Ilk; Lord Mountbatten; Paul Officer, royal protection officer; Stephen O'Brien, chief executive, Business in the Community, 1983–92; George Pratt, founder-director of the Prince's Trust; (Lord) Richard Rogers; Michael Shea, press secretary to the Queen, 1978–87; Tom Shebbeare, director of the Prince's Trust, 1978–; Lord Snowdon; Nicholas Soames MP; the late Viscount Tonypandy; the late Lord Wilson of Rievaulx, prime minister 1964–70 and 1974–6; the Rt Revd Robert Woods, Dean of Windsor, 1962–70.

Among experts in the prince's specialist fields, some of them his close friends, who have helped me to a better understanding of his preoccupations, I must thank: Peter Ahrends, Ashley Barker, Christopher Booker, Tony Clegg, Phil Collins, Theo Crosby, Dan Cruickshank, Sir Philip Dowson, Trish Evans, Richard Frewer, Paul Greetham, Ernest Hall, Stuart Lipton, John Lockwood, Jules Lubbock, John Simpson, Deyan Sudjic, John Thompson, Richard Wade, Dr Elizabeth Whipp and Lady Roisine Wynne-Jones.

Among writers, journalists and photographers, some of whom earn their living watching the prince's every move, and other friends and colleagues whose assistance has informed this book, I thank: Bryan Appleyard, (Lord) Jeffrey Archer, Harry Arnold, Michael Barratt, Richard Barber, Sally Bedell Smith, Tony Benn MP, Ross Benson, the late Basil Boothroyd, William Boyd, Sarah Bradford, Tina Brown, Beatrix Campbell, Nigel Dempster, Peter Dunn, Anne Edwards, Bob Edwards, Kent Gavin, Tim Graham, John Grigg, Philip Hall, Prof. Stephen Haseler, Prof. Peter Hennessy, Christopher Hitchens, Anthony Howard, Anwar Hussein, Robert Jobson, Richard Kay, Kitty Kelley, Robert Lacey, Elizabeth Longford, Brian MacArthur, Stryker McGuire, Suzy Menkes, Peter Osnos, John Pearson, Prof. Ben Pimlott, Howell Raines, Charles Rae, Fiametta Rocco, Anthony Sampson, Alan Scales, Ingrid Seward, Andrew Stephen, David Thomas,

Hugo Vickers, James Whitaker and Christopher Wilson.

It is customary in books like this to thank the Prince of Wales's office for its courteous co-operation, etc., as I myself have done in the past. On this occasion, alas, it is not appropriate.

At the time of my previous volumes, the press office of Buckingham Palace was more than helpful. Over the years I have enjoyed close relations with a succession of press secretaries to the prince, some of whom have become my close friends: John Dauth, Warwick Hutchings, the late Victor Chapman, Philip Mackie and Dickie Arbiter. This time around, however, I have reason to thank few beyond Geoff Crawford, formerly press secretary to HRH the Princess of Wales, now press secretary to HM the Queen, who has remained his unfailingly courteous self, despite my occasional public criticisms of his employers. Only two others have consistently displayed the same civility: Sir Robin Janvrin, private secretary (designate at the time of writing) to the Queen, and Patrick Jephson, formerly private secretary to the Princess of Wales.

A charm offensive of my own, at much the same time as the prince's with the media in the wake of his ex-wife's death, meanwhile failed to soften the hearts, or clear the heads, of Charles's current staff, who have rejected all my proffered olive branches: Stephen Lamport, private secretary; Mark Bolland, deputy private secretary; and Sandy Henney, press secretary. Henney went to some lengths, in vain, to prevent me joining the Prince of Wales's 1997 trip to South Africa, despite my accreditation on behalf of a national newspaper, and was as obstructive as possible while we were there, excluding me from the chartered aircraft on which the prince chatted with other members of the press for the first time in ten years. The most recent, and most sophisticated, member of the prince's private staff, Mark Bolland, declined my invitation to lunch on the grounds that it would be a waste of my time. 'I come with no axes to grind,' he wrote, 'but . . . we do not start from the best of wickets. I am sorry not to be more positive.' Translating this as 'Sod off', the *Guardian* of 26 May 1998 further reported Bolland as having told royal reporters two months earlier, while on tour in Canada, 'We are always polite when someone approaches us with a book project. Except for Tony Holden. We don't bother being polite to him.'

The Prince's ex-wife was rather more gracious. In all three of her incarnations, as Lady Diana Spencer, HRH the Princess of Wales and subsequently ex-HRH Diana, Princess of Wales, I am lucky enough to have known the mother of Charles's children – to the point of enjoying several candid lunches with her, in public and private places, over the last five years of her life. After careful thought, I have decided to include in this book some of her confidences at those times, which began with a meeting at the Knightsbridge restaurant San Lorenzo in 1993 while I was writing *The Tarnished Crown* ('Perhaps,' she giggled, 'it should be called *The Tarnished Tiara*') and ended with a long lunch at Kensington Palace – just the two of us – in October 1996, ten months before her death. The various different conversations, dates and venues are clearly flagged in the source notes.

That last Kensington Palace lunch, which would not have been possible before her divorce became final, was a very happy occasion; relaxed, gossipy, full of laughter. Her habitual candour was delightful. The princess had recently returned from a trip to Washington, and was full of praise for her hostess, Katharine Graham, and for Hillary Clinton, with whom she was planning a series of joint initiatives. Her cattiest remarks were reserved for the Queen Mother, with whom she had come to share a strong mutual antipathy. She spoke with distaste of Kevin Costner, who had just been on the phone trying to persuade her to appear with him in a movie, and with admiration of General Colin Powell, who had recently talked her out of launching a Margaret Thatcher-style foundation ('too much bureaucracy'). In a conversation which ranged far and wide, high and low, we also spoke at length of the nuances of bringing up children after divorce. She permitted herself a few withering remarks about her ex-husband, and the 'third person' in their marriage – referred to throughout as 'you-know-who' – but tended by then to err on the side of generosity. She spoke with great passion of her public work, and with adoration of her children.

In the absence of any input from the prince or his staff – if not of other friends and associates sensible enough to realize that whatever I wrote might make some impact – Diana's memory has been my guiding star in the writing of this third and, I devoutly hope, last in my series of interim reports on the man who would be king.

CHARLES AT FIFTY

PART ONE

Winning His Spurs

CHAPTER ONE

'IT WAS NOT TO BE'

SOON AFTER MIDNIGHT ON SUNDAY, 31 AUGUST 1997, AS FORTY-EIGHT-
year-old Charles, Prince of Wales slept at Balmoral Castle, the rest
of his life was being brutally rewritten by a freak sequence of
events 1,000 miles away in Paris. At 12.45 a.m. Charles was
awoken by a phone call telling him that his former wife, Diana,
had been gravely injured in a car crash that had instantly killed
her companion, Dodi Fayed. By dawn the prince was waking
his sons, William and Harry, to tell them that their mother was
dead.

The scale of the ensuing public grief took Britain and the world,
especially Charles and the Windsor family, utterly by surprise.
During the week leading up to Diana's funeral, amid scenes
unprecedented in modern British history, daily life ground to a halt
as millions made flower-laden pilgrimages to Kensington Palace to
pay their last respects in wholly unEnglish ways: publicly weeping
and wailing; sobbing in the arms of total strangers; lamenting the
loss of a tragically young mother as vulnerable as she was inspirational, dead at the age of only thirty-six.

Four months after the landslide election of a populist new
government, the mass mourning betokened the loss of a public
figure who had somehow remained 'one of us', while ready to rock
the boat to knock some sense into 'them'. Diana's crusades for the
sick, the suffering and the underprivileged had contrived to trans-
cend politics, and indeed her own fallibility, striking a chord in
all but the hardest of hearts. Even those who had never met her

felt personally bereaved. Many families the world over mourned as if they had lost one of their own.

At first, Diana's death looked like very bad news for Charles. As he and his family remained in seclusion at Balmoral, apparently reluctant to share the nation's grief, the crowds outside Buckingham Palace grew angrier by the day. This, after all, was the princess the Windsors had banished a year earlier, stripping her of her royal rank and expelling her from the family when her divorce from Charles had become final. Far from retreating in disarray, Diana had since carved her own niche in the life of the nation, leaving Charles an almost marginal figure, rapt in puzzled contemplation of an uncertain future, with only his mistress to console him.

Diana had shown that royalty could be human, could move among its people, could even touch them by way of lending solace to their woes. So stark was the contrasting silence from Scotland that events soon moved beyond royal control. Even when the prime minister persuaded the Windsors finally to come south, after five days of mounting public unrest, and the Queen made an emergency broadcast to show her subjects that she cared, 'Diana's Army' – the millions who loved her even more in death than in life – found it hard to forgive. From the beginning of the week, Charles had been the main target of their rage. 'How dare he?' asked one woman in the crowd outside Buckingham Palace on the very day of Diana's death, when her ex-husband flew to Paris to escort her coffin home. 'How dare he go to Paris? He's the man who ruined her life.'[1]

Charles's problems were largely of his own making. Only six weeks before Diana's death, he had taken his public life in his hands with an overt demonstration of his affection for the woman he had loved before, during and after his marriage – the 'third person' in their marriage, as Diana herself had famously called Camilla Parker Bowles. On the evening of Friday 18 July the prince hosted a fiftieth birthday party for Camilla at his Gloucestershire home, Highgrove, where she had long since replaced Diana as chatelaine. Was she also to replace the princess on the future King's arm, perhaps even on the throne? The party was the climax of a long-term strategy to win public acceptance for Camilla as his consort, dating back to his televised confession of adultery with her in June 1994.

Mrs Parker Bowles had since become the most reviled woman in the land, so unpopular that fellow housewives pelted her with bread rolls in their local supermarket; but there were signs that Charles's game plan was finally beginning to work. With unfortunate timing, as it transpired, the Camilla question had been manipulated to the top of the national agenda during the weeks before Diana's death. It became the subject of opinion polls, radio phone-ins and TV debates, and it dominated public discussion in bars, pubs and clubs, even after Diana herself took up with the scion of one of the country's most controversial families.

The polls still showed a large majority against Camilla replacing Diana as Charles's future queen, but the tone of the debate was beginning to soften. As one participant put it in a BBC television debate, 'If the state of the nation prevents the marriage of two fifty-year-old divorcees, who have apparently been in love for some twenty-five years, when other such couples get married every day, then there is something wrong with the state of the nation.'[2]

But Diana's death changed all that. Camilla, as one friend put it, promptly 'crawled under her bed with a bottle of whisky and a packet of cigarettes, and wondered when, if ever, she would be able to come out again'.[3] Charles had long since declared Mrs Parker Bowles a 'non-negotiable' part of his life. Even during the week of Diana's funeral, he called her several times a day on his mobile phone, and told friends he needed her 'now more than ever'. But his first priority then, and for the foreseeable future, had to be his two bereft sons.

For the first time in his life, to warm public approval, the prince began to cancel or postpone public engagements to be with them. That November, during the half-term break Prince Harry had been due to spend with his mother, Charles took him to South Africa to meet Nelson Mandela and the Spice Girls. There, for the first time, Charles paid brief tribute to his ex-wife's public work, and for the second time thanked the world for its expressions of condolence. To his surprise, he found himself riding a wave of public sympathy – directed primarily at his sons, but washing over him as their father – which saw his public popularity begin to climb for the first time in nearly two decades. By Christmas 1997, four months after Diana's death, a poll for *The Times* officially declared him as popular as prime minister Tony Blair, then still enjoying an extended honeymoon with the electorate after his historic election victory the previous May.[4]

Still the old, insular Charles would occasionally resurface – defiantly going out fox-hunting, for instance, within days of a huge parliamentary vote for its abolition, amid polls showing overwhelming opposition among his future subjects. But the plight of his sons was disarming criticism. By February 1998 he was cutting back on his charity work to devote more time to them. The following month he took them with him to Canada to brave their first public engagements, amid scenes of mass hysteria, before a photocall on the ski slopes. Prince William, it became clear, could bring his mother's charms to the rescue of the ailing British monarchy. At the age of only fifteen, 'Wills' – far more than his father – was the House of Windsor's hope for the future. Or was it the House of Spencer's?

Charles looked on happily as William donned a back-to-front baseball cap and played to the cameras. This time around, he did not resent the comparisons. Where once he had been jealous of Diana's greater popularity, now he could only breathe a huge sigh of relief as their son picked up where she had left off. At the supreme court of the House of Windsor – his mother, also his monarch – Charles might at last be relieved of the blame for bringing the Crown into such disrepute.

In his ex-wife's lifetime, Charles would have been appalled at the idea of a 'Dianified', baseball-cap monarchy. Deep down, he still was; but even he could see that this was the only realistic way forward, the key to the monarchy's survival in an increasingly sceptical age. It was time, he was advised, to assert a leadership role by appearing to become the family's prime 'modernizer'. If that involved public disagreements with his father, who had caused him such grief over the years, then, as far as Charles was concerned, so much the better. It was time for him to escape from Philip's shadow – the bullying father of his childhood, whom he had blamed for 'pushing' him into his luckless marriage, and whose wrathful disapproval could still, even as he approached fifty, reduce him to tears.

Diana's disappearance from the scene, in short, was proving Charles's salvation. Now he could reclaim the role of 'caring, compassionate' prince, in which he had been cast before Diana arrived in his life, but which she had hijacked and played so much better. Suddenly there was a spring in the prince's step, despite another painful knee operation, as he chatted amiably with the 'reptiles' of the press for the first time in ten years. In their instinctive decency, the British people were giving him another chance. Moreover, in their loyalty to the monarchy, they were allowing the Windsors surreptitiously to reclaim in death the princess they had banished in life. Even the excesses of the posthumous Diana cult, with her Memorial Fund sanctioning her autograph on margarine tubs and scratch cards, began to work in the prince's favour. All that was left was to win public acceptance for Camilla.

On the weekend of 14–15 March 1998 – after his return from Canada, and with the boys safely back at boarding school – Charles hosted a 'cultural' weekend for a dozen loyalists at Sandringham, his mother's country estate in Norfolk, and let it be leaked that Camilla had acted as hostess. The tacit approval of the Queen, who tactfully spent the weekend at Windsor, could be assumed. Among the guests was Peter Mandelson, the government's master manipulator, who was helping his friend Charles to assume the guise of a leadership role in the battle to modernize the monarchy.

To those who knew the private prince – whose true conservatism in matters royal had been laid bare by his attitude to his marriage – it seemed wholly out of character that he would wish to preside over a slimmed-down, Scandinavian-style monarchy bereft of the splendour of its post-imperial rituals. It was he, after all, who had led the vain fight to save the royal yacht *Britannia*, long after the polls had showed a daunting majority of taxpayers unwilling to finance such post-imperial extravagances. But the fortunes of the House of Windsor had sunk so low that both the Queen and the prince were forced to adapt to Tony Blair's newly 'cool' Britannia, gritting their teeth through walkabouts and photo opportunities with pink-haired, nose-ringed rock stars.

And the tactic seemed to be working. On her golden wedding anniversary, ten weeks after Diana's death, a 'rebranded' Queen walked around Whitehall laughing and chatting, even clutching a heart-shaped balloon for photographers. New Labour, new monarchy. By February 1998, when Britain was contemplating war with Iraq and the Northern Ireland peace talks seemed in danger of collapse, the television news and newspaper front pages were dominated by the Queen Mother's hip operation and Princess Margaret's stroke. Normal British values seemed to have been restored.

*

Over the last century, since Disraeli masterminded the widowed
Queen Victoria's rebirth as Queen-Empress, the British monarchy
has survived as the world's pre-eminent hereditary institution by
continually reinventing itself. In a secular age, when constitutional
monarchs were obliged to sign government legislation whether
they liked it or not, the Saxe-Coburg-Gothas changed their awkwardly German name to the cosier-sounding Windsor and cast
around for a new role. During the reign of the present Queen's
father, King George VI, they found their twentieth-century niche as
a 'family' monarchy – a living exemplar of Christian family values,
strong enough to survive another world war.

Charles's own mother has played a major part in the royal
family's iconography, sitting for portrait painters over tea at
Windsor with her father, mother and sister – for all the world like
any other British nuclear family, albeit a pampered and privileged
one that seemed to speak a different language from its subjects, as
well as living a different way of life. As Elizabeth II, fast approaching Victoria's record as Britain's longest-reigning monarch, she has
kept the theme going strong, encouraging the nation to bill and coo
over her children, surrogate offspring of every house in the land.
As *ex officio* head of the Church of England, the monarch was
content with the role of custodian of the nation's moral values, and
the job of setting an exemplary model for decent-minded citizens
to follow.

Throughout the 1980s, as the younger generation came to the
fore, the British love of its royals – reflected in the slavish
sycophancy of the press – reached a crescendo with a succession of
royal weddings and births. Amid the harsh realities of Thatcher's
every-man-for-himself, devil-take-the-hindmost Britain, the royals
fulfilled their primary function by offering some much-needed
good news amid all the bad. No wonder, when all those marriages
collapsed within a decade, the backlash was all the mightier. The
British people had made a huge investment of affection and goodwill – not to mention money – in Charles and Diana, Anne and
Mark, Andrew and Fergie. As they abused their privileges, broke
the sacred vows of marriage, then offended bedrock monarchists
by opting for divorce, all viewers of the royal soap opera felt
cheated, even angry. What was the royal family for, if not to provide a symbol of stable family life?

Charles took the brunt of the backlash. He was, after all, the future king; but he had also two-timed Britain's most popular princess, the world's most famous woman, loved as much for her faults as for her strengths. The prince who at thirty had promised to be a 'New Age' husband – present at the birth of his sons, changing his fair share of nappies, sharing the upbringing of the children – had reverted to royal type, marrying Diana as a brood mare, and expecting her to take charge of the nursery while he openly kept a mistress. Had Diana been the brainless bimbo he thought he had married, so in love with being a princess that she would turn a blind eye, Charles might have got away with it. But she turned out to be a thoroughly modern woman, and at the same time a deeply traditional one, by insisting on her own rights within the ideal of a strong family unit. Unlike some of her predecessors as royal brides, she was not prepared to look the other way. When this Cinderella stamped her glass slipper, with a crash that echoed around the world, she transformed herself from mere jet-set clothes horse to potent feminist icon. Diana became the potential instrument of Charles's destruction.

Now, realizing the scale of the mistake he had made, the prince looked on helpless as his wife set about attempting to remove him from the line of succession, winning public support for a direct transition from his mother to their son. The law, of course, was on the prince's side; it would take a constitutional upheaval, plus his mother's agreement, for the succession to be altered. But he was in serious danger of losing the public consent by which any monarch reigns. He had forfeited respect and affection – the two public gifts indispensable to a successful monarch. Diana was at her most vengeful in the second half of 1991, when she made the tape recordings that blackened Charles's name via Andrew Morton's book *Diana: Her True Story*. Since the divorce she had softened, working out a *modus vivendi* with her ex-husband for the sake of their sons. She had agreed to make a joint appearance with him aboard *Britannia*, the scene of their ill-fated honeymoon, during the royal yacht's poignant farewell voyage around Britain in the autumn of 1997. It would have symbolized the civilized way in which they were rebuilding their separate lives; and it would have boosted Charles's public ratings, then largely in Diana's control. But Dodi Fayed and fate intervened.

Now that she is dead – and Charles has a chance to regain the respect, if not the affection, of the nation – it becomes forlornly clear what might have been, what Britain and the Commonwealth might have had. 'We would have been the best team in the world,' as Diana herself put it, only weeks before her death. 'I could shake hands till the cows come home. And Charles could make serious speeches . . . But' – she shook her head sadly – 'it was not to be.'[5]

What kind of man could throw away such a pearl, such a rare combination of private happiness and public triumph? Even before her death, a friend of Diana spoke with equal eloquence of what might have been:

> His indifference pushed her to the edge, whereas he could have romanced her to the end of the world. They could have set the world alight. Through no fault of his own, because of his own ignorance, upbringing and lack of a whole relationship with anyone in his life, he instilled this hatred of himself.[6]

The turnaround in the fortunes of the monarchy during the half-century of Charles's lifetime is stark to behold. Three weeks before Diana's death, during the dog days of August 1997, an ICM opinion poll showed its popularity at an all-time low, commanding the support of less than half the Queen's subjects for the first time in British history. 'Solid support' for the royal family, according to the poll, would 'literally die out' with the over-sixty-fives, the only age group to show a clear majority in believing that Britain would be worse off without them.[7]

Yet when Charles was born, in November 1948, the thousand-year-old institution was as popular as it ever had been, with a third of Britons believing the monarch was personally chosen by God. The prince himself must shoulder much of the responsibility for the decline in the fortunes of the institution that he was born to serve. Another poll in August 1997, just before Diana's death, showed 46 per cent of Britons were 'dissatisfied' with his performance as Prince of Wales, 4 per cent more than professed themselves 'satisfied'.[8] A majority wished him to step aside, for the throne to pass to his son Prince William.

They will, more or less, get their wish. The best Charles can hope for is a brief reign as a caretaker king for the last decade or so of his life. As he turns fifty, his mother is seventy-two years old, twenty-six years younger than her own mother, who is as old as the century and showing every sign of making it to the millennium. All his life Charles has known he will spend most of it waiting in the wings – 'the longest apprenticeship ever', as it has been called[9] – and has consequently tried to win his place in history as a crusading Prince of Wales.

He can point to a record of achievement in helping disadvantaged youth via the Prince's Trust. His admirers would point to his campaigns for more traditional architecture, alternative medicine, the environment, ecumenism, literacy standards; his detractors would say they have achieved little, and in some cases done positive harm. Here, it appears, is a well-meaning man, decent and civilized, anxious to make something of his position rather than merely living a life of idle self-indulgence, like many of his predecessors. Yet he has made minimal impact, and is best known for two-timing one of the most-loved women of the twentieth century.

What is it about Charles that seems to have made him his own worst enemy? The seeds of the introspective, melancholy soul with a depressive streak, intensely proud of his heritage, yet unable to adapt it to a changing world, can be traced to his childhood and youth in a cold, distant family, bereft of the normal human interaction which fuels most mortal lives. Add the privilege that went with his birth, a cocoon of deference and sycophancy blocking out the real world, and you have all the ingredients of a tortured soul unable to treat other human beings as equals, to appreciate his own frailties, to understand that he can occasionally be wrong.

But if the public Charles has been undone by the private Charles, it is really because he has never been in sympathy with the age in which he lives. Beam the prince back to any previous century and he would be entirely at home, capable of appreciating its public and private values, its art and architecture, its morality and Zeitgeist – a popular future King with a beautiful wife and two fine sons, whose mistress would have remained a well-kept secret among his intimate circle. Land him in the twentieth century, where he has the misfortune to belong, and Charles is a displaced person, restless and discontented, out of synch with his contemporaries, unhappily resigned to being unappreciated and misunderstood.

The outstanding princes of Wales in British history have been those in tune with the spirit of their times – patrons of the arts, public benefactors, inspirational and much-loved figures, regardless of their private lives. Charles, by contrast, stubbornly resists even understanding the notion. 'Whatever that might be!' he has said of the phrase 'the spirit of the times', just as he famously said 'Whatever that means!' of another notion he took too casually – marital love.[10]

During his one brief spell in the real world, at university, he was 'proud to be square', regarding his fellow undergraduates as 'hairy unwashed student bodies . . . long-haired, bare-footed and perspiring'.[11] Has Charles ever been a man of his time? Even his most sympathetic and like-minded biographer, granted access to his private journals and correspondence, seems confused. At one point the prince is dubbed 'a child of his times' (by virtue, ironically, of not wishing to be unfaithful to his wife); at another he 'stands outside the age in which he lives', raging 'too much at the folly of the world to be wise'.[12]

As Charles himself put it on entering his forties:

> The fear of being considered old-fashioned seems to me to be so all-powerful that the more eternal values and principles which run like a thread through the whole tapestry of human existence are abandoned under the false assumption that they restrict progress.[13]

Has Charles's contrary pride in being considered old-fashioned hampered his own progress through the twentieth century? Has the institution he embodies – clinging defiantly, like him, to the past – outlived its rational lifespan? Can Diana's death now help him, via his sons' popularity, to find his feet in a new century, a new millennium, bringing new meaning to his birthright as a successful, if short-lived, king? Perhaps. But can Charles manage all this, unlike his great-uncle David, Duke of Windsor, without the 'help and support' of the woman he loves?

CHAPTER TWO

'NO, NOT YOU, DEAR'

THE ODDS, PERHAPS, WERE AGAINST HIM FROM THE START. NO previous Prince of Wales has been obliged to act out the office's ancient duties in the age of the mass media – self-appointed tribunes of the people – whose criteria of what is interesting or important rarely coincide with his. This uniquely twentieth-century accountability, as unwelcome as it is unwonted, has shaped his life so completely as to transform it.

Had he lived in an earlier age, when he could have retained greater control of what remained private and what became public, the world might now have very different perceptions of Charles Philip Arthur George, Prince of Wales and Earl of Chester, Duke of Cornwall and Rothesay, Earl of Carrick and Baron Renfrew, Lord of the Isles and Great Steward of Scotland. But even before he was born, even before his gender was known or his name chosen, he was the object of global speculation and media curiosity. Even as an embryo, back in glamour-starved, rationed and couponed, post-war 1948, the child growing inside twenty-two-year-old Princess Elizabeth, Duchess of Edinburgh, excited the world and its press to fever pitch.

Charles's story begins, as almost fifty years later it will climax, outside his future kingdom, in Paris. During a visit in May 1948 by Princess Elizabeth, elder daughter of King George VI, those who saw her told each other she did not seem herself. At Divine Service in the British church she looked tired and listless, rarely raising her eyes from the ground. At a British Embassy reception in her honour that evening, she had met only half the guests when her husband led her from the room to rest. It was less than six months since she had married Lieutenant Philip Mountbatten RN, the former Prince Philip of Greece, but that was time enough. Paris decided that Elizabeth, heir presumptive to the British throne, must be pregnant.

Back in the reign of her father, King George VI, pregnancy was still a word Buckingham Palace could not quite bring itself to utter. A coded announcement on 4 June, the eve of Derby Day, stated simply that 'Her Royal Highness The Princess Elizabeth, Duchess of Edinburgh, will undertake no public engagements after the end of June.' Left to draw its own conclusions, the public remembered that the same wording had been used eighteen years earlier of the Duchess of York, Elizabeth's mother, four months before she had given birth to Princess Margaret Rose. No announcement at all had been made during the Duchess's previous pregnancy; the first Britain had known of Princess Elizabeth Alexandra Mary, whom it little thought would one day be its Queen, was when she entered the world by Caesarean section on 21 April 1926.

With Elizabeth's baby expected in mid-November, the princess and her husband were still living in Buckingham Palace while Clarence House was made ready for them, but much of their time was spent at Windlesham Moor, their rented country house near Sunningdale, Berkshire. There were those who suggested this might be the most peaceful place for her accouchement, but the princess herself decided she would like to have her baby at the Palace.

On the first floor, overlooking the Mall, a suite centres on the Buhl Room, which the Windsor matriarch Queen Mary, widow of George V, had converted into a makeshift surgery. Within a few months, this was to be the scene of the first of her son George VI's arterial operations, saving him the loss of his right leg. During the latter stages of his daughter's pregnancy, the King was first made aware of the seriousness of his condition: arteriosclerosis, with a grave danger of gangrene. He was diagnosed in the Buhl Room only two days before Charles's birth, but he gave strict instructions that his daughter was to be told nothing. For the time being, it was thus for a happy event that the room was transformed into a lavishly equipped operating theatre.

By 14 November 1948, the comings and goings of a posse of distinguished doctors at Buckingham Palace were the only clues that the birth was imminent. Crowds lingered outside the Palace throughout that rainy Sunday, the lack of news doing little to dampen their ardour. But some spirits within the Palace itself did begin to flag. By early evening the expectant father had grown impatient; Prince Philip took his private secretary and close friend, Lieutenant-Commander Michael Parker, for a game of squash on the Palace court. After a swim in the adjacent pool, they were back on the squash court at 9.15 p.m. when the King's private secretary, Sir Alan Lascelles, ran in with the news that a prince had been born.

Shortly before midnight, an announcement was secured to the Palace railings by the Colville cousins: Sir John ('Jock'), private secretary to Princess Elizabeth (and previously to three prime ministers: Neville Chamberlain, Winston Churchill and Clement Attlee, at No. 10 Downing Street), and Commander Richard, press secretary to the King, and later to Elizabeth II. Richard Colville had proudly written the announcement in his own precise hand-writing:

> Her Royal Highness the Princess Elizabeth, Duchess of Edinburgh, was safely delivered of a Prince at 9.14 o'clock this evening. Her Royal Highness and the infant Prince are both doing well.

By that time, word of mouth had already drawn Londoners from their homes, restaurants and nightclubs to swell the crowd outside the Palace to some 3,000. The announcement on BBC radio had been nicely timed to launch closing-time celebrations in pubs all over the country, to start guns firing and bonfires blazing, to turn the fountains in Trafalgar Square blue for a boy (as they stayed for a week) and to draw 4,000 telegrams of congratulation to the Palace post office that night.

The first the growing crowd outside the Palace knew of the birth came very soon after it happened, when those who had climbed to the top of the Victoria Memorial saw a blue-liveried footman emerge to whisper in the ear of a policeman – one of the many trying (ironically enough) to protect the Palace guard, then still on the pavement outside the railings, from being trampled underfoot. Every car going in and out was fiercely scrutinized, none more so than that of the King's formidable mother, the eighty-one-year-old

Queen Mary, who arrived at 11 p.m. to inspect her first great-grandchild. Despite the after-effects of a bout of influenza, the old lady stayed until after midnight, by which time the crowd outside had grown larger and noisier than ever.

Up on the first floor of the Palace, on the Mall frontage, was a young woman exhilarated by the birth of her first child and the enthusiasm of her family, but in need of sleep. The well-wishers outside were keeping her awake. At the princess's behest, Mike Parker and a colleague walked across the forecourt to try to quieten them. As they struggled to make themselves heard over the hubbub, the first recipient of the princess's message was none other than the film star David Niven, a friend of Prince Philip. 'I was pinned against the railings and, being unable to move, I was the recipient of the message hissed in my ear by the man from the Palace. I had my coat collar turned up and was huddled inside the garment, hoping not to be recognized and asked for autographs at that particular location. However, I turned round and did my best to shush those nearest to me, which did little good as everyone was far too excited and happy.'[1] The crowd was eventually dispersed by loudspeaker vans – a bizarre lullaby for the exhausted princess.

The 7lb 6oz infant so warmly welcomed was the first royal child to be born at Buckingham Palace for sixty-two years, and the first royal baby in direct succession to the throne since the birth of the future King Edward VIII in 1894. Princess Elizabeth was only the fourth heiress presumptive in British history to have given birth to a male child. The prince, as yet unnamed, was fifth in descent from Queen Victoria, thirty-second from William the Conqueror and thirty-ninth from Alfred the Great. He was the most Scottish prince since Charles I and the most English since Henry VIII. Eleventh in descent from the Electress Sophia, through whom the present royal family's title to the throne is established under the 1701 Act of Settlement, he could claim descent from the Yorkist kings through Richard II and the Lancastrian kings through John of Gaunt. Thirteenth in descent from James I and VI, his Scottish ancestry included Robert the Bruce and St Mary of Scotland through James's mother, Mary Queen of Scots; through Henry Tudor, his Welsh ancestry could be traced back to Llewelyn-ap-Gruffydd, the last native prince of all Wales. Through his maternal grandmother, he was the first potential Prince of Wales ever to be a direct descendant of Owen Glendower; through his father, he had the blood of Harold, last of the Anglo-Saxon kings. Genealogists stretched the line almost to the crack of doom: on one side Charlemagne, Cadwallader and Musa ibn Naseir, an Arab sheikh born in Mecca in 660; on the other plainer names such as John Smith, Frances Webb, Mary Browne and Peter Checke, a sixteenth-century innkeeper.[2]

The following morning's events are a striking reminder of how much the world has changed in the intervening fifty years, as Charles's birth was heralded rather more extravagantly than that of another potential king, his own son William, would be some three decades later. The British fleet, wherever it happened to be, was dressed overall; in Australia, the Melbourne town hall carillon somewhat prematurely played 'God Bless the Prince of Wales' (not yet among his titles); forty-one-gun salutes and peals of bells awoke New Zealand and South Africa; in Kenya the news was broadcast in seven native languages; from Key West, Florida, President Truman sent a message of congratulations; and from South Africa, President Jan Smuts cabled, 'We pray that the prince will be a blessing to our Commonwealth and to the world.' In republican America, radio stations across the nation interrupted their programmes with the news; in New York, the *Herald Tribune* declared that freedom in Britain had 'grown and been safeguarded under the ancient institution of the monarchy'. In Athens, where it was not forgotten that Philip had been born a prince of Greece, hundreds of his compatriots carried their greetings to the British Embassy; on the island of Tinoa, where she was engaged on charitable work, his mother, Princess Andrew of Greece, was aroused from sleep by the arrival of her telegram.

In London, the King's Troop, Royal Horse Artillery, rode in full dress from St John's Wood to Hyde Park, drawing six guns to fire a forty-one-salvo salute. The bells of St Paul's pealed almost without interruption from 9 a.m.; those of Westminster Abbey took three hours to complete a peal of 5,000 changes, then did it all again. On the Thames, barges and small craft were gaily festooned with flags and bunting; at the top of the Mall, cars and taxis passing the Palace kept up a constant hooting of horns. At Plymouth, the US warships *Columbus* and *Hamel* joined with the battleship *Vanguard* in a twenty-one-gun salute; guns were fired in Edinburgh and Rosyth, Cardiff and Windsor; a chain of beacons was lit along the mountain ranges of Wales. In towns the length and breadth of the kingdom, the day was marked by the constant firing of guns and pealing of bells.

The BBC marked the event by commissioning 'Music for a Prince' from three prominent British composers, Gordon Jacob, Herbert Howells and Michael Tippett, to be performed at a Royal Albert Hall concert two months later. No less speedy in his inspiration was the Poet Laureate, John Masefield, whose quatrain 'A Hope for the Newly Born' bore the Laureateship's authentic limp:

> May destiny, allotting what befalls,
>   Grant to the newly born this saving grace,
> A guard more sure than ships and fortress-walls,
>   The loyal love and service of a race.

Hearing a news vendor's cry of 'It's a boy!', the Labour politician Hugh Dalton, then chancellor of the exchequer, presciently wrote in his diary: 'If this boy ever comes to the throne . . . it will be a very different Commonwealth and country he will rule over.'[3] Other political reflections were more conventional. The prime minister, Clement Attlee, rose in the Commons to speak in sombre tones of the 'great responsibilities' ahead of the young prince, adding sentiments with which not even Labour's republicans were going to quibble in the mood of national exhilaration: 'We shall watch him growing to manhood with lively interest, knowing that in his own home he will receive a training by example rather than mere precept, in that courtesy and in that gracious and tireless devotion to the manifold duties of constitutional monarchy which have won the hearts of the people.'[4] The moment was then marked in rather more ringing terms, as was his wont, by the leader of His Majesty's opposition, Winston Churchill:

> Our ancient monarchy renders inestimable services to our country and to all the British Empire and Commonwealth of Nations. Above the ebb and flow of party strife, the rise and fall of ministries and individuals, the changes of public opinion and fortune, the British monarchy presides ancient, calm and supreme within its functions, over all the treasures that have been saved from the past and all the glories that we write in the annals of our country. Our thoughts go out to the mother and

father and, in a special way today, to the little prince, now born into this world of strife and storm.[5]

A week after the prince's birth Palace staff were allowed in to inspect him in groups of five, as were select members of the Privy Council. His mother had already begun to breastfeed him, as she did for several weeks. Though the princess did not leave her bed for ten days, her son was soon being walked in a second-generation pram, which Elizabeth had sought out in Royal Lodge, her parents' Windsor retreat. It was so enormous that Charles claims he can still remember lying in its vastness, overshadowed by its high sides.[6]

Information as to his looks was at a premium. The first word came from the Queen's sister, Countess Granville, who told a convention of Girl Guides in Northern Ireland that 'he could not be more angelic looking. He is golden-haired and has the most beautiful complexion, as well as amazingly delicate features for so young a baby ... The Queen says that she thinks the baby is like his mother, but the Duke is quite certain that the baby is very like himself.'[7] Princess Elizabeth, whom the Countess described as 'wonderfully well and radiantly happy', wrote to her former music teacher:

> The baby is very sweet and we are enormously proud of him. He has an interesting pair of hands for a baby. They are rather large, but fine with long fingers quite unlike mine and certainly unlike his father's. It will be interesting to see what they will become. I still find it hard to believe I have a baby of my own![8]

The photographer Cecil Beaton, commissioned to take the first official photos of mother and child, noted that the infant prince was 'an obedient sitter ... He interrupted a long, contented sleep to do my bidding and open his blue eyes to stare long and wonderingly into the camera lens, the beginning of a lifetime in the glare of public duty.'[9]

Not for a month, until the day of his christening on 15 December, was any announcement made about the child's names. The unusual delay prompted some criticism – it was a first move, pleaded his parents, to protect him from undue publicity – which quickly turned to surprise when the names were revealed.

Elizabeth and Philip were the first royal generation in a hundred years to defy Victoria's wish that all her descendants should bear her or her husband's name.* Though said by the Palace to have been made for 'personal and private reasons', the choice of Charles Philip Arthur George, with the emphasis on Charles, caused widespread surprise. The two English kings of that name had enjoyed such miserable reigns that it had been abandoned by the royal family for nigh on 300 years; its only other royal holder, Bonnie Prince Charlie, was notorious for his insurrection against the House of Hanover. The choice was widely interpreted, especially when the prince's younger sister was christened Anne almost two years later, as a deliberate revival of the names of the royal Stuarts; to the Queen's sister, Princess Margaret, one of the godparents, it meant something else entirely: 'I suppose I'll now be known as Charley's Aunt.'

The names were duly registered by Prince Philip with Mr Stanley Clare, senior registrar of Caxton Hall in the City of Westminster, who called at the Palace on the morning of the christening. The ceremony that afternoon would have been held at Windsor, where all such family occasions usually take place, had it not been for the King's health. As it was, the Palace Chapel had been destroyed by Nazi bombers in 1940, so the baptism was performed in the white and gold Music Room, whose great crimson-curtained bow windows looked out on to a wintry Palace garden.

The ceremony was followed by tea in the White Drawing Room, where the guests presented their lavish array of christening presents. Queen Mary's gift seems (no doubt as intended) to have stolen the show: 'I gave the baby a silver gilt cup and cover which George III had given to a godson in 1780, so that I gave a present from my great-grandfather to my great-grandson 168 years later.'[10]

The Archbishop of Canterbury, Dr Geoffrey Fisher, officiated, assisted by the Precentor of the Chapels Royal. The golden Lily Font, designed by Prince Albert for the christening of his and Victoria's children, had been brought up from Windsor for the occasion. By Dr Fisher's account, the infant prince, dressed in a robe of Honiton lace and white silk, again used by all Victoria's children, remained 'as quiet as a mouse' as he was bathed in water

---

*They remedied the matter in 1960 by naming their second son Andrew Albert Christian Edward.

specially brought from the River Jordan. Apart from his aunt and grandparents, the King and Queen, Charles's godparents were the Queen's brother, David Bowes-Lyon; the King of Norway; the Duke of Edinburgh's grandmother, the Dowager Marchioness of Milford Haven; his uncle, Prince George of Greece; and his cousin, Earl Mountbatten's elder daughter, Lady Brabourne.

Thus Prince Charles of Edinburgh formally entered the Protestant Church of England, of which he was destined one day to become Supreme Governor, and with which he would be drawn into a series of uncomfortable conflicts in middle age. At the same time, as a newborn, post-war 'baby boomer', he was duly allotted his state ration card and milk allowance.

The new Prince Charles's first few years were to be acted out against two dark and dismal backdrops, which were to make a lasting impression on his psyche: the constant absence of his parents, and the worsening health of his grandfather, the King. The boy's first Christmas and New Year, for instance, six weeks after his birth, were the last for several years he would spend with both his parents at his side. It was the first, and hardest, lesson in learning that he had not been born as other boys.

Before Charles's birth, Elizabeth had said, 'I'm going to be the child's mother, not the nurses.' Even before she became Queen, however, Charles's mother was always wife first, mother second. The midwife's work complete, she was replaced in the nursery by two Scottish-born nurses, Helen Lightbody and Mabel Anderson. Miss Lightbody had been recommended to the princess by her aunt, the Duchess of Gloucester, whose two sons she had brought up; as the senior of the two Palace nurses, she was given what was then quaintly considered the courtesy title of 'Mrs'. Miss Anderson, the daughter of a policeman killed in the Liverpool blitz, had placed an advertisement in the situations wanted column of a nursing magazine, only to find herself summoned to Buckingham Palace for an interview with the princess. In time she was to find herself in charge of Anne, Andrew and Edward as well, and later of Anne's own children, Peter and Zara.

Five days after the christening, Dr Jacob Snowman of Hampstead, London, then in his eighties, visited the Palace to circumcise the baby. On his doctor's advice, the King had cancelled a projected Commonwealth tour of Australia, New Zealand and

Canada. Christmas, most unusually, was spent in London, also on medical orders. By January, however, the King was sufficiently recovered to lead a family shooting expedition to Sandringham, so Miss Lightbody found herself back in familiar territory, having spent hours in the country nursery with Charles's cousins, the princes William and Richard of Gloucester. For three weeks she was in sole charge of Charles as his mother succumbed to a bout of measles.

By March the family was back in London, and the princess was able to resume her round of engagements. For her father, however, the prognosis was more dispiriting. Since the November diagnosis he had led the life of a virtual invalid; his doctors now advised that he must continue to do so, or face an immediate operation to ease blood constriction in his right leg. George chose the operation, which was performed in the Buhl Room on 12 March and which proved so successful that two weeks later he was able to preside at a meeting of the Privy Council, and by May he was back on a full schedule of public duties. But he and his wife, if not their daughters, now realized that he could not have long to live.

By July, when her father seemed in much better spirits after a week's rest at Balmoral, Princess Elizabeth was at last able to move out of Buckingham Palace with her husband and child and into their first family home. The renovation of Clarence House, a few hundred yards away down the Mall, had dragged on much longer than expected, and it was a great relief to leave the draughty vastness of the Palace for a more compact, centrally heated home with all mod cons. The former home of the Duke of Clarence, before his accession as William IV in 1830, the house had been used as Red Cross offices during the war. Now it boasted a chintz-curtained nursery, with white walls and blue-for-a-boy mouldings, which looked out across its own walled and private garden over the Mall to St James's Park, around which the two nurses could wheel the infant prince with little fear of recognition, or, in that era of respectful restraint, much press intrusion.

Though the infant prince's daily routine has been described in meticulous detail, it comes down to an unsurprising round of playpens, teddy bears, torn-up books and regally soiled nappies. One of its few distinguishing features was that enormous pram, which would sometimes be wheeled to nearby Marlborough House, where visits to Queen Mary (whom he called 'Gan-Gan', as

Edward VIII had called Queen Victoria) provide another of Charles's earliest memories. He has a vivid picture of the dignified old lady sitting bolt upright, her legs culminating on a footstool, surrounded by the array of precious objects which formed her famous collection (much of it filched from subjects too timid to say no). Whereas the previous generation of royal infants, even Elizabeth and Margaret, had never been allowed to go near the jade, the silver and the crystal in their splendid display cabinets, Charles was allowed to play around with whatever priceless object took his fancy. Since her grand-daughters' infancy, the *grande dame* of Windsor had lived through the deaths of her husband and two sons, and had seen another abandon the throne for an American divorcee. Now another son, she knew, lay dying. In the child by her footstool lay all her hopes for the dynasty of which she was undisputed matriarch.

Only for the first year of Charles's life was his mother spared most royal duties, while his father was based at the Admiralty in London rather than on active naval service. By his first birthday in November 1949, however, the normal working life of what the King called 'the family firm' had been resumed. Charles's father was away in Malta, where his mother flew to join him less than a week after their son's birthday. Both his parents were also away for Christmas, which Charles spent with the King and Queen at Sandringham. Over six weeks away from her infant son, Elizabeth missed out on his first steps and his first teeth. His first word was not 'Mama' but 'Nana', as in the person closest to him, his nanny. It was a depressing portent of what was to come: the most solitary of childhoods, deprived of a large degree of the parental love and warmth that most children enjoy, to the lasting benefit of their sense of self and security.

Even when Elizabeth returned to London at the end of December 1949, she seemed in no particular hurry to see her year-old son. Just as the long separation had not caused her 'any obvious consternation', in the words of the best of her biographers, nor did she 'find it necessary to rush back to him' as soon as she returned home. Instead, she spent four days at Clarence House, apparently 'attending to engagements' and 'dealing with correspondence' before going to the races to watch a horse she owned jointly with her mother. 'Only then was she reunited with her son, who had been staying with her parents at Sandringham.'[11]

For another six months, Charles's parents kept to themselves a new family secret: that during her wedding-anniversary visit to her husband in Malta, spent at the Mountbattens' Villa Guardamangia, Elizabeth had conceived her second child. Charles was one year and nine months old when his sister arrived the following summer, on 15 August 1950. Photographs of the period show the signs of bewilderment on the face of a young boy no longer the centre of his parents' intermittent attention. Charles's young world was already, as it was to remain throughout his childhood, a world much more of adults than of children his own age; and it may not have been merely wishful thinking on his parents' part that credited him with 'a most watchful, protective interest' in his sister from the first.

With two children installed, and their parents' lives again busy and public, the royal nursery settled into a rigid daily regime in the care of the two nannies, 'Mrs' Lightbody and Miss Anderson. Charles and Anne were got up each day at 7 a.m. sharp, dressed, fed and played with in the nursery until nine, when they enjoyed a statutory half-hour with their mother. They rarely saw her again until teatime, when Elizabeth would try to clear two hours in her day. She liked to bath the children herself whenever her schedule permitted, after which they were often dressed up again to be introduced to distinguished visitors. Even before his third birthday, Charles had learned to bow before offering his cheek for a kiss from 'Gan-Gan', Queen Mary, and not to sit down unbidden in the presence of his grandfather. It was a formidable introduction to the complexities of any child's life – basking but sporadically, and unpredictably, in the attentions of his mother, with his father all but a stranger.

Already a pattern was being set that would come to haunt Charles's life even in adulthood, even at times of his greatest need. Neither of his parents saw any great problem or indeed emotional wrench in leaving him to the care of his nannies for the majority of the time. Philip assumed there was little he could contribute at this stage of his son's life; that would come later. Elizabeth, meanwhile, was merely raising her child the way she herself had been brought up by her own parents: putting duty first, withholding physical affection as somehow demeaning, and trusting in the servants.

Given the values of the age, and her class, she knew no better. But it would deprive Charles of the intimacy with his parents on which most children are able to rely, not just in childhood but throughout life. Even in adulthood Charles would communicate with both his parents largely by letter or internal Palace memo; few topics of any substance were felt appropriate for discussion face to face, in the family context. The coldness and distance in Charles's lifelong relations with his parents were sown at this tender age, when he was far too young to grasp what was happening – thus preventing him at a maturer age, when most men can finally work such things out, from understanding or appreciating the lasting effect upon him.

Charles's third Christmas, in 1950, saw his father still stationed in Malta, now with his own naval command. His mother chose to spend the holiday alone with her husband, again leaving her children behind in the care of their grandparents at Sandringham. Even their attention, however, was frequently denied Charles. The young prince enjoyed an early and somewhat brutal experience of constitutional monarchy that Christmas, when the Lord President of the Council, Herbert Morrison, shut the door of a Privy Council meeting in his face. 'Sorry, young fellow-me-lad,' said Morrison, 'but I'm afraid you can't go in there. We've got a meeting with your grandfather and it's very, very secret.'[12]

Charles was visibly happier when the domestic routine settled back to comparative normality at Clarence House that spring. And so might what passed for family life have continued for another ten or fifteen years, before being further blighted by the burden of monarchy. But the King's health was growing worse. His wife and daughter now knew, though as yet he did not, that he had cancer. By July, an increase in the young couple's royal duties on the monarch's behalf forced Philip to give up his one brief naval command. In October, their departure delayed for two weeks by another operation on the King, Charles's parents left for a tour of North America and Canada. Included in Princess Elizabeth's luggage was a sealed envelope of documents, which she would have to sign if her father died during her absence.

So Charles's parents now missed his third birthday, which was spent with his grandparents and Aunt Margaret at Buckingham Palace. On their return the King made the Duke and Duchess of Edinburgh members of the Privy Council. It was all by way of momentous preparation, which to Charles only meant another

Christmas spoilt by the news that his parents would soon be off
travelling again. At the time of his birth, his grandfather's health
had forced him to cancel a Commonwealth tour; by Christmas
1950 it had been rescheduled for early 1952. Now, because of the
King's increasingly rapid decline, it was to be undertaken by his
daughter and her husband. The pictures of George VI waving them
off at London airport, a frail and shadowy figure seemingly
buffeted by the breeze, were a shock to his affectionate subjects.

On 6 February 1952, at Treetops, a hunting lodge overlooking
the Sagana River in Kenya, Charles's mother learnt that overnight
she had become Queen. Monarch at twenty-five, Elizabeth that
day lost what little there was of her restricted freedom and family
life. Her father was dead at only fifty-six – fourteen years younger
than his own father, George V, and, as it was to prove, twenty-two
years younger than his brother, Edward VIII – though both were
equally heavy smokers. Less prepared for accession than on her last
tour, Elizabeth left for the urgent flight home in a brightly
patterned dress and hat. As she said goodbye to the servants at
the door of the lodge, her chauffeur knelt on all fours to kiss her
shoes.

Heir apparent at three years old, Prince Charles was not yet Prince
of Wales, but already Duke of Cornwall, Duke of Rothesay, Earl of
Carrick and Baron of Renfrew, Lord of the Isles and Great Steward
of Scotland. 'That's me, Mummy,' he was heard to whisper when
the Duke of Cornwall's name was mentioned in church among the
prayers for the royal family. But, from his point of view, little else
had changed. He was scarcely aware that flags would now fly
throughout the land on his birthday. His daily routine was much
the same, apart from the absence of his grandfather, from whose
funeral rites he was carefully excluded, though he had been staying
with him at Sandringham on the night he had abruptly
'disappeared'.

Soon after Easter 1952, a subdued holiday with the court still in
mourning, Charles was confronted with the first outward sign of
change in his family life. His grandmother and aunt moved into
Clarence House, the family home refurbished only two years
earlier for him and his parents, who in turn moved back into
Buckingham Palace. The second-floor nursery suite had been carefully redecorated to seem as much like the Clarence House nursery

as possible. There was his box of toy soldiers, his cuckoo clock, his ten-foot-high mock-Tudor doll's house, his toy cupboard, and he had a new, full-sized bed, made for him by students of the Royal College of Art. But his mother's study on the floor below was now declared out of bounds.

Passing it one day, Charles urged his mother to come and play. 'If only I could,' said the Queen, gently closing the door against him. As the months went by, this was not the only reason he had to think his childhood different from that of other boys. When he joined his family on the Palace balcony, or at the Trooping the Colour, Charles's eyes were those of an excited member of the crowd, watching the colourful displays. What puzzled him was that some people seemed to prefer to look at him.

As far as they knew how, his parents tried to mitigate the potential corruptions of privilege. All the Palace staff, at the Queen's insistence, called the prince simply 'Charles' (as indeed they did until his eighteenth birthday). When he misbehaved he was duly punished, the palm being administered to the royal hindquarters as much by his nannies as by his father. Philip once spanked him for sticking his tongue out at the crowd watching him drive down the Mall. In such painful ways did Charles begin to learn about the accident of his birth.

Nor was he allowed to take deference for granted. When the prince omitted to call his detective 'Mister', simply using his surname, as he heard his mother and father do all the time, he was told to apologize. When he slipped an ice-cube down a footman's back he was punished. When he left a door open and a footman rushed to shut it, Philip stopped the servant, saying, 'Leave it alone, man. The boy's got hands.' His father also found Charles pelting a Sandringham policeman with snowballs, while the hapless officer silently took his punishment, unsure whether to reply in kind. 'Don't just stand there,' shouted Philip, 'throw some back!' It was also at Sandringham that the Queen once sent Charles back out of the house, not to return until he had found a dog lead he had lost in the grounds, with the memorable royal rebuke, 'Dog leads cost money.'

Such was the pattern throughout his childhood. But in the later months of 1952, as he began to master the rudiments of the Queen's English, Charles began, almost by accident, to discover the meaning of the lavish home life he otherwise took for granted. No

longer could he ride around London in the back of the family car
with his father at the wheel. These popular excursions had
suddenly stopped, and now, aged three, he had his own car and
chauffeur. He also had his own footman, an eighteen-year-old
Palace servant called Richard Brown (whom he once 'knighted'
with his knife when Brown stooped to pick up some food Charles
had dropped). 'Why haven't you got a Richard?' Charles asked
when visiting the home of another well-born boy his own age. His
friend didn't have a Mr Kelly, either – Sergeant Kelly, to be precise,
Charles's newly assigned private detective, the first in a long line
who would shadow him for the rest of his life. It was thanks to
Kelly that Charles soon had another change of routine: he could no
longer go for walks through Green Park and St James's Park,
across the road from his home.

Part of growing up, as Charles's character began to emerge, was
to develop some sort of working relationship with his sister. The
Queen, looking back, is emphatic that all four of her children
showed very different personalities at the earliest ages, and it was
already clear that Charles and Anne were totally unalike. Charles
was much more like his father in appearance, already aping some
of Philip's public mannerisms: the hands behind the back, the erect
bearing, the habit of looking an interlocutor fixedly in the eye,
often causing a certain unease. Anne was much more like her father
in character: extrovert, self-confident to a fault, occasionally
temperamental. Charles took after his mother, who in turn took
after her father: instinctively shy and retiring, yet overcoming it
with an effort of will, which in time sowed the seeds of a driving
sense of duty.

The solemnity of Charles's face in some early photographs, contrasting with the mischievousness of Anne's, is that of the shy, not
of the humourless, child. It was Anne, the crowds in the Mall
noticed, who waved confidently, after the fashion of her mother,
long before her older brother could summon the confidence to do
the same. It was Charles, by contrast, who kept reminding his
sister, often in vain, that she must curtsey when entering their grandmother's drawing room. It was Charles who pulled Anne along the
platform to say thank you to the engine driver when the royal train
delivered them to Sandringham. But it was Anne who first discovered, and duly exploited, the wonderful Palace game discovered by
her aunt and mother before her: if you walked past a sentry, he

would make a satisfying clatter coming to attention and presenting arms. To walk back and forth past a sentry box provided hours of childish entertainment (to the chagrin of the long-suffering guards on duty). When he discovered that he, too, was one of the privileged few who could produce this startling effect, Charles steered clear of sentry boxes. As yet, he found it embarrassing.

The prince's fourth birthday was the first his father ever spent with him. Preparations were already under way for the Queen's coronation the following June. Ancient ritual called for the Duke of Cornwall, as senior royal duke and head of the peerage, to take an oath of allegiance to the new monarch; but it was the first time in British history, at least since the creation of the dukedom in 1337, that a sovereign with so young an heir was to be crowned. With his mother reluctant to put Charles through such an ordeal, he instead watched with his grandmother from a gallery of the Abbey. That afternoon, when his parents returned home after a triumphant progress through London, they led their son onto the balcony of Buckingham Palace, to a wave of renewed cheering. It was Charles's first experience of mass adulation, which might be thought to have turned the head of a four-year-old child. But scarcely anything of that day has lodged vividly in his memory.

For the bewildered young boy, all the coronation really meant was that his parents would soon be going away again – this time, for longer than ever. For a few months his mother's presence was interrupted only by trips around the country to show herself to her new subjects. But in late November, soon after Charles's fifth birthday, she and Philip were again to undertake that interrupted Commonwealth tour, this time in their own right. They would be away for six months.

The coronation had led to the first full flush of publicity about the royal children, which their mother decided was not in their best interests. Charles and Anne had never been allowed to see many of the newspapers that carried their photographs; now the Queen began to impose further restrictions, for her children's own good. In late June, following an absurd number of requests for his presence, the Palace officially announced that Prince Charles, still only four, would not yet be undertaking any official engagements. By way of confirmation, the Queen cancelled plans for the youngest member of the Duke of Cornwall's Light Infantry to present him with a set of model soldiers to mark the regiment's 250th anniversary.

No more photographs of the royal children were issued for several months. There had been criticism that they were already becoming overexposed to the public's unremitting interest; the *Daily Express* calculated that in the twenty-three weeks of 1953 up to June, it alone had published fifty pages of royal pictures, (suggesting, *en passant*, that today's tabloid obsession with the royal family, especially its younger members, is nothing new).[13] Nor was there any special celebration of Charles's fifth birthday that November. His parents stayed away at Sandringham, finalizing their plans for the tour, while the crestfallen boy spent the day at Windsor with his grandmother and Aunt Margaret.

A week later – once the Queen had ordered some toys from Harrods, to be stored away for her son's Christmas presents – came the moment of parting. Charles wept copiously; but as much as he disliked these separations, he was already aware of the need for them. 'Mummy has an important job to do,' he told a friend who asked where she was. 'She's down here.' He pointed out Australia on the globe that had been newly installed in the nursery, on which he followed his parents' progress around the world. His nannies testified that he felt his mother's absence very keenly. Upon their reunion aboard the royal yacht at Tobruk, it was only with difficulty that Charles was restrained from joining the line of dignitaries waiting to shake hands with the Queen as she was piped aboard. 'No, not you, dear,' were his mother's first words to her son after six months apart.[14]

After this latest prolonged separation, the young prince seemed to his mother to have grown up almost beyond recognition. For a five-year-old he was still very shy, woefully unsure of himself and almost impossibly serious. As they sailed home, the Queen decided it was time for her son's education to begin in earnest.

CHAPTER THREE

'A THOROUGHLY AVERAGE PUPIL'

'FROM HIS CHILDHOOD THIS BOY WILL BE SURROUNDED BY SYCOPHANTS and flatterers by the score, and will be taught to believe himself as a superior creation.'[1] The words of the Labour leader James Keir Hardie, on the birth of the future King Edward VIII in 1894, have echoed with equal resonance through the life of the next Prince of Wales.

Even as a child, Charles was insulated from life's verities by the in-built deference of life at court, to the point where his distaste for his schooldays can be seen as that of a superior being compelled to fend for himself amid the lower orders. As an adult, his many qualities have always been tempered by unseemly expectations of those around him, eminent or menial, who displease him at their peril. No-one, in short, can be considered his equal. In middle age, Charles's central, and somewhat surprising, flaw is that he has come to take his unearned station in life as his due, permitting the ex officio respect he requires to override normal, civilized human values. In this respect, as in so many others, his troubles stem from a conscious, almost wilful, failure to adapt to changing times.

As a child, still comparatively unspoilt, he seems to have been rather charming. The main force in shaping his young character, and thus those emergent values, was much less his mother than his father. If this seems ironic in hindsight, as Charles has embraced spiritual values so alien to the less reflective Philip, it is due partly to a hereditary stubborn streak, partly to his father's crude attempts to stiffen the spine of a young son who seemed to him

distinctly unmanly. Even as a small child, Charles already appeared
to his father to lack his sister Anne's 'panache'; the boy was 'soft',
and needed toughening up.[2] Boarding school might do the trick –
preferably, to Philip, the same ones he himself had attended – after
a brief induction at a local day school.

On his fifth birthday, in the November following his mother's
coronation, Charles had reached the age at which English law
requires every child to begin a formal education. Although his
parents had already discussed altering the traditional patterns of
royal tutelage – strictly in private, behind Palace walls – their plans
as yet remained secret. Philip was not alone in worrying about his
son's gentle, rather repressed nature. Even to his mother Charles
did not seem ready to be sent to school with other children, let
alone, as some Labour Members of Parliament were demanding, to
the nearest state primary school. For a five-year-old, the rather
plump little boy was socially mature, as was only to be expected of
one living in a world of formal adult behaviour. But he did not
seem particularly bright.

He could write his own name, in carefully etched capital letters;
he could count to a hundred; and he could tell the time. But he
could scarcely read at all, despite hours of enjoyment being read –
and committing to memory – the works of Beatrix Potter, A. A.
Milne and the *Babar the Elephant* books. The prince liked his
dancing classes, for which a mixed group of young aristocrats
joined him at the Palace each week, and his riding lessons at
Windsor, though he was already displaying less enthusiasm than
his sister. He attended a London gym class and had started piano
lessons, showing promise of some musical aptitude. But, as yet,
the only formal instruction Charles had received for the arduous
royal years ahead was to be made to stand still for long periods of
time.

Before leaving for her Commonwealth tour, the Queen had
engaged a governess for her son – a spry Scotswoman in her mid-
forties named Catherine Peebles. Though Miss Peebles had
previously had charge of the widowed Duchess of Kent's two
younger children, Princess Alexandra and Prince Michael, she had
no formal training, no degree and no revolutionary ideas on the
upbringing of children. It was enough for the Queen to have
noticed in 'Mispy' a mixture of common sense and strictness that
echoed her own instincts. The one rule Charles's mother imposed

on her son's governess, knowing the child's in-built uncertainty of himself, was 'No forcing'.

The Queen had considered inviting other children to join Charles's classes, but decided that his temperament urged against it. If the boy's world so far had been one of adults, it had also been one of female adults, and distinctly genteel ones at that. Apart from his father, who was so often away, Charles had spent most of his time with the Queen, the Queen Mother, Princess Margaret, his two nurses and his sister. The difficulty of establishing normal dealings with other children just now might distract him. It was decided that Charles would, for the present, take his lessons alone. Even Anne was forbidden to disturb her brother's mornings with Miss Peebles in the Palace schoolroom, where a desk and a blackboard had now joined the more familiar globe. When the time came for 'Mispy' to teach Charles's three young siblings, other children did join the classes. Looking back, the Queen felt sure she judged the difference in Charles correctly.

Miss Peebles now became one of the select few to receive a copy of the Queen's daily engagement card. Each morning at nine o'clock, when possible, Charles still spent half an hour with his mother. Then the day's instruction began, lasting initially until eleven-thirty; noon when he was a little older. Miss Peebles confirmed the Queen's own concern that Charles's unnatural start in life had rendered him a nervous, highly strung child of unpredictable sensitivity. 'If you raised your voice to him, he would draw back into his shell, and for a time you would be able to do nothing with him.' His nurse, Mabel Anderson, agreed: 'He was never as boisterous or noisy as Princess Anne. She had a much stronger, more extrovert personality. She didn't exactly push him aside, but she was certainly a more forceful child.' Anne could always find some way to amuse herself, while Charles always needed to be entertained. She was also better with her hands; Charles, as yet, was 'all fingers and thumbs'.[3]

Charles's shy, almost timorous nature was due in part to his growing awareness of his position. He knew how he was expected to behave, if not yet exactly why. When he visited a friend's farm, it was noticed that he took a polite interest in everything to be seen – almost as if he were on a royal visit – rather than showing a child's quick and selective enthusiasms. At times the spectacle of a little boy so aware of proprieties became almost pathetic: when encouraging his corgi or another of his many pets to perform their tricks, he would always add a most polite 'please'.

On a rewards-for-effort system, Miss Peebles began to draw out the boy's special interests. After beginning each day with a Bible story, Charles was allowed to indulge his fondness for painting. Geography was another natural source of fascination; thanks to the globe on which Charles followed his parents' travels, he was soon able to tell visiting ambassadors the whereabouts of their country. History was more of a problem, when trying to educate a potential king to think of himself as a normal child. But the canny Miss Peebles developed a course she called 'Children in History', in which great figures were traced right back to their origins, whether regal or humble. The only subject that completely baffled Charles, as it has done ever since, was maths.

The afternoons were taken up with educational excursions: down the Mall to the shipping offices in Cockspur Street, for a talk from Miss Peebles on the trade routes; up Highgate Hill to trace the steps of Dick Whittington and his cat before a visit to the pantomime; to the Tower, to be shown round by the Beefeaters; to St George's Chapel, Windsor, to see Winston Churchill installed as a Knight of the Garter; to Madame Tussaud's, to laugh at the wax effigies of himself and his parents.

In that first year Charles quickly learnt to read, but he still had some difficulty with his writing. After Christmas 1955 – celebrated with a party for forty children at the Palace, and a visit to Harrods to ask Father Christmas for a bicycle – he began to learn French. The afternoon excursions became overtly instructive, with visits to the various London museums. But by now the press had caught on to the routine, and the outings had to be abandoned for a straight-forward nature walk through Richmond Park. Even they, in time, became uncomfortable obstacle courses.

The Queen began to doubt whether it was possible for her son to enjoy anything approaching a normal education. If the press would not allow him to visit the British Museum in peace, what chance of privacy would he have at a 'normal' school? And would his presence disturb the education of the other children? Her plans seemed in danger, but she was determined not to abandon them lightly. On 11 April 1955 her press secretary, Richard Colville, sent the first in what was to prove a long series of such messages to British newspaper editors:

> I am commanded by the Queen to say that Her Majesty and the
> Duke of Edinburgh have decided that their son has reached the
> stage when he should take part in more grown-up education
> pursuits with other children. In consequence, a certain amount
> of the Duke of Cornwall's instruction will take place outside his
> home; for example, he will visit museums and other places of
> interest. The Queen trusts, therefore, that His Royal Highness
> will be able to enjoy this in the same way as other children,
> without the embarrassment of constant publicity. In this
> respect, Her Majesty feels it is equally important that those in
> charge of, or sharing in, the instruction should be spared undue
> publicity, which can so seriously interrupt their normal lives. 4

The request caused a lull, albeit temporary, in press attention.
Charles and 'Mispy' remained unmolested when they visited
London Zoo and the Planetarium; the boy was soon an expert in
recognizing constellations, proof to his mother that, like her, he
was 'at heart a country person'. They even managed a ride on the
underground, the prince passing unrecognized as the son of
inconspicuous parents (Miss Peebles and Sergeant Kelly). Extra-
curricular activities now included charades, field sports, more
riding and Charles's first games of cricket and soccer – neither of
which, though the national sports of his future subjects, was to
prove an abiding enthusiasm. Team sports, apart from polo, have
never much appealed to him. It is striking that even at so young an
age, he took with much more passion to the solitary pursuit of fly-
fishing, under the guidance of one of the Balmoral stalkers. His
father also began to teach him boxing, but reluctantly, and with
some irritation, abandoned the idea after a chorus of public
protest.

By the autumn of 1956 the Queen was sufficiently pleased with
Charles's progress to take the next major step she had in mind. In
October, soon after the start of the school term, Colonel Henry
Townend, founder and headmaster of a smart London day school
for boys, was pleasantly surprised to find himself invited to tea
with Her Majesty at Buckingham Palace. Hill House, the Colonel's
small establishment in Hans Place, just behind Knightsbridge (con-
veniently near the Palace), had been recommended to Charles's
parents by friends and acquaintances who had sent their own sons
there. One Hill House mother had particularly pleased the Queen

by informing her that it was the only school in London outside
which the pavement was washed and the railings dusted every day.
The school's rather spartan manifesto – very much that of Charles's
father – was trumpeted on the busy noticeboard beside its front
steps, open for inspection to any casual passer-by:

> A sense of rivalry has to be encouraged and a boy must be led
> to discover something in which he can excel. He must be trained
> to react quickly in an emergency, have a good sense of balance
> and control, have the strength and ability to extract himself
> from a dangerous situation, and the urge to win.

Though naturally flattered when the Queen asked him to accept
her son as a pupil, Colonel Townend was alarmed by the daunting
double responsibility, both to the heir to the throne and to his other
pupils. It was mutually agreed that, for the present, Charles would
join the other boys only for their afternoon recreation. Lessons
with 'Mispy' continued in the mornings; Charles would then don
his school uniform and be taken to Hill House to join the crocodile
along the King's Road into Chelsea. School games were played in
the grounds of the Duke of York's Headquarters, the military depot
named after that very duke who marched his men to the top of the
hill and marched them down again. Newspaper editors, of course,
also marched their men towards the playing fields, once the
prince's new afternoon schedule was discovered. But one picture of
Charles playing soccer looked much like another, especially as he
didn't join in with much enthusiasm, and the novelty soon wore
off.

As his mother and headmaster had hoped, Charles soon merged
into the crowd of schoolboys walking in line down the street,
recognizable only when politely raising his school cap to passers-
by. His eighth birthday passed unremarked; it was not as if he were
yet a fully fledged schoolboy. That, amid tight security, was being
planned for the New Year.

Christmas, which again saw his father abroad on official duties,
also marked the end of Catherine Peebles's supervision of Prince
Charles. Although 'Mispy' would stay at the Palace to take charge
of Princess Anne, Charles was to miss her sorely. With the
retirement not long after of Helen Lightbody – Miss Anderson also
stayed on to look after Anne – he was suddenly deprived of the two

main guardians of his childhood, with whom he had spent considerably more time than with his parents. As he moved into a suite of his own in the Palace, Charles kept in close touch with both, but the shock of their departure renewed his sense of isolation. The approach of that first day at school with other children, away from the security of home, is difficult enough for any child, most of whom face it at the age of five. For eight-year-old Charles the prospect became positively awesome. Although his parents had striven to prepare him for it, the young prince was simply not equipped to be wrenched from his sheltered environment.

For all his parents' good intentions, by no stretch of the imagination was Prince Charles an ordinary child. He had grown up in palaces and castles. Ships and soldiers, objects of fantasy to other boys of his age, were to Charles everyday realities. British history was the story of his own family. He had seen his parents, often himself, treated with awe and reverence even by the high and mighty. People became nervous and ill at ease in their presence. At the ring of a bell, his nanny – and he had no reason to suppose that all children didn't have nannies – would drop whatever was happening and take him to see his mother. At the age of four he had been named one of the world's Top Ten Best-dressed Men, alongside Marshals Tito and Bulganin, Adlai Stevenson, Billy Graham, Fred Astaire and Charlie Chaplin.

The prince had never handled money; when occasionally he saw some, this supposedly potent substance turned out to be pieces of paper, or lumps of metal, bearing a picture of his mother. He had never been shopping. He had never been on a bus. He had never got lost in a crowd. He had never had to fend for himself.

Nevertheless, on 28 January 1957 Charles made royal history by becoming the first heir to the British throne ever to go to school. At 9.15 a.m. a black Ford Zephyr driven by a Palace chauffeur, with Charles and his governess (not his mother) in the back, pulled up at the school entrance, where Colonel Townend was waiting to greet him. In the school uniform of cinnamon-coloured jersey and corduroy trousers, Charles ran up to the man he had previously known as a football referee. Inside he hung up his coat – distinctive for the velvet collar so admired in his Best-dressed Man citation – and plunged with stiff upper lip into the morning's routine.

The new boy was number 102 on the school roll of 120, the sons of well-to-do professional men, lawyers, doctors, military men and politicians. One fellow pupil was the grandson of the new prime minister, Harold Macmillan. There were a number of foreign children, the sons of diplomats stationed in London; the school, which boasted a sibling establishment in Switzerland, aspired to share its places equally between English and non-English pupils. Hill House was a school for privileged children, still young and self-interested enough not to be too much in awe of the prince. The headmaster had warned them to make no special fuss of the familiar new face in their midst, who would be required like everyone else to wash up and sweep the classroom floor; but their upbringing had anyway taught them otherwise. Charles's new peers were more than equipped to take his arrival in their stride.

Opened only five years before, Hill House very much reflected the personal philosophy of Colonel Townend, a former Gunners officer in his late forties who had been an Oxford football blue and England athlete. There was no corporal punishment, and the predominately female staff taught a syllabus broad by pre-preparatory school standards. It even included elementary anatomy lessons from Townend's wife, Beatrice, a state-registered nurse, who had once been theatre sister to Sir John Weir, an assistant at the prince's birth. The doors were equipped with automatic devices to prevent trapped fingers, all the furniture had rounded edges and the school motto was taken from Plutarch: 'A boy's mind is not a vessel to be filled, but a fire to be kindled.'

It had been decided that the new boy would be 'Prince Charles' to the staff, but plain 'Charles' to his fellow pupils in Form Six of Middle School. Given no special escort that first morning, but left to make his own way, he decided that the highlight was a visit to the school 'madhouse' – a gymnasium with padded walls – for a game of basketball. After a lunch of boiled beef and carrots followed by apple pie, he painted a picture of Tower Bridge and signed it Charles. At three-thirty it was time to go home, and the chauffeur-driven Zephyr was waiting at the door. As Charles told his mother all about it, she felt a great sense of relief. The experiment, it seemed, was going to work.

Next morning, however, the crowd outside Hill House was so enormous that she hesitated to let him go. It wasn't just that the press had set up a constant vigil; local residents who had read of the new recruit in their morning papers were all but choking the street. After telephone consultations with Townend the Queen relented, and Charles arrived at school thirty-five minutes late. He had to run the gauntlet of sightseers and photographers to get inside. It was the same when he left, and again the next morning. Already it was clear to both the headmaster and the royal parents that this could not go on. Unless the newshounds and thus the gawpers could be moved on, the monarchy's bold experiment in liberal education would have to be called off.

The Queen kept her son at home while her press secretary again went into action. A detective reported back to him with the identities of all the journalists waiting outside the school, and their stated intention to wait all day. Colville then telephoned each of the newspaper editors involved, reminding them of the Queen's plea of eighteen months before. Within an hour Fleet Street had recalled its hounds and Charles was able to get on with his education.

Before long he had settled into everyday school routine more smoothly than those watching over him had reason to hope. Swimming and wrestling – which took the place of boxing at Hill House – became his favourite pastimes, and he continued to show promise with watercolours. In the classroom he remained something of a plodder, which worried nobody. The purpose of sending Charles to school was not to sow the seeds of a giant intellect, but to help him meet people his own age and learn to live among them. His parents would be more than happy with merely 'ordinary' progress.

His end-of-term report was certainly ordinary. Hill House made a practice of not sending exam results to parents; they were posted on the board and could be viewed by those who wished. The royal parents refrained, but it is the unenviable fate of princes to have their school reports preserved for posterity. Apart from arithmetic, where the verdict was still 'below form average, careful but slow, not very keen', Charles's report for the Lent term of 1957 contained its standard quota of 'fair', 'good', 'shows keen interest' and 'made a fair start'.[5] Hidden behind the vernacular of the schoolteacher, anxious not to cause too much trouble at home, was what appeared to be a reassuringly average start.

The summer term began, like the first, with an attack of tonsillitis, but this time the tonsils lost. After their removal in the Buhl Room at the Palace by James Crooks of Great Ormond Street Hospital for Sick Children, Charles insisted on keeping them in a jar on his bedroom mantelpiece. By the end of term, despite further absences through illness, the assessment remained much the same: determined but slow. Charles was, perhaps generously at that stage, credited with 'above-average intelligence', and showed continuing signs of a creative bent scarcely evident in either of his parents.

By August he was enjoying his first yacht racing at Cowes, though seasickness made his first outing in his father's yacht, *Bluebottle*, something of an ordeal. Once he got over it, however, he shared Prince Philip's exhilaration at the closeness to sea and wind – and the distance from the press. Earlier that summer his father had stumped up ten shillings (50p) after betting Charles that he couldn't swim two lengths of the Palace pool; later that summer he ticked him off, in front of a crowd of 20,000 people, for fidgeting at the Highland Games at Braemar. The prince was wearing his first kilt, of Balmoral tartan – to the Scots a sure sign that he was growing up. The nation received another sign of his maturity that summer, with the announcement that HRH Prince Charles of Edinburgh was soon to be sent away to board at a preparatory school.

Well aware that she herself had met few beyond the Palace walls before the age of eighteen, when she had persuaded her father to let her sign on as a second subaltern in the wartime ATS, the Queen was conscious of the disadvantages of sequestering her son at home. But she and her husband had equal evidence that it was no use expecting him to blend inconspicuously into the life of a boarding school, like any other child. Simpering royal commentators were already cooing that Charles and Anne were 'ordinary' children being brought up in a 'normal' way; but it was now obvious, even to their parents, that this was impossible.

'The Queen and I', said Philip, during a visit to the USA in 1956, 'want Charles to go to school with other boys of his generation and learn to live with other children, to absorb from childhood the discipline imposed by education with others.' The royal couple had already been making a series of visits, private and public, to British boys' schools, and had entertained a number of headmasters socially at Buckingham Palace. But Philip's announcement brought forth a predictable shower of advice.

In the forefront was the writer Lord Altrincham, whose attack on the monarchy in the August 1957 edition of his journal, the

National and English Review, earned him a televised slap in the face, excrement through his letterbox and lasting public obloquy. His title, which he later disclaimed, to revert to plain John Grigg, became synonymous with sedition; but it is now forgotten that Altrincham wrote as an ardent monarchist, protesting that he made his loyal criticisms in the Queen's own interests. There were few who bore this in increasingly apoplectic mind as they read how the monarchy had 'lamentably failed to live with the times', and that the court, unlike the society it was supposed to reflect, remained 'a tight little enclave of English ladies and gentlemen'.

The Queen's decision that her son would go to a private 'prep' school was another topic to which Altrincham addressed himself:

> Will she have the wisdom to give her children an education very different from her own? Will she, above all, see to it that Prince Charles is equipped with all the knowledge he can absorb without injury to his health, and that he mixes during his formative years with children who will one day be bus drivers, dockers, engineers etc., not merely with future landowners or stockbrokers?[6]

A minority of Labour MPs used Altrincham's strictures to renew their plea that the heir to the throne should attend a state school, to mix with the less wealthy and privileged of his future subjects as a symbolic beneficiary of the welfare state. But his parents were adamant: a boarding school, and a private one, it was to be. Charles was too young to be consulted about the choice of his first school, and had anyway made it more than clear that he was reluctant to leave home at all. Besides, his lack of self-confidence was 'so inhibiting that . . . [his] qualities were not yet easy to discern behind the carapace of diffidence and reserve with which he habitually protected himself'.[7]

The Queen and Prince Philip had looked over a number of preparatory schools, including the one Philip had himself attended. It had moved since the 1930s, and was scarcely the same place, but it seemed to provide everything they were looking for. Like many other conservative-minded British fathers, Philip found the idea of sending his son to his old school downright satisfying. He was also pleased of the chance to offer a posthumous salute to a favourite

ancestor. Just before the First World War, Prince Louis of
Battenberg, then First Sea Lord, had occasion to be impressed by
the polished manners of two midshipmen under his command. On
discovering that they were both ex-pupils of Cheam preparatory
school, the Duke of Edinburgh's grandfather decreed that henceforth all male members of the Battenberg family would go there.

Cheam claims to be England's oldest prep school, founded in
1645 'for the sons of noblemen and gentry'. Its long roll of headmasters included William Gilpin, the model for the schoolmaster in
Smollett's *The Adventures of Peregrine Pickle*, and one Robert
Stammers Tabor, who in the mid-nineteenth century devised
intriguing modes of address for the aristocratic pupils the school
has always attracted: a peer was called 'my darling child', the son
of a peer 'my dear child' and a commoner 'my child'.[8] Tabor would
have enjoyed working out a new category for the eight-year-old
pupil who joined the school on 23 September 1957: Charles, Duke
of Cornwall, the first heir apparent to have been sent to a preparatory school in British history. At his mother's request the joint
headmasters, Peter Beck and Mark Wheeler, continued the style
established at Hill House: the new pupil would be 'Charles' to his
fellow pupils and 'Prince Charles' to members of staff, whom he in
turn would address normally as 'Sir'.

The school's most distinguished old boy was the new recruit's
father, whose educational credo later prefaced its official history:
'Children may be indulged at home, but school is expected to be a
spartan and disciplined experience in the process of developing
into self-controlled, considerate and independent adults. The
system may have its eccentricities, but there can be little doubt that
these are far outweighed by its values.'[9] Philip's cousin, the
Marquess of Milford Haven, had also been there. Among other
former pupils were one prime minister, Henry Addington (later
Viscount Sidmouth); one speaker of the House of Commons; two
viceroys of India; Sir Iain Hamilton, military commander of the ill-
fated Gallipoli expedition; Lord Dunsany, the Irish writer; and
Lord Randolph Churchill, father of Sir Winston, who, according to
his son, was 'most kindly treated and quite contented' at the
school.[10]

Charles had already visited Cheam with his parents and his
sister. 'You won't be able to jump up and down on these beds,' his
mother had told him as he gazed with dismay upon the 200-year-

old springless wooden frame and its unyielding hair mattress. As the royal family roamed the school grounds, the peace disturbed only by jets from the nearby US airbase, they felt reassured that Cheam's sixty-five acres should offer due insulation from the outside world of sightseers and pressmen. Its copious undergrowth, however, would also provide excellent cover for intruders, so it was decided that the young prince's detective should accompany him and live in the grounds.

Before term the headmasters had sent a letter to all parents, noting the 'great honour' Charles's parents had conferred on Cheam, while passing on their wish that there be 'no alteration in the way the school is run'. Charles was to be treated in 'exactly the same way as other boys'.[11] Again, however, it was impossible to expect Charles to merge inconspicuously into the beginning-of-term throng. As a young man, he remembered those first few days at Cheam as the most miserable of his life. His mother recalls him shaking with horror as they began the long overnight train journey from Balmoral to London, to be followed by the sixty-mile drive to Headley. On arrival, in his grey school uniform, Charles raised his blue school hat politely to Mr Beck, then watched his parents drive away. A few hours later the maths master, David Munir, who had been detailed to keep a special eye on the prince, looked out into the school grounds. One small boy, 'very much in need of a haircut', stood conspicuously apart, a solitary and utterly wretched figure.[12]

Cheam boys were that much older than Charles's fellow pupils at Hill House. Despite – perhaps because of – their parents' urgings, they simply could not accept the heir to the throne as just another of the twelve new boys. Charles himself had no experience at all of forcing his way into a group of strangers and winning the acceptance of his peers. For his first few nights at Cheam he cried himself to sleep. Like most other boys sent away to school at so tender an age, he was desperately homesick.

Cheam had 100 pupils between the ages of eight and fourteen; Charles's school number was eighty-nine. For the first time in his life he was sharing an uncarpeted room with other boys, making his own bed, cleaning his own shoes, waiting on others at table and keeping his clothes in a wicker basket under his bed (known to the boys as 'the dog basket'). The day began at 7.15 a.m. with the rising bell, followed by Matron's cleanliness inspection, prayers at

7.45 and breakfast at eight. Lessons began at nine, and continued with one break until lunch at one. There were half-holidays on Wednesdays and Saturdays, and on Sundays there was an extra half-hour in bed before the school parade to the nearby parish church of St Peter's.

Charles wrote the obligatory minimum of one letter home per week, and was always among the first to snap up his weekly half-pound allowance of sweets. Though he was losing his puppy fat, he was still a plumpish boy. When the change to the school diet prompted a few stomach upsets, he confided to his first-year teacher, Miss Margaret Cowlishaw, that he wasn't used to 'all this rich food' at home.

According to Peter Beck, Charles's unwonted need to fend for himself soon helped him become a good mixer. In fact, Charles's loneliness may have been partly in his own mind. He was already aware that other children might befriend him for the wrong reasons. It was often the nicest boys, he recalls, who hung back, not wishing to be seen to be 'sucking up' to him; those who forced their attentions on him were often those he liked least. His peers soon marked him down as a bit of a lone wolf – a description he would not himself deny. He seemed happier on his own or with just one other person rather than as part of a group. By his own account and that of others, he did not find it easy to make friends.[13]

As a schoolboy, furthermore, Charles was haunted by another shadow which has pursued him ever since: that of his father, an outgoing, gregarious man who had never had to cope with such problems. At Cheam, after all, Philip was Prince of Greece and Denmark, not of England or Wales. The press were not pursuing him from bush to bush, and the boys looked on him with no awe. While academically undistinguished, Philip had shone on the sports field – First XI goalkeeper and captain of the cricket team – and Charles knew all too well that his father was looking for similar achievements from him.

The prince's lessons at Cheam were geared to the Common Entrance exam taken before admission to most British public schools (although, as it transpired, he was to attend one that didn't require it). History remained an abiding interest, not least because he now knew that it largely concerned his ancestors, and was uneasily aware that it might be waiting to receive him. In geography he also shone, again because his parents' tours had made the globe a familiar place. Maths remained an utter mystery, closely followed by Latin and Greek. Before the afternoon lessons there were games, about which he remained unenthusiastic – despite evidence to the contrary in his end-of-term reports – or other outdoor activities, such as camping or wildlife study.

As at Hill House, the gym became one of his favourite haunts, where athletic rough-and-tumble often developed into a mild schoolboy fracas. Charles soon had a reputation for giving as good as he got. He was particularly sensitive to jokes about his plumpness, and took days to recover after hearing the boy beneath a collapsed rugby scrum cry, 'Oh, do get off, Fatty.' The school was visited regularly by a barber from Harrods, Cecil Cox, who once saw an older boy douse Charles's head under a cold tap; the visitor watched impressed as the prince filled a bath with cold water, wrestled with his assailant and finally forced him in fully clothed, only to be pulled in himself.

This was one of many Cheam anecdotes, some truer than others, which found their way into the press during Charles's first term. 'Even the school barber was in the pay of the newspapers,' snorted Prince Philip.[14] It did not help the 'normality' of Charles's education, or his standing among his peers, that all too often there had to be complex inquiries before school crimes, apparently to be laid at his door, were found to be the work of others. Within a week of his arrival, for instance, Charles's name had been carved in the back of a pew in the parish church. This was one story the papers did get hold of; with help from the Palace, Beck persuaded them to print corrections when other boys eventually admitted their guilt.

In an attempt to head off journalists' intrusions, Beck and Wheeler had held a press visit to the school before term began and made a special plea to be left in peace thereafter. But of the eighty-eight days of term, there were stories in one newspaper or another on sixty-eight. Again the effects were unpleasant, not least for the pupil at the centre of it all. Rumours abounded of boys and staff accepting bribes from pressmen. They were never proved true, but a tense atmosphere of mutual suspicion developed, and morale at the school began to suffer. Although the prince's detective coped with most intruders, there were occasionally more dramatic incidents. One night he aroused the headmaster after seeing a prowler on the roof of Charles's dormitory; a lengthy search was conducted, but no-one found. Only much later did a boy confess to getting back into bed seconds before the search party arrived. Even schoolboy pranks were becoming worthy of the police incident book. Once again, the Queen decided to safeguard her son's education, not to mention his sanity, by direct action.

In the Christmas holidays her press secretary invited all British newspaper editors to a meeting at Buckingham Palace. Peter Beck told the gathering of the disruption their employees were causing at his school. Bribes had been offered, though none, to his knowledge, had been accepted. Everyone felt themselves under constant surveillance. Charles's first term had ended unhappily for all, not least for the boy himself. Recalling the pleas he had made before and during Charles's time at Hill House, Colville spoke plainly to the editors. Either it stopped, and the press printed only stories of genuine significance, or the Queen would abandon her plan to educate her son outside the Palace, and withdraw him behind its walls and into the care of tutors. History would record that the failure of the great royal education experiment had been entirely the fault of the press.

Years later, it would become apparent that this moral blackmail of the press was somewhat unfair on the Palace's part. If Charles had been withdrawn from Cheam, it would really have been because he was 'utterly miserable' there. As the Queen wrote to her former prime minister, Sir Antony Eden, early in 1958: 'Charles is just beginning to dread the return to school next week. So much worse for the second term!'[15]

Six months later, Charles's mother herself brought down blanket press coverage on her nine-year-old son's head. It was the summer term of 1958, the end of Charles's first year at Cheam, and the Commonwealth Games were being held in Cardiff. The Queen had been due to perform the closing ceremony at Cardiff Arms Park on 26 July, but a sinusitis operation enforced her absence. Her husband took her place and introduced a tape-recorded message from the monarch, which was played over the loudspeakers of the packed stadium.

Charles and a few friends, who had filed into Peter Beck's study to watch the event on television, heard the Queen's disembodied voice say:

I want to take the opportunity of speaking to all Welsh people, not only in this arena, but wherever they may be. The British Empire and Commonwealth Games in the capital, together with all the festivities of the Festival of Wales, have made this a memorable year for the principality. I have therefore decided to mark it further by an act which will, I hope, give as much pleasure to all Welshmen as it does to me.

There was a buzz of anticipation as many in the arena had guessed what she was going to say: 'I intend to create my son Charles Prince of Wales today.' The tape had to be stopped as an enormous cheer convulsed the stadium and 36,000 Welsh voices broke into 'God bless the Prince of Wales'. When the clamour died down, the Queen's voice continued: 'When he is grown up, I will present him to you at Caernarfon.'[16]

The scene in Beck's study at Cheam might have given her a moment's pause. The headmaster, who had known what was coming, watched a look of dire unease cloud the prince's face as the other boys spontaneously joined in the clapping and cheering. Charles himself remembers being 'acutely embarrassed . . . I think for a little boy of nine it was rather bewildering. All the others turned and looked at me in amazement. And it perhaps didn't mean all that much then; only later on, as I grew older, did it become apparent what it meant.'[17]

For a mother trying to bring up her son as far as possible like other boys, aware that his own emergent character was far from self-confident and far from mastering its environment, it was an odd piece of timing. The Queen has since confessed that she now numbers this moment among the few mistakes she made in Charles's upbringing.[18]

In the headmaster's study that afternoon Charles also automatically became Earl of Chester and Knight Companion of the Most Noble Order of the Garter. They go, as it were, with the job. The earldom of Chester is the oldest of all the dignities of the heir to the throne, dating from 1254, when it was bestowed on the future Edward I. Since then it has always been conjoined with the title of Prince of Wales, though both, unlike the dukedom of Cornwall, are life peerages, which merge into the Crown when their holder becomes monarch, to be bestowed at his discretion upon his eldest son.

The monarch and the Prince of Wales are the only two ex officio of the twenty-six Knights of the Garter, Europe's oldest order of chivalry. Reflecting that her son was still young for his years, Elizabeth decided that it was too soon for the formal ceremony installing Charles in his Garter stall at Windsor; this ancient ritual was, in fact, to wait ten years, by which time it was part of the build-up to another major ordeal – his investiture as Prince of Wales at Caernarfon – and thus his emergence into full-time public life.

Those days remained mercifully distant as Charles enjoyed his summer holidays at Balmoral before continuing his steady if undistinguished progress at Cheam. 'He is still a little shy,' his first end-of-term report read, 'but very popular . . . passionately keen on and promising at games . . . academically, a good average.' Beck later summed up with the verdict that the prince was above average in intelligence, but only average in attainment. By this he did not mean that the boy was bright but idle; he was pointing out the natural advantage Charles possessed in general knowledge. The new Prince of Wales was much better informed about the outside world and its ways than his contemporaries. By this time, after all, he had met many of the people who ran it, and engaged them in polite conversation.

This strange species of maturity, fostered by the formal conduct around him at home, also meant that Charles spoke and wrote the Queen's English with above-average clarity and style, at times tending to a precocious use of long words. In other ways, he was much less mature than his fellows, and remained so for many years. But he joined with a will in many of the school entertainments devised by David Munir; like his mother, who with her sister had starred in the wartime Windsor pantomimes, he seemed to find such enforced public display one method of conquering his shyness. In a way, it was an apt preparation for many of the more bizarre public roles required of royalty.

One such Cheam production certainly was: a Shakespeare compilation under the title 'The Last Baron', which told the tale of the Duke of Gloucester, later King Richard III. The time-honoured understudy's dream came true when the boy cast as Richard fell ill and Charles hurriedly took over the part. In front of an audience of parents, he had to deliver with due gravity such lines as, 'And soon may I ascend the throne.' The drama critic of the *Cheam School Chronicle* wrote, 'Prince Charles played the traditional Gloucester with competence and depth; he had a good voice and excellent elocution, and very well conveyed the ambition and bitterness of the twisted hunchback.'[19]

The Queen was not in the audience that night, 19 February 1960, as she had been the previous Christmas for her son's minor début in a Munir entertainment called *Ten Little Cheam Boys*. The headmaster interrupted the performance to come onstage and announce that Richard III's mother had given birth to another son, Prince Andrew. Cheam staff were accustomed to boys being somewhat dashed by the news of the arrival of a younger sibling. They were struck by Charles's delight at having a baby brother and the almost excessive enthusiasm with which he relayed the latest news from home – evidence to the teachers who now knew him well that he would always be much happier in the protective bosom of his family. As Mabel Anderson said of Charles, 'He felt family separation very deeply. He dreaded going away to school.'[20]

His only link with home was the unlikely figure of his detective, DC Reg Summers, who provided a reassuring presence around the school grounds and behind the Sunday crocodile to church. Though the Queen largely resisted the temptation to call her son home for royal occasions, a special dispensation was granted that summer for him to attend the wedding, in Westminster Abbey, of his aunt Margaret to the photographer Antony Armstrong-Jones (later ennobled as the Earl of Snowdon).

The Queen visited her son no more frequently – three times a term – than other parents, and asked for no special privileges beyond cameras being put away in her presence. Princess Anne enjoyed coming for the annual sports day and always entered the younger sisters' race, unfortunately achieving no higher a position than fourth. But she could take comfort in her brother's generally undistinguished record on the sports field. Never much of a team player, Charles was bored by cricket, although he eventually made the First XI, and not the most mobile of rugger players. 'They always put me in the second row,' he complained, 'the worst place in the scrum.'

His reluctant best was soccer, and in his last year at Cheam he was made captain of the First XI. Unhappily, the team lost every match that season, with a final tally of four goals scored against their opponents' eighty-two. This time, the *Cheam School Chronicle* was not so kind: 'At half,' wrote the soccer coach, 'Prince Charles seldom drove himself as hard as his ability and position demanded.'[21]

Looking back, the staff remember Charles primarily for his uncertainty of himself and for a few little incidents that showed promise of the reflective man in the making. 'Most of the time,' said one of Charles's teachers, 'he was very quiet. He never spoke out of turn. Sometimes his voice was so low that it was difficult to hear him. But he was a boy who preferred action to noise. When there was a task to do, he got on with it quietly. No fuss.' David Munir remembered once catching Charles downstairs, finishing off his daily chores, when he should long since have been in bed. Munir warned him that he would get into trouble with Matron. 'I can't help that, sir,' the boy replied. 'I must do my duties.'[22]

Charles's extreme gentility was particularly marked on the football field, where he caused amusement by his habit of apologizing chivalrously to anyone he felled with a perfectly proper tackle. But it was endearing to find him so embarrassed by the standard prayer for the royal family, including the Prince of Wales, at Sunday morning service in St Peter's. 'I wish', he said, 'they prayed for the other boys, too.' He took his corporal punishment with the self-discipline of one who would rather get things over with. 'I am one of the people for whom corporal punishment actually worked,' he said years later. 'We had two headmasters [who] took turns at beating us . . . I didn't do it again.'[23] On at least one occasion, his crime was experimentation with cigarettes in the Cheam hedgerows – the beginning of a lifelong aversion to smoking.

By the end of his time at Cheam, despite such unnerving distractions as an IRA plot to kidnap him, which had the school grounds swarming with police, Charles had emerged a thoroughly average pupil. That he was made head boy says more about his standing in the outside world than within the school itself, although his good manners and sense of decorum may in themselves have been cause enough. In the holidays, meanwhile, his father encouraged his enthusiasm for field sports. From taking him out shooting to teaching him to drive a Land-Rover while still only twelve, Philip was intent on advancing his son beyond his years. At Christmas 1958 they went off on their first expedition together, to a coot shoot at Hickling Broad, near Sandringham. It turned into a minor rite of passage when their rented bungalow was flooded, and the royal pair caused some local excitement by applying for a room at the nearby Pleasure Boat Inn.

That same Christmas, Charles toured the British Sugar Corporation plant in King's Lynn – his first look inside a factory, and his first solo public engagement. His parents were pleased with his progress, if concerned about his continuing shyness and lack of self-confidence, especially in contrast with his sister. In the spring of 1962, in his father's absence abroad, the Queen asked Charles to take Philip's place as host at one of the luncheon parties she had introduced as a way of meeting a broader cross-section of her subjects. The thirteen-year-old prince, earnest for his years, held his own in conversation with a dozen guests, including the editor of the *Church Times*, an industrialist, a trade-union leader, a choreographer and the chairman of the BBC.

While at Cheam, Charles had disposed of a number of childhood's other chores: his first broken bone (his ankle, falling down the school stairs), measles, chickenpox and his appendix. But the school had never quite won his wholehearted enthusiasm. The jolt of leaving home bequeathed bruises he still nursed. If he had grown accustomed to life away from home, he was still miserably aware that he was not, and never could be, one of the boys. Beck emphasized that 'the job of a preparatory school is what it says: to prepare and not to produce a finished product'.[24] But Charles had only just mastered his new environment when he was abruptly removed from it. Even his mother acknowledged, via the Arundel Herald of Arms, that 'his first few years at Cheam had been a misery to him'.[25] The last thing Cheam had prepared him for, in short, was an unwelcome translation even further from home, to the chilly wastes of the north of Scotland.

CHAPTER FOUR

'HE HASN'T RUN AWAY YET'

PRINCE CHARLES WAS 'A VERY SENSITIVE LITTLE BOY, VERY KIND, VERY
sweet', according to friends and relatives of his parents. But they
worried that the Queen was too distant a mother. 'She's not very
tactile. A child wants a mother to be emotional, hugged, kissed –
and that's not what the Queen is good at.' But if his mother was
'tough, totally unsentimental', his father could be brutal. 'Philip
misinterpreted Charles on many occasions. His attitude was based
on himself. Here was this child – he would have to make his way
in the world. People spoiled him. He needed to counteract the
spoiling.'[1]

At the age of thirteen Charles had little choice but to gratify his
father's whims by following in his footsteps. At twenty-one he felt
bound to justify it: 'He had a particularly strong influence, and it
was very good for me. I had perfect confidence in his judgement.'[2]
But bringing up Charles in Philip's mould was not a logical exercise. Where Philip was outgoing, Charles was introspective; where
Philip was gregarious, Charles was awkwardly sociable; and where
Philip had been an obscure European prince, of the kind not
unfamiliar to many British public schoolboys, Charles was the heir
to the British throne, the first to be sent away to any school, let
alone his father's remote alma mater on the Moray Firth. Charles's
fears that Gordonstoun sounded 'pretty gruesome' were confirmed
shortly before his arrival when Lord Rudolph Russell, son of the
Duke of Bedford, ran away from the school, declaring,
'Gordonstoun is no place for me.'

Was it the right choice of school for a shy and hesitant child, in most respects a late developer? Those involved in the decision, among them the Queen Mother, Lord Mountbatten and the Dean of Windsor, Dr Robin Woods, remained divided ever after. Charles himself, though he tactfully opined in later life that Gordonstoun had been 'good for me', absolutely hated the place.

The school has been painted as a remote spartan outpost providing some sort of Germanic assault course towards manhood. Its life is tough, to be sure, with an unusual emphasis on outdoor and physical attainment. Its pupils are drawn more heavily than those of most comparable schools from a curious mix of the old-school upper classes and the social-climbing self-made. But Gordonstoun's ideology is based on a rigorous ethical code, founded in pacifism – formulated in the wake of the First World War by Prince Max of Baden, last chancellor of the Kaiser's Imperial Germany, and refined by his private secretary and disciple, Kurt Hahn. It may provide a more eccentric, narrowly aristocratic education than most other British public schools, but Gordonstoun parents are well aware of what they are letting their sons in for.

The school is modelled on that founded in 1920 by Prince Max in his castle-monastery at Salem, on the north shore of Lake Constance, in southern Germany. Max, who had been intimately involved in the collapse of Germany, set himself the personal task of rebuilding his nation's manhood. 'Let us train soldiers,' he said, 'who are at the same time lovers of peace.' The prince was given to somewhat grandiose statements, which he expected Hahn to put into effect as the school's first headmaster: 'Build up the imagination of the boy of decision and the will-power of the dreamer, so that in future wise men will have the nerve to lead the way they have shown, and men of action will have the vision to imagine the consequences of their decisions.'

In the Germany of the 1930s, after the death of Prince Max, Hahn was accused of anglicizing German education. He also happened to have been born Jewish. In 1933, when Hitler took power, he was arrested and the school closed. He took up an uncompromising stand, calling on all old boys active in the SA or SS to 'terminate their allegiance either to Hitler or to Salem'. The rise of Nazism made Hahn feel more urgently 'the need to educate young people in independence of judgement and in strength of purpose when following an unfashionable cause, to teach the protection of the weak, the recognition of the rights of the less fortunate, and the worth of a simple human life'.

On his release Hahn fled to England, where he fell ill. An Oxford friend invited him to recuperate on his estate in Morayshire, where he met up again with another university contemporary, Evan Barron, owner-editor of the *Inverness Courier*. When Hahn told them of his plans to recreate the Salem experiment in Britain, they took him to see the Gordonstoun estate, near Elgin. A lease was available on the eighteenth-century mansion house and its 300 acres. Hahn took it, and in the summer of 1934 opened the school with a clutch of masters and just thirty boys, among them Prince Philip.

Although the Gordonstoun philosophy was overtly based on that of Salem, Hahn added two significant new dimensions. One was to import from Germany the altruistic traditions of the Cistercian monks, who had ministered to the vicinity of Salem centuries before. The other was to counteract the scholastic emphasis of other British schools. 'I estimate', he said, 'that about sixty per cent of boys have their vitality damaged under the conditions of modern boarding schools.' His aim was 'to kindle on the threshold of puberty non-poisonous passions which act as guardians during the dangerous years'.

To protect his pupils from their increasingly urbanized home environments, he also wanted them to pit their young physical resources against the forces of nature on land and sea. Like Baden-Powell, he aimed to inspire a sense of purpose and self-reliance, aligned with one of duty and service. Boys, said Hahn, should be taught 'to argue without quarrelling, to quarrel without suspecting and to suspect without slandering'. Apart from a special concern for late developers – a boon to its new recruit – the school's purpose, enshrined in its motto, *Plus est en vous* ('There is more in you'), was not markedly different from the traditional British public school ideal.

But its methods were – as were the fees, higher even than Eton. Physical fitness was something of a cult; it remains so with the Prince of Wales to this day. Boys were frequently dispatched on testing expeditions, over land and water, designed to stretch initiative and physique to their limits. A sense of public service was instilled by joining in four local activities: fire fighting (the school's auxiliary service is a recognized branch of the Elgin fire service);

manning a coastguard station, complete with rockets and life-saving equipment; a mountain-rescue team, which has in its time saved climbers' lives; and an ocean-rescue team. Hahn introduced the Moray Badge as a selective reward for achievement in these fields. It proved the inspiration for the Duke of Edinburgh's own nationwide award scheme, whose silver medal Charles was to win in his last term.

Hahn's precepts are now as evident in Charles's beliefs and pronouncements as in his father's. It was a bold Prince of Wales, for instance, who suggested in 1987 that a form of compulsory community service might take the place of national service in Britain, the only European country in which it had been abolished. As the leader writers sharpened their pens, none traced the notion back to the immense influence of Kurt Hahn on both father and son. On the very day that it was announced that Charles was going to Gordonstoun, Hahn was delivering a lecture in Glasgow: 'A sick civilization', he said, 'is throwing up five kinds of young people: the lawless, the listless, the pleasure and sensation addicts, the angry young men and the honourable sceptics.' The antidotes were 'simple physical training, expedition training and rescue-service training'.[3]

Uncannily similar phrases can be found – increasingly, as he grows older – in many of Charles's own speeches. Back in 1962, with garbled versions of Hahn's philosophy and Gordonstoun's regime appearing in the British press, it was no wonder the teenage prince felt daunted. On a visit to the school with his parents, he found conditions even more spartan than at Cheam: unpainted dormitories with bare floorboards, naked lightbulbs and spare wooden bedsteads. Life appeared to be lived in huts, as exposed to the North Sea gales as were the boys' knees in their short trousers. Inside each pupil's locker was a chart, to be filled in each evening, with daily columns for 'Teeth Brushed, Rope Climbed, Skipping, Press-ups, Shower' etc. All in all, it was a cheerless place, leaving Charles distinctly unenthusiastic about what he called his 'imminent incarceration'.

Philip flew his son north on the first of May. The locals could tell they were coming; on the school gates stood naval guards with fixed bayonets, who required tradesmen (and parents) to produce passes to gain admission. The Queen's consort, not the new boy, was accorded an official welcome by the school's headmaster,

Robert Chew, a founder-member of Hahn's Gordonstoun staff, who had previously taught at Salem, flanked by the chairman of the governors, Captain Iain Tennant, and the head boy, Peter Paice. The only privilege accorded the new boy was a quiet lunch with his father and the headmaster before Philip left. He drove back to his aircraft at Lossiemouth, then flew over the school before heading south again, dipping his wings in a farewell salute to his son, who watched with sinking heart.

Charles's arrival at Gordonstoun, he remembers, was even more miserable than at Cheam. As he was shown to Windmill Lodge, the asbestos-roofed stone building he was to share with fifty-nine of the 400 other boys, the prospect seemed even worse than he had expected. One Gordonstoun old boy, the novelist William Boyd, has written with 'retrospective revulsion' of 'the concrete and tile washrooms and lavatories, the pale-green dormitories with their pale wooden beds'.[4] One of Charles's contemporaries, the journalist Ross Benson, reports that the windows were 'kept open throughout the night, which meant that those closest to them were likely to wake up with blankets rain-soaked or, in winter, covered with a light sprinkling of snow'.[5]

Not only had Charles been rudely yanked from the one external environment to which he had grown accustomed; all his dogged progress up the Cheam hierarchy had now come to naught. He was an unprivileged new boy again, at a school where the boys' older years altered their attitude to him. Where at Cheam he had found diffidence, at Gordonstoun he came up against adolescent malice. Boyd paints a vivid picture of a 'reign of terror', with gangs of marauding thugs 'beating up smaller boys' and 'extorting food and money'. New boys, according to Benson, were welcomed 'by taking a pair of pliers to their arms and twisting until the flesh tore open. In all the houses boys were regularly trussed up in one of the wicker laundry baskets and left under the cold shower, sometimes for hours'. Although apparently spared this indignity, Charles was immediately picked out for bullying 'maliciously, cruelly, and without respite . . . He was crushingly lonely for most of his time there'.[6]

The only boys he knew, apart from Lord Mountbatten's grandson, Norton Knatchbull, were his cousins Prince Welf of Hanover, whom he had recently visited with his father in Germany, and the exiled Prince Alexander of Yugoslavia. Even they, for befriending him in his first few days, were labelled 'bloodsucker' and 'sponge' by their contemporaries.

The Gordonstoun day began with the cry of the 'waker' at 7 a.m., followed by a run around the garden in shorts and singlet. Then came the first of the day's two cold showers; Charles and his fifty-nine housemates shared a washroom containing six showers and one bath. He had to make his own bed and clean his own shoes before breakfast. The rest of the new boys' day, in an official summary prepared for public consumption by the headmaster, went beyond the normal stint of classwork to 'a training break (running, jumping, discus- and javelin-throwing, assault course, etc.) under the Physical Training Master' and 'seamanship, or practical work on the estate'. They would also see active service as coast-guard watchers, sea cadets, army cadets and scouts, with the fire service, mountain rescue and/or surf life-saving teams.

When not occupied by this formidable schedule, boys were at liberty to wander at will around the countryside and down to the sea, though the nearby town of Elgin was strictly out of bounds. Charles eagerly took full advantage of this freedom; visitors noticed with interest that he tended to take them for walks round the countryside rather than show them round the school. He developed nodding acquaintanceships with the fishermen and shopkeepers of the village of Hopeman, and occasionally, but only occasionally, for fear of singling himself out, he accepted invitations to Sunday lunch or a day's shooting with family friends among the local worthies, such as Captain Tennant, who doubled as the Lord-Lieutenant of Morayshire.

Charles desperately wished he could use his position to bend the rules and escape more, but this would have involved braving the wrath of his father as much as the staff and fellow pupils. Conforming to the school regime, like any other underprivileged member of its society, was gradually to become claustrophobic. It was in the countryside that Charles preferred to relax; he didn't much enjoy school games, and he felt obliged to shun his peers' illicit activities in Elgin's Pete's Café.

But he quickly took to all maritime activities. He and Welf teamed up as a life-saving unit, receiving their proficiency certificates on Charles's fourteenth birthday in November 1962. One of his earliest exercises, a canoe expedition from Hopeman Beach to Findhorn Bay, turned ugly even by Gordonstoun standards when a storm blew up shortly after they were out at sea. The twelve-mile journey took all day, and the prince arrived back at school exhausted. In true British public-school spirit he recovered in time to go out to dinner that night with Captain Tennant, and mustered enough sang-froid to claim he was eager to repeat the adventure as soon as possible.

Other early duties included emptying the school dustbins and tidying up their trail of refuse. By the end of his first term Charles had qualified (in one of Gordonstoun's many unique hierarchical rituals*) to wear the standard school uniform of grey sweater and shorts, rather than the blue uniform that distinguished new boys. He also qualified for a ritual ducking, fully clothed, in yet another cold bath; but the prince was apparently spared this ordeal. It may seem strange that Gordonstoun boys hesitated to put the heir to the throne through a ritual humiliation; but Charles's limited success at 'blending in' – or, perhaps, the full extent of what he was up against – was soon evident from the testimony of one school-leaver, who was not slow to sell his story to a Sunday paper:

> How can you treat a boy as just an ordinary chap when his mother's portrait is on the coins you spend in the school shop, on the stamps you put on your letters home, and when a detective follows him wherever he goes? Most boys tend to fight shy of friendship with Charles. The result is that he is very lonely. It is this loneliness, rather than the school's toughness, which must be hardest on him.[7]

It was. 'It's near Balmoral,' his father told him. 'There's always the Factor there. You can go and stay with him. And your grandmother goes up there to fish. You can go and see her.'[8] Charles did, whenever he could. At Birkhall, her home on the Balmoral estate, the Queen Mother listened to Charles's plaintive outpourings about his loneliness, his homesickness, the impossibility of blending into school like other boys. She provided a sympathetic shoulder to cry on, often literally, and was especially moved by the

---

* Upward progress at Gordonstoun is a process so arcane that it may best be summarized by Prince Charles's graduation through all stages: School Uniform, Junior Training Plan, Senior Training Plan, White Stripe, Colour Bearer Candidate, Colour Bearer, Helper, Guardian. Colour Bearers (prefects) are elected by their fellows; from their number housemasters appoint Helpers (heads of houses), from whom the headmaster chooses the Guardian, or head boy.

gentle qualities of her late husband so evident in her favourite grandchild. More than either of Charles's parents, perhaps, his grandmother understood the ordeal of the quiet, uncertain child in a harsh and alien world. 'He is a very gentle boy, with a very kind heart,' she said, 'which I think is the essence of everything.' But she would not, as he asked, intercede with his parents to take him away from Gordonstoun. She would try, she said, to help him through a trial he must face. It was another early lesson in the duty which went with his birth.

Charles was utterly miserable, and did not hide the fact, even from a father unlikely to feel, let alone show, much sympathy. 'Well, at least he hasn't run away yet,' was all Prince Philip would say, asked how his son was getting on at Gordonstoun. At the end of Charles's first term, however, the headmaster was able to report to his parents that their son was 'well up . . . very near the top of his class'. The Christmas holidays, after family festivities at Sandringham, provided the first in a new and traumatic wave of trials-by-press. It was New Year 1963, and Charles travelled alone to Bavaria for a winter-sports break with his 'uncle', Prince Ludwig of Hesse, and his family. But the crowd of press photographers, which in turn attracted crowds of sightseers, ruined it for him. After two or three chaotic days in the resort of Tarasp, he was forced again to retire into an artificial world: the private slopes of the Hesse *Schloss*. Even there, he needed a bodyguard of Swiss police, themselves patrolling the property on skis.

His resentment was forgotten only the following summer, when a much greater ordeal overwhelmed him. The Cherry Brandy Incident, now a fondly remembered, mildly amusing milestone in Prince Charles's childhood to most Britons, was much more than that to the boy at the time. It upset him deeply, leaving scars which lasted several years – notably a bewildered mistrust of the press which has never left him, though it is now more contemptuous than bewildered.

On his arrival at Gordonstoun another appeal had been made for the press to leave him in peace:

> The added strain and burden of publicity upon a young boy of
> the Prince of Wales's age, on joining a public school for the first
> time, can readily be understood by all parents. For this reason,
> Her Majesty and His Royal Highness hope that editors

personally will be able to cooperate ... When publicity was
reduced at the end of the first term at Cheam School, it became
possible for the whole school to function in the normal way,
and therefore the Prince of Wales was able to receive a normal
education. This was only possible because neither he nor any of
the other boys and staff were subjected to publicity, which is
most unsettling and which, of course, singles His Royal
Highness out as different in the eyes of all other boys of the
school.[9]

By his third term at Gordonstoun Charles remained utterly unrec-
onciled to the place. 'It's absolute hell,' he wrote home,[10] but at
least press coverage of his progress was minimal. By then, June
1963, he had won further promotion within the school, entitling
him to more freedom of choice over outdoor training activities,
including expeditions aboard the school yacht, Pinta, one of which
took him to Stornoway, on the isle of Lewis, on Monday 17 June.
As usual his detective, Donald Green, accompanied the party of
Charles and four other boys ashore. Green went off to make
arrangements at the local cinema – Jayne Mansfield was to be the
subject of their scholastic attentions that evening – leaving the boys
to wait in the Crown Hotel. Once word of the prince's arrival got
around, a crowd quickly gathered, and Charles found a sea of faces
pressed against the hotel windows, peering and pointing at him.

> I thought 'I can't bear this any more' and went off somewhere
> else. The only other place was at the bar. Having never been
> into a bar before, the first thing I thought of doing was having
> a drink, of course. And being terrified, not knowing what to do,
> I said the first drink that came into my head, which happened
> to be cherry brandy, because I'd drunk it before when it was
> cold out shooting. Hardly had I taken a sip when the whole
> world exploded around my ears.[11]

Into the bar, as he took that first sip, had walked Frances
Thornton, a young freelance journalist known ever after to Charles
as 'that dreadful woman'. At fourteen, unknown to him, the Prince
of Wales was under the legal age for purchasing alcoholic liquor.
Within twenty-four hours the story had gone round the world.
Coming soon after other public criticisms – of Charles shooting his

first stag and 'invading the Lord's day' by skiing in the Cairngorms on a Sunday – it caused uproar. Even the Profumo Affair, the government sex scandal then at its height, could not keep the unfolding saga of Charles's misdemeanour off the front pages. To make matters worse, Buckingham Palace at first issued a denial, after misunderstanding Green's telephoned account of the incident. The following day, after further inquiries, the Palace press office was forced to retract the denial, thus keeping the story bubbling along. There followed the carpeting of Green by the Queen's senior detective and his subsequent resignation, while the entire nation felt entitled to discuss the question of suitable school punishment for Charles. Even *The Times* felt moved to inform its readers that the headmaster of Gordonstoun kept a cane in his study, at the ready, for just such moments.

As leading articles called on the head to act, Mr Chew summoned Charles to his study and withdrew his recent school promotion. It was a punishment much more devastating than the cane. Reduced to the ranks, Charles had again had his life complicated by undue and unwelcome attention. For so trivial an incident to have had so disproportionate an effect now seems absurd. The Queen was able to laugh it off; but Charles, though a more human and endearing figure to most newspaper readers, was thoroughly unsettled and unable to laugh about it for several years. When boys made puns on the name of the school yacht, *Pinta* – 'Drinka Pinta Milka Day' was then the Milk Marketing Board's popular slogan – he somehow failed to appreciate the joke.

As his Gordonstoun life grew more varied – a stint at HMS *Vernon*, the naval training camp at Portsmouth, his first archaeological digs around Morayshire, a bout of pneumonia after a fishing trip – he won his way back up the Junior Training Plan and further up the scale. A year later he proved something to himself and his family by passing five GCE O levels, in Latin, French, history, English language and English literature, though maths and physics still eluded his grasp. The summer of 1964 was a particularly happy one, at Balmoral and Cowes, with the bonus of an excursion to King Constantine's wedding in Athens, where Charles had the satisfaction of ducking a raftload of French photographers. By the time he returned to school that September, his life seemed to have found a new equilibrium. But it was very soon to turn sour again, as an exercise book went missing from his classroom.

This sort of thing had happened before: forgeries had been hawked around Fleet Street, and one genuine one, culled from a waste-paper basket, had turned out to be the work of another boy. Name tags from Charles's clothes had proved popular on the school's 'black market', and textbooks inscribed with his name had disappeared. These were the everyday realities of his 'normal' school life, with which he had learned to live, albeit uncomfortably. But this time the olive-green book in which Charles wrote his essays had been stolen from the pile on his form-master's desk. The headmaster issued an appeal for what he called 'a collector's item'.

It was too late: the book had already reached Fleet Street. A Gordonstoun boy (who was never identified) was reputed to have got £7 for it from an old boy, an officer cadet, who had then sold it on to a Scottish journalist for £100. Rumours of offers as high as £5,000 abounded in London until it was traced to St Helen's, Lancashire, and the offices of Terence Smith of the *Mercury Press*. It took Scotland Yard six weeks to get the book back, by which time the German *Der Stern*, the French *Paris-Match* and the American *Life* magazines all possessed photocopies. Convinced by the Scotland Yard seizure of the document's authenticity, *Stern* published the essays in full, in German, illustrated by the hand-written text in English, complete with the form-master's comment: 'Quite well-argued.' It was 'highly regrettable', said Buckingham Palace, 'that the private essays of a schoolboy should have been published in this way'.[12]

So it was; but it could have been much worse. Charles emerged with credit from worldwide exposure that would have daunted any schoolboy. Though published under the lurid headline THE CON-FESSIONS OF PRINCE CHARLES, what little the essays revealed showed the sixteen-year-old prince a liberal and original thinker, mature for his age. *Stern* managed to miss the point of the piece about which it got most excited: a dissertation on the corrupting effects of power. Its views were not those of the future King, but of the nineteenth-century historian William Lecky, a section of whose *History of England in the Eighteenth Century* the class had been told to précis.

The Times quoted with approval from another piece on the sub-ject of democracy. Charles professed himself 'troubled by the fact that the voters today tend to go for a particular party and not for the individual candidate, because they vote for the politics of a party'. He thought it wrong, for instance, that a below-par Conservative candidate should win votes simply because he toed the party line against nationalization or the abolition of public schools. In another essay, on the press, he emerged from his recent ordeals surprisingly unsoured, arguing that a free press was essential in a democratic society 'to protect people from the government in many ways, to let them know what is going on – perhaps behind their backs'.

A fourth essay was a ten-minute exercise to name the four items he would take to a desert island if – a sign of the times – evacuated during a nuclear crisis. Charles opted for a tent, a knife, 'lots of rope and string', and a radio, both to keep in touch with developments and to monitor any hope of rescue. He did add, with his now familiar archness, that such an emergency would have him 'in a frightful panic'.

The matter might have ended there, had not *Stern* thought of adding a last, gratuitous passage: 'Prince Charles became short of pocket money at Gordonstoun at the end of August. It then occurred to him that some collectors paid good money for original hand-written manuscripts and sold the work to a schoolmate for thirty shillings.' *Time* magazine decided to follow up this intriguing titbit, and the following week published its version of the saga under the headline THE PRINCELY PAUPER. Now the Palace lost patience and issued one of its extremely rare denials. Colville wrote to *Time*:

> There is no truth whatsoever in the story that Prince Charles sold his autograph at any time. There is also no truth whatever in the story that he sold his composition book to a classmate. In the first place he is intelligent and old enough to realize how embarrassing this would turn out to be, and second, he is only too conscious of the interest of the press in anything to do with himself and his family. The suggestion that his parents keep him so short of money that he has to find other means to raise it is also a complete invention. Finally, the police would not have attempted to regain the composition book unless they were quite satisfied that it had been obtained illegally.

Far from printing a retraction, the editors of *Time* headlined the letter MONEYED PRINCE CHARLIE, with the rider, 'The royal family's press officer mounts a princely defence in his belated offer to clarify the case.'[13]

Charles's national notoriety did nothing to endear him to the school bullies. During his second year he was still pleading for release from the 'hell' that was Gordonstoun. Charles's letters home about his night-time ordeals, and his suffering at the hands of the 'foul' people in his dormitory, make grim reading. He complained that he had slippers thrown at him, and was hit with pillows and punched at all hours of the night. He hated the school, which he called a 'HOLE', and his school fellows. He longed to go home.[14]

For the first, if by no means the last, time in his life, Charles was also subjected to merciless teasing about his large and prominent ears. Mountbatten had already urged his parents to get Charles's ears 'fixed', bluntly telling the boy, 'You can't possibly be King with ears like that.' But nothing had been done. Now he found himself the mortified victim of newspaper cartoonists as much as his Gordonstoun contemporaries. In the most affecting terms, he bemoaned the bad manners of his contemporaries, who had the 'foulest natures' he had ever come across. He was stunned to find that people like them existed.[15]

The school rules were widely ignored. Smoking and drinking, even openly in the pubs of Elgin, were as 'commonplace' as pilfering from the local shops, even 'joy riding' in 'borrowed' cars. All mention of sex was taboo at Gordonstoun, naturally encouraging a thriving trade in pornographic magazines, sexual banter 'of the vilest and coarsest sort' and 'male lust at its most dog-like and contemptuous' when it came to the local girls, including 'consenting kitchen maids'.[16] Ever the innocent, and already rather priggish about the ways of his contemporaries, Charles does not seem to have got involved. Far from cavorting in Elgin with his peers, Charles was even shocked by their 'horrid' language, which he attributed to lazy-mindedness.[17]

The following month, March 1964, saw the birth of another brother for Charles, Prince Edward. The Gordonstoun inmate tried to use it as an excuse to escape for a few days. His hopes that his mother would ask the headmaster to let him return to London to meet his new brother proved vain. But that autumn offered a different diversion from Gordonstoun's routine strains in the shape of a 'mock' election – a common practice in many British schools – to coincide with the general election of October 1964. Charles was to be seen wearing a Scottish Nationalist Party rosette around Gordonstoun, and speaking vehemently in favour of devolution. When one opponent gently reminded him that he was Prince of Wales, he cried, 'Independence for Wales, too! That's for the next election!' It is a measure of the background of British public schoolboys that the Conservative Party romped home with 140 votes; the Scottish Nationalists polled 129; but Labour, with a mere sixteen votes, trailed way behind the Liberals and the Irish Independents, at a time when the party was winning its first British general election for thirteen years.

The Christmas holidays were marked by the delivery to Windsor Castle of a 'beat group kit' – an electric guitar with amplifier, and an electric organ – to complement Charles's 'much-worn' Beatle wig; at this early stage of his life, he was not yet entirely immune to the tastes of his contemporaries. After New Year at Sandringham, he and Anne were again dogged by the press on a skiing holiday in Liechtenstein. Through his hosts, Prince Franz Josef and Princess Gina, he reached an accommodation with the photographers, who were mostly foreign; British editors were still attempting to respect the Queen's wishes. They would be welcome on the slopes in the afternoons if they would leave him alone in the mornings. To universal surprise, it seemed to work, and he was able to continue his progress towards becoming the proficient skier he is today.

Back at Sandringham it was the usual round of field sports, in unusually severe winter weather. 'The whole family', said Miss Anderson, 'goes out in weather most would think mad.' That Easter, Charles was due to be confirmed at Windsor. Though his young seriousness took on, for the first time, a contemplative air which today is very familiar, the episode is primarily remembered for the attitude of his father, who took a dim view of the entire proceedings.

Prince Philip thought his son too young, at sixteen, for solemn acceptance into the Church of England, and had indeed been undergoing a period of doubt about his own religious beliefs. Philip's tortured progress from the Greek Orthodoxy of his childhood through Salem's German Protestantism to the formal Anglicanism of his adopted life had bred a disenchantment, even a cynicism; there had been a time, though he had now in middle age reverted to Anglican orthodoxy, when he had classed himself agnostic, perhaps even atheist. Again, Charles was in a different mould. During pre-confirmation talks with the Dean of Windsor, Robert Woods, he displayed a sound grasp of his undertakings – and his faith, while becoming more complex, has not wavered since. His father, at the time, was intent on making his protest felt, and considered the then Archbishop of Canterbury, Dr Michael Ramsey, a very tiresome preacher. Throughout his son's confirmation service in St George's Chapel, Windsor, Philip conspicuously read a book. 'Come and have a drink,' said Woods to Ramsey afterwards. 'Thank you,' said the outraged Archbishop. 'Bloody rude, that's what I call it.'[18]

Charles's progress at Gordonstoun had been interrupted by only one recall to London on official duty that year, for the state funeral of Sir Winston Churchill. He was nearing the end of his fourth year, had advanced from Senior Training Plan to Colour Bearer (prefect), and had finally managed to satisfy the O level examiners of a modest grasp of mathematics. He had graduated from piano to trumpet, taking part in several concerts in Elgin town hall and St Giles's Cathedral, Edinburgh. He had also enjoyed his first taste of two contradictory passions, polo and the cello, only the first of which was to prove enduring. He was to crown his last full year at the school with boldness in a field in which his father had never shone. For the school play at Christmas 1965, Charles undertook the role of Shakespeare's Macbeth; thirty years before, Prince Philip had qualified only for the role of an attendant lord.

The production was to be directed by Eric Anderson, a new arrival from Fettes School in Edinburgh – where he had recently directed the future prime minister, Tony Blair, as Mark Antony in *Julius Caesar*. Later headmaster of Eton and rector of Lincoln College, Oxford, Anderson and his wife Poppy were to become close lifelong friends of the prince, sharing his secrets with a sensitivity apparent from their first encounter. On his arrival at Gordonstoun the previous year, Anderson had pinned up a notice seeking volunteers for a production of *Henry V*. At auditions, in his view, the best candidate for the title role was the Prince of Wales. But Anderson was reluctant to take such a risk with the prince's fragile self-confidence; the production would be attended by the Morayshire squirearchy, and any embarrassment might well reach the press. After talking it over with his wife, he had instead cast the prince in the lesser role of Exeter. Twelve months on, Anderson decided that the prince had matured enough for them both to take the risk of a truly royal Macbeth.

Charles took the part very seriously, treating his six weeks of research into the character as a further expedition into those realms of human nature explored at the time of his confirmation. A fortnight after their son's seventeenth birthday, his parents flew north to see Charles strut and fret his few hours in the Gordonstoun art department's re-creation of Glamis Castle (ancestral home of his maternal grandmother's family, the Strathmores). A schoolboy's photo of the false-bearded prince performing the famous dagger soliloquy went around the world, swelling the coffers of the school's Photographic Society.

Anderson deemed it necessary to make one small amendment to Shakespeare's text. Out of consideration for the Queen, it was decided to dispense with the stage direction 'Enter Macduff, with Macbeth's head.' Otherwise, Charles's satanic thane stoutly endured the eloquent nagging of fourteen-year-old Douglas Campbell as Lady Macbeth, and raised an inappropriate laugh only when the three witches cried, 'All hail, Macbeth, that shalt be King hereafter!' The *Gordonstoun Record* did him proud:

> Prince Charles was at his very best in the quiet poetic solilo-quies, the poetry of which he so beautifully brought out, and in the bits which expressed Macbeth's terrible agony of remorse and fear. In the second part of the play, he equally well expressed the degenerative hardening of Macbeth's character, the assumption of cynicism in an attempt to blunt the underly-ing and too painful moral sensitivity.

A local triumph, it was the high point of a year during which school life had become, after those early trials, merely monoton-ous. That Christmas, the question of a university career was already under discussion in royal circles. Charles had not yet com-pleted his span at Gordonstoun; but he was in the mood for a change, the familiar mood of school-leavers who take a year out in the wide world between school and university. As this would not be available to him, his parents for once agreed that his position

might now be used to afford him a privilege allowed few other
schoolboys. On condition that he would return to Gordonstoun to
finish the work he had begun there, he could take a break at a
school somewhere in the Commonwealth.

During her coronation tour of Australia, the Queen had promised
that she would 'send my son to visit you too, when he is older'. The
promise seemed long overdue in that autumn of 1965, when the
Australian prime minister, Robert Menzies, seized the chance of a
visit to London to persuade the Queen that the ideal choice would
be Geelong Grammar School – the so-called 'Eton of Australia'
near Melbourne, in his own state of Victoria. It was the Australian
high commissioner, Sir Alexander Downer, himself a Geelong old
boy, who suggested the idea of Timbertop, Geelong's mountainside
outpost 200 miles to the north of Melbourne and 2,000 feet above
sea level, in the remote but accessible foothills of the Victorian
Alps.

All Geelong boys undergo a year of exercise and 'self-reliance' at
Timbertop, which at first made Charles fear that it sounded like an
Australian Gordonstoun. In fact, the school's philosophy is far less
heavy-handed, more homespun. By self-reliance, Geelong meant
literally that: there was a handful of masters *in loco parentis*, but
the boys were mainly younger ones in the care of their seniors, who
would appeal to the staff only in the event of emergency. Theirs
was a rural life of comparative self-sufficiency, each boy having
considerable freedom to spend his time as he pleased. It was above
all an exercise in getting to know people and displaying leadership
qualities, from which the young Prince of Wales, still far from sure
of himself, could only benefit. Being of the age of the older boys,
he would undertake the responsibility of having a younger group
in his care. Unlike his fellows, he would have to spend some time
working for his GCE A levels in history and French, scheduled for
his return to Gordonstoun, but the rest of the time would be more
or less his own, in fine fishing and walking countryside. Though
made famous by Neville Shute in *The Far Country*, the gum-tree
forests around Mount Timbertop were otherwise relatively
uncharted territory.

In December 1965 Charles had received a letter at Gordonstoun
from a man he knew well, his father's equerry, thirty-five-year-old
Squadron Leader David Checketts, who had been chosen to escort

him to Australia. 'You are probably, and quite naturally, apprehensive about going to Australia, and if I can be of any help with
any doubts or fears you might have, please let me know. I give you
my word they will go no further than me.' Though hand-picked for
the role by Philip, Checketts clearly knew of the tensions between
father and son, and was going to kindly pains to reassure Charles
that he would be more approachable, and more sympathetic to
doubts and fears. 'I couldn't be more delighted to be going with
you,' he added, 'and sincerely hope you will feel free to ask me any
questions and for any advice or help, which, unless you wish
otherwise, will remain purely between us.'[19] Again, Charles could
be in no doubt that it was not the press to whom Checketts was
referring, but his father. The boy need be in no fear that any signs
of human frailty would be relayed home.

Charles flew out to Australia with Checketts at the end of
January 1966. Though just seventeen, he had still not entirely conquered his fear of new, unknown situations, and again remembers
feeling highly apprehensive. He had heard that Australians were
'critical' and expected a mixed reception. Even more unnervingly,
it was his first trip abroad without either of his parents, though he
had reassuring company in the shape of Checketts and Detective
Inspector Derek Sharp.

A former public relations man with a distinguished RAF record,
Checketts was to prove a mainstay of Charles's life for the next
thirteen years. He set up home with his wife and family at Devon
Farm, 120 miles from Timbertop, and acted as a kind of business
manager to the prince. The farm became a headquarters for dealing with press enquiries, and for entertaining Charles over many a
down-to-earth weekend. The prince would muck in like a member
of the family, making his own bed, coming down to breakfast in his
dressing gown, doing his share of the household chores and acting
as an elder brother to the Checkettses' young children. It was the
beginning of a lasting friendship; in time Checketts was to become
his equerry, and later his first private secretary.

Checketts has said of those seven months in Australia, 'I went
out there with a boy and came back with a man.'[20] Many others,
including Charles himself, have since testified that this was the
period in which he at last shed his perennial burden of 'late
development' and grew into manhood. If the Australian public at
first received him warily, it was the acceptance of his schoolmates

Lord Mountbatten, his 'honorary grandfather', was the mainstay of the young Charles, briefly bearded like his great-grandfather, King George V.

'Sowing wild oats': Pre-marital girlfriends Lady Jane Wellesley (*above*), Davina Sheffield (*opposite*, *above*) and Lady Sarah Spencer, sister of his wife-to-be.

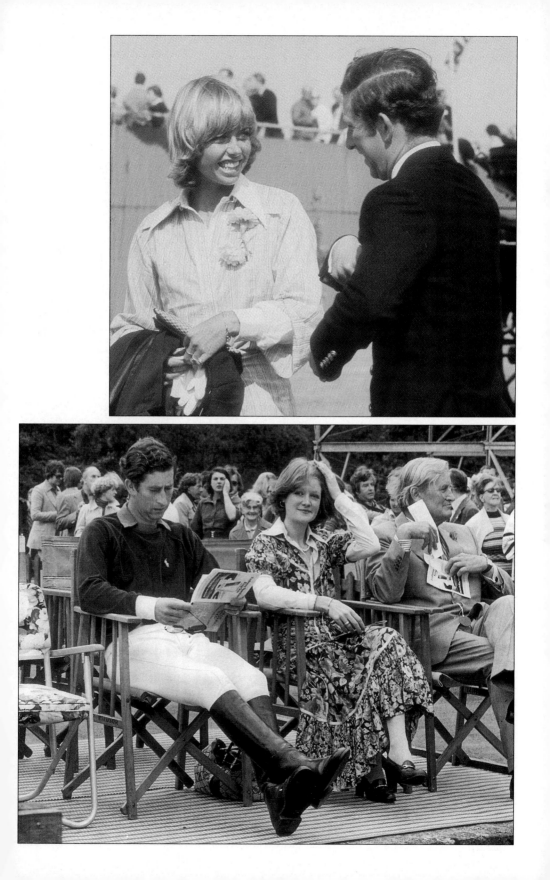

'My great-grandmother was your great-great-grandfather's mistress – so how about it?' said Camilla Parker Bowles (with Charles, *below*) of Edward VII and Mrs Alice Keppel (*above*).

'Whatever love means,' said Charles at the announcement of his engagement to Lady Diana Spencer in February 1981.

'Don't worry, it will get a lot worse,' Princess Grace of Monaco told Diana at her first public engagement at Goldsmiths Hall in the City of London. Before they arrived, Charles had upset Diana by declaring her low-cut black dress unsuitable for a member of the royal family.

The 'fairytale' wedding at St Paul's on 29 July 1981 was sealed by the first kiss ever seen on the balcony of Buckingham Palace.

(*Opposite*) While Charles was courting Diana, he introduced her to his close friend Camilla Parker Bowles.

'To this day, you know – vivid memory,' said Diana of the sight of Camilla Parker Bowles among the VIP guests at her wedding (*above*).

Diana's bulimia grew worse on the honeymoon aboard *Britannia*, when pictures of Camilla fell out of Charles's diary.

The couple's apparent marital bliss at Balmoral (*overleaf*) was already a tragic sham.

early September, for the annual centrepiece of the Windsors' ten-week summer holiday, the Highland Games at Braemar. The pace of Charles's pursuit was suddenly intense and relentless.

'Intimidated' by the atmosphere at Cowes, where all the other guests, including Charles's friends, seemed so much older than her, and all of them, this time, were over her 'like a rash', Diana confessed herself 'terrified' of her début at Balmoral, which amounted to a thinly disguised royal inspection of Charles's latest potential bride. Meeting the Queen, she said in retrospect, was 'no big deal'; she had been 'around the royals' since childhood. But she wanted to 'get it right'. So she knew, unlike Sabrina Guinness, not to sit in Queen Victoria's chair.

But the ordeal was nonetheless unnerving, so she was delighted to be able to stay not in the main house but with her sister Jane, whose husband Robert now enjoyed the use of a grace-and-favour cottage on the estate. In a prim twentieth-century version of courtly love, Charles would telephone each morning to suggest a walk or a picnic, and Diana found herself having a 'wonderful' time. Other house-guests that weekend included the prince's skiing friend Charles Palmer-Tomkinson and his wife, Patty, who recalled being 'particularly taken' by the carefree young Diana:

> We went stalking together, we got hot, we got tired, she fell into a bog, she got covered in mud, laughed her head off, got puce in the face, hair glued to her forehead because it was pouring with rain ... she was a sort of wonderful English schoolgirl who was game for anything, naturally young but sweet and clearly determined and enthusiastic about him, very much wanted him.[7]

As Charles taught Diana to fish, and his brothers fought to sit next to her at dinner, the prince told his intimate circle that weekend that he did not yet love her, but felt that in time he might learn to. She was full of gaiety and good humour; she had no 'past'; she was young enough to be 'moulded' to the role of wife and mother according to the 'special needs' of his position; and, as her first love, he could have every reason to hope, as Mountbatten had once advised him, that he would also be her last. Charles began to take Diana very seriously, while she made no secret of her feelings for him. But these few days, less than two months since the spark had been ignited on that Sussex hay-bale, were to prove their last chance to get to know each other in private, free from public pressure.

Beside the river Dee one day that week, their idyll was suddenly shattered by the glint of a pair of high-powered Nikon binoculars. The indefatigable James Whitaker, whose self-imposed duty each summer was to perch himself all day on a rock above Balmoral to see what happened, had spotted the latest love interest in the life of his prime target. With a photographer in tow, he did some human stalking of his own, creeping ever closer to the coy couple on the riverbank until they themselves were spotted. Taking the initiative, significantly enough, Diana told Charles to go fishing alone while she hid behind a tree, cunningly using the mirror from her powder compact to track the journalists' movements while staying out of sight. Even Whitaker was impressed: 'She was very clever that day, much more so than any of his previous girlfriends.'8 Diana managed to make her escape incognito, by hiding her head in a scarf and Charles's cap while walking away through the trees. But it was only a matter of time before she was identified as the Prince of Wales's secret new love.

It was the end of the only private life Diana would ever know. Within days an army of reporters was camped on the doorstep of Coleherne Court, following her wherever she went in her red Mini Metro, pursuing her even to the Young England kindergarten, where eventually she was persuaded to let them take their first photograph of her – too innocent, as yet, to know that standing with her back to the sun would treat the world to its first close-up, through her ankle-length skirt, of her long and elegant legs. 'I knew your legs were good, but I didn't realize they were that good,' Charles teased her. 'But did you really have to show them to everybody?'9

These few tender words amounted to the only encouragement, let alone assistance, Diana was to receive as her ordeal-by-press escalated. Showered with questions each time she emerged from her front door, she was careful to give monosyllabic, non-committal answers about her feelings for Charles – well aware that one word out of place could consign her, like her sister before her, to the royal out-tray. While endearing herself to the watching world, perfecting her famous art of grinning coyly through her eyelashes, the innocent, naïve Diana was under enormous stress. In private, she admitted, 'I cried like a baby to the four walls. I just couldn't cope with it.' When she sent out an SOS to the Palace press office, she was told there was nothing they could do to help her. Charles, similarly, was 'not at all supportive'. All Diana could do in her distress was hope he would 'hurry up and get on with it'.[10]

Still intent on behaving correctly to her prince, she bit her tongue and said nothing when his phone calls mentioned only his concern about Camilla Parker Bowles. Poor Camilla, he would complain, had all of 'three or four' photographers hanging round outside her home; Diana forbore to mention that the rest of Fleet Street was camped on hers. Already, unsurprisingly, she was beginning to wonder about the precise nature of Camilla's role in Charles's life. The Parker Bowleses had been among the house-guests that recent weekend at Balmoral; indeed, Andrew, together with Nicholas Soames, had been delegated to escort Diana home to the press furore, leaving Camilla behind with the prince in splendid Scottish isolation. Whenever Charles invited Diana to dinner at Buckingham Palace, the Parker Bowleses were usually there, too, and Camilla always seemed to know everything that had passed between Charles and Diana.

So she was far from surprised, the following month, when a trip to Ludlow to watch Charles ride in an amateur race turned into a weekend as the Parker Bowleses' house-guests. The only photographs of Diana and Camilla together date from that October day in 1980 when Charles's long-term lover 'looked after' his potential fiancée while their mutual hero came second in the Clun Handicap Stakes on his favourite horse, Allibar. The next day Charles and Andrew went out hunting, leaving Diana and Camilla to get better acquainted. So well did things go, as far as Camilla was concerned, that Charles and Diana were back to stay with them again the following weekend.

Now Charles drove Diana the short distance to show her round Highgrove, the new home he had just acquired. When he asked her to take charge of the interior decoration, she was excited but baffled. The prince said he liked her taste; but he had never been to her flat, never once picked her up himself on one of their evenings out. She was also, rather charmingly, somewhat shocked, thinking it a 'most improper' suggestion as they were not yet so much as engaged. Camilla's enthusiasm for the idea that evening told Diana just how well Mrs Parker Bowles already knew the inside of the house. Fourteen years her junior, Charles's girlfriend began to harbour suspicions about her suitor's closest confidante. But she bit her tongue and hoped for the best, confident that, were Charles eventually to propose, he was a moral enough man to leave his past behind.

The well-brought-up young girl was being careful to play the game by the rules as she saw them, not wishing to appear too eager, remaining scrupulous about what was proper and what was not. So she was genuinely distressed a few weeks later when the *Sunday Mirror* carried a front-page story proclaiming that on 5 November she had secretly driven from London to spend the night with Charles aboard the royal train in a rural Wiltshire siding.[11] Now at last, for the first time, Buckingham Palace intervened on her behalf with an angry denial; the story was 'wholly false . . . a total fabrication', protested the Queen's press secretary, Michael Shea, demanding a front-page retraction. But the paper's experienced editor, Bob Edwards, defiantly stood by his story, which was 'very reliably' sourced. In vain did Diana plead that she had spent that evening at home with her flatmates, watching TV before an early night, exhausted after escorting Charles to Princess Margaret's fiftieth birthday party at the Ritz the night before.

She even went to the lengths of speaking directly to the man she had nicknamed the 'wicked' James Whitaker, telling him, 'I am not a liar. I have never been on that train. I have never even been near it.' The vehemence of the Palace's denial, meanwhile, intrigued Edwards, weighed against his own solid evidence (later said to have come from the security services) that a blonde woman had been seen boarding the train, and had stayed 'several hours' before departing 'in the most furtive manner'. As the Palace pressed its case all the way to the Press Council, the editor remained puzzled; when the Palace suddenly backed off, saying it had no wish to pursue the matter further, he became yet more intrigued. But neither he nor the rest of the national press saw the alternative explanation staring them in the face. So in love with Diana was the whole of Fleet Street, so intent that Charles should make her his bride, that it did not cross the collective mind of the royal-loving British press that there might have been another 'mystery blonde' in the prince's life, whom he entertained aboard the train that night.

The story eventually evaporated in the euphoria of ensuing events. As the fairy tale sought by Fleet Street began to unfold, it took some years for the journalists involved to realize the truth of the story they had got so nearly right, and yet so badly wrong – the truth that Diana realized at the time, to her horror, but which Fleet Street comprehensively missed. Charles had entertained three Duchy of Cornwall officials to dinner aboard the train that evening; the telephone records also showed that a call had been made to Bolehyde Manor. Six years later, when the retired Bob Edwards was awarded the CBE in the New Year honours list – a token, as he took it, of royal forgiveness – a card from the late Lord Wyatt of Weeford, an establishment figure close to the royal family, carried the simple message: 'I think you'll find it was Camilla.'[12]

At the time, Diana had no chance to take up the matter with the prince himself. On the morning the story broke, he had left for an official visit to Nepal and India. In New Delhi, as the stand-off continued back home between Palace and paper, he chose to denounce the 'sensationalism' of the British press, bewailing the 'lack of moral values' it displayed. 'Honesty and integrity are vital factors in reporting,' he told (rather incongruously) members of the Indian Institute of Technology, 'and often get submerged in the general rush for sensationalism.' Whatever may have passed between himself and Mrs Parker Bowles on the train that evening, this was hypocrisy of truly princely proportions. 'Insofar as personal integrity goes,' as one commentator later observed, 'this was a low water mark in Charles's life.'[13]

With Diana's honour left undefended, her mother now chose to go to battle on her behalf. In early December Mrs Shand Kydd wrote a letter to *The Times* protesting at the 'lies and harassment' her youngest daughter had been forced to endure. 'May I ask the editors of Fleet Street', she continued, 'whether, in the execution of their jobs, they consider it necessary or fair to harass my daughter daily, from dawn until well after dusk? Is it fair to ask any human being, regardless of circumstances, to be treated in this way?'[14] Sixty Members of Parliament then tabled a motion 'deploring the manner in which Lady Diana Spencer is being treated by Fleet Street', precipitating an emergency meeting between national newspaper editors and the Press Council. But the siege of Coleherne Court continued unabated.

For all his indignant remarks in India, it was noticeable that

Charles seemed to avoid Diana on his return. He spent Christmas and New Year at Sandringham, she at Althorp and her London flat. Relations between the press and the royals sank to an all-time low over the festive season, as one by one the Windsors lost their composure when confronted by crowds of reporters. 'A very happy New Year to you,' yelled Charles sarcastically at a posse of reporters, 'and a particularly nasty one to your editors.' His younger brother, Edward, appeared to have fired a shotgun over the head of a *Daily Mirror* photographer. Even the Queen's patience snapped; she broke years of silence to shout, 'Why don't you go away?' That, at least, is what she was reported as saying. James Whitaker, as so often, had a slightly different version. 'Her Majesty, if you'll excuse me, behaved like a fishwife,' he recalls. 'I've never heard her use such strong language.'[15]

Such was the climate in which Diana was finally invited to join Charles at Sandringham, driving herself to Norfolk on New Year's Day. By now she was becoming skilled at evading pursuit by the press outside her front door in Chelsea, laying false trails and sneaking through side exits, even, on one occasion, knotting the sheets from her bed to lower her suitcase out of a rear window before going to meet Charles at Broadlands. On this occasion she drove herself to Kensington Palace, behind whose walls she swapped her now famous Metro for her grandmother's silver Volkswagen Golf, in which she managed to slip away undetected, only to drive into a sea of journalists at the other end of her journey.

Given her suspicions about Mrs Parker Bowles, and the true identity of the 'mystery blonde' on the royal train, Diana was in an unusually pensive mood during her reunion with Charles, already beset by the doubts that would haunt her marriage. There is no question that she was desperate to marry him, that she harboured lofty ambitions forgivable in one so young; so it appears that she now bent over backwards to give him the benefit of the doubt. The shy, rather prim teenager felt motherly towards the prince, whom she had so often heard complaining about his lot.

Friends of the period say that she echoed Charles's self-pitying strains, telling them that his parents and their staff 'work him too hard' and 'push him around'. To her, he seemed the loneliest of men; as she had told him during their first real conversation, he was in urgent need of someone to 'look after' him, and the ambitious nineteen-year-old could think of no more suitable candidate than herself. Whatever part Camilla Parker Bowles had played in Charles's life to date, she was married to another, and would surely disappear after Charles too had wed. Mrs Parker Bowles had, after all, shown nothing but kindness to Diana, who chose to ignore warnings from Anna Wallace and others that Camilla was the only woman the prince would ever really love.

If Charles, too, was assailed by doubts, he was unprepared to listen to the well-intentioned warnings of friends who could already see the scale of the mismatch. His mother, as always in personal matters, felt it inappropriate to offer an opinion; but everyone around her was enthusiastic about Diana, including, significantly, the Queen Mother and her friend Ruth, Lady Fermoy. Diana's grandmother concealed her doubts about the couple's compatibility until she was on her deathbed, thirteen years later, contenting herself at the time with telling Diana, 'Darling, you must understand that their sense of humour and their lifestyle are different, and I don't think it will suit you.'[16]

But two of Charles's closest friends were adamant that he was making a mistake: Nicholas Soames and Penny, Lady Romsey, the former Penny Eastwood, now wife of Mountbatten's grandson Norton Knatchbull. Quite apart from the twelve-year age gap, she argued, Charles and Diana had very little in common. To her it seemed that Diana had fallen in love with an idea rather than a person, that she acted as if she were 'auditioning for a central role in a costume drama . . . quite unaware of the enormity of the real undertaking that she seemed to contemplate so light-heartedly'. When her husband endorsed his wife's views, arguing the case against Diana with more vigour but less tact, Charles was moved to an outburst of indignation. He was 'not willing or – at this time – able to loosen, let alone sever, so precious a bond merely because of the anxiety of those about him'.[17]

By now, sensing that the all too public melodrama was in urgent need of some denouement, the prince also felt himself under intense pressure from his father, who issued a stern warning about Diana Spencer's honour, which Charles interpreted, rightly or wrongly, as 'an ultimatum'. Ominously, he described to friends the prospect of marriage to Diana as a leap into the dark. It was in his nature, he knew, to be hesitant about giving undertakings which might return to haunt him.

In what he confessed was a 'confused and anxious state of mind', he went skiing with the Palmer-Tomkinsons to steel himself to taking the plunge. It was barely six months since his first real chat with Diana in Sussex; the speed with which Charles had reached this point of no return was almost as if he feared this eminently suitable candidate, like so many others, might slip through his fingers. Already, in the cabbage patch behind the Parker Bowles house, he had ventured an informal enquiry, along the lines of, 'If I were to ask, might you consider . . .' But he had yet to make a formal proposal. Now, from the Palmer-Tomkinsons' Klosters chalet, he telephoned Diana to set up a meeting on his return. He had 'something important' to ask her.

Coleherne Court held its collective breath, her flatmates reassuring Diana that the prince would surely now abandon any other women in his life, as Charles returned to London on 3 February, only to disappear on manoeuvres aboard HMS *Invincible*. He was back at the Palace two nights later, having arranged to meet Diana at Windsor Castle on the Friday, 6 February. Late that evening, in the castle's nursery, he formally proposed marriage. 'I've missed you so much,' Diana remembered him saying, none too convincingly. He did not go down on his knees, or even take her hand, just came straight out with, 'Will you marry me?'

Diana's immediate response was a fit of the giggles, which did not please him at all. Charles reminded her that he was in deadly earnest, and that his offer meant she would one day be queen. While 'a small voice inside my head', according to Diana, told her she would 'never become queen', she accepted the prince without the slightest hesitation, telling him repeatedly how much she loved him. 'Whatever love means,' he replied, by her account, even then.

Charles went upstairs to telephone the Queen, and then Earl Spencer to ask formally for his daughter's hand, leaving Diana alone with her thoughts. Her natural elation, fuelled by her love for the prince and her inbred sense of duty, was only slightly tempered by anxiety. Even that was forgotten when she got home and broke the news to her flatmates, who had put champagne on ice. After excited celebrations, they took a drive around London for the heck of it, revelling in their secret.

Diana had fallen deeply in love. Few girls her age could have resisted the attentions of the world's most eligible bachelor. Whatever Charles's reasons for choosing her, she was prepared to put up with all the flummery – even to look on as the antique absurdities of the contemporary British monarchy obliged her uncle to reassure the press that she was a virgin. 'Charles's parents!' says one friend of the Windsors, looking back to that moment. 'They should have known that he needed someone more experienced than that . . . To hell with being a virgin. That was the least important consideration.'[18]

Diana was young for her years, Charles old for his. But she had every reason to hope that together they could create the happy family life she herself had been denied, the happy family life that he told her he too wanted. There are those who believe, not without reason, that Diana had set out to 'get her man' with all the determination of the proverbial Canadian mountie. But those who knew her well, from her former nanny, Mary Clarke, to her girl-friends at Coleherne Court and her sisters, also believed that Diana would never have agreed to marry Charles unless she was convinced that he loved her in return.

Two days later, her days of freedom numbered, Diana flew off to Australia with her mother and stepfather for a ten-day break at his farm in New South Wales, decamping to its nearby beach house for extra security. One of the few who knew her precise whereabouts was the Prince of Wales, for whose telephone calls his fiancée waited in vain. 'I pined for him,' as she put it, 'but he never rang me up.'[19] After several days' trying to be understanding, telling her mother to put it down to pressure of work, she could bear it no longer, and telephoned Charles at the Palace, only to be told that he was not there. Later, he did return her call. It was the only one she received from him during those ten days. On her return home, she was thrilled to answer the door to a member of his staff bearing a bunch of flowers. But there was no note from Charles, and Diana wistfully decided that they could not have come directly from her fiancé. It must have been merely a considerate gesture by his office.

Only a few days were left before the world shared their secret, as plans were discreetly laid for the engagement to be announced from the Palace the following Wednesday, 24 February. They met just once, when Diana rose at dawn to drive down to the Berkshire stables of Nick Gaselee, Charles's friend and racehorse trainer, to see him put Allibar through his paces. As she watched with his detective, the horse suddenly reared its head and collapsed beneath the prince after suffering a massive heart attack. Diana rushed to Charles's side, but the horse was dead within minutes. There was little time for her to comfort the distraught prince, as he had to leave for engagements in Wales. After a hasty farewell, Diana was smuggled away in the Gaselees' Land-Rover, with a rug over her head, to dodge the lurking photographers.

On the following Thursday, the eve of the announcement, she packed a bag, said a tearful goodbye to her flatmates, and left the real world behind at Coleherne Court to move into Clarence House, the Queen Mother's London residence. As she drove through its gates with the armed police bodyguard assigned to protect her, Inspector Paul Officer, he said, 'This is the last night of freedom in the rest of your life, so make the most of it.' His words, said Diana, 'went like a sword into my heart.'[20]

There was no-one else – no-one from the royal family, least of all her fiancé – to welcome her. 'It was', she said, 'like going into a hotel.' Far from the Queen Mother fluttering around and giving her 'a crash course in the art of being royal', as Fleet Street legend has it, Diana was shown by a servant to her first-floor room, where she found a letter waiting for her on the bed. Dated two days earlier, it was from Camilla Parker Bowles.

How did Camilla know she would be at Clarence House? Even Diana herself had not known until a few hours earlier. 'Such exciting news about the engagement. I'd love to see the ring!' gushed the letter, suggesting lunch while the prince was away. With what would turn out to be extremely bad timing, Charles was due to go on an official visit to Australia and New Zealand, returning via Venezuela and the United States. He would be gone all of five weeks. First, at least, Diana could enjoy sampling the engagement rings sent round for her inspection, in a briefcase supposedly containing a choice of signet rings to mark Prince Andrew's twenty-first birthday. She chose the biggest: 'Along came these sapphires. I mean *nuggets*! The Queen paid for it.'[21]

Diana waltzed through the engagement rituals as if in a dream. When asked in her first television interview if they were in love, she responded with a smile and an instinctive 'Of course!' to Charles's grim encore of, 'Whatever love means.' Did he make this subsequently celebrated response because he knew Camilla would be watching? If so, the supreme irony is that, thanks to Camilla, the real Charles knew just what love meant.

As Diana moved into Buckingham Palace, and realized how inadequate was her meagre wardrobe for the rigours of royal life, she sought help from a friend of her sisters, Anna Harvey, fashion editor of *Vogue* magazine. Over the days that followed, while laying the foundations of a collection versatile enough for all royal requirements, she commissioned her wedding dress from David and Elizabeth Emanuel, to whom she had been introduced by Lord Snowdon. She also asked them to design 'something special' for her first official engagement on Charles's arm – a reception at Goldsmiths Hall, in the City of London, where the guests were to include Princess Grace of Monaco.

Diana was thrilled with the black silk ballgown that the Emanuels produced, strapless and backless with a daringly deep neckline. Come the evening, and her arrival in all her finery at Charles's study door, it did not win her the compliments for which she was hoping. On the contrary, the prince was moved to spluttering protests, declaring her décolletage unsuitable for a member of the royal family. Black, the colour Diana thought 'the smartest you could possibly have', was to him to be be reserved for times of mourning. Fighting back tears, she replied simply and honestly that she possessed nothing else suitable for the occasion. So off they went in a mutually sullen silence, shattered only by the roar of the crowd and excited shouts of photographers as Diana made her highly dramatic, and typically distinctive, exit from the car and entrance into public life.

Thrilled to meet the former Grace Kelly, whom she had always admired, Diana was surprised to be taken aside by the princess and led off for a friendly chat in the powder room. The sympathetic Grace had noticed Diana's unease on her first big night out, and sensed the fuss her choice of dress was causing not just the party guests, but the watching world. She encouraged Diana to share her doubts and fears, and proved a good listener as the teenager poured her heart out about the press, the coldness of her royal reception, the constant absence and distance of her future husband. 'Don't worry.' Princess Grace finally smiled. 'It will get a lot worse!'

Days later, at the end of March, Diana drove with Charles to Heathrow Airport to see him off to Australia. As he climbed the steps and turned to wave, she was pictured through the window of the VIP suite brushing away her tears. At the time, this was taken as a touching glimpse of the love at the heart of the unfolding fairy tale. In truth, as she herself later revealed, she was weeping because her last minutes alone with the prince at the Palace had been interrupted by a phone call. It was Camilla, wanting her own fond farewell. So tender was the conversation that Diana had felt obliged to leave the room.

That moment, she said ten years later, 'just broke my heart'. Left alone in the vast emptiness of Buckingham Palace, she went into a spiral of decline from which she was never really to recover throughout the fifteen years of marriage ahead. Once it was over, she recalled, 'I missed my girls so much I wanted to go back there and sit and giggle like we used to, and borrow clothes and chat about silly things, just being safe in my shell again.'[22]

Since her arrival at Clarence House, Diana's friends had worried that she seemed to be growing dramatically thinner. They were not to know that she was already visiting the royal kitchens, making new friends among the backstairs staff as she gorged herself on whatever was to hand, only to vomit it up again later. Her increasingly regular routine, by one particularly vivid account, ran as follows:

> At lunchtimes when she did not have guests, Diana would go into the nursery kitchen. She would take down a large glass bowl engraved with the EIIR cypher which held just over half a packet of breakfast cereal. She would fill it with Kellogg's Frosties and several chopped bananas, strawberries and sometimes pieces of apple. She would add tablespoons of caster sugar and pour on Windsor cream, a thick double cream from the Jersey herd at the Home Farm at Windsor. She would then sit down on top of the spin-dryer to eat her way through the mess which she washed down with fresh orange juice. When she had finished, she would go to her lavatory, lock herself in and spew up what she had just forced down. This pattern of gorge and regurgitate would happen twice and sometimes three or four times a day.[23]

Bulimia nervosa, the eating disorder that would haunt her marriage, had already taken hold, brought on, her friends will always believe, by acute anxiety about Charles and Camilla. The prince's camp – typified by the less than sympathetic note of distaste in the description above – will always maintain the opposite: that Diana's bulimia was the 'canker' within the marriage. Friends of the Queen, such as her biographer Elizabeth Longford, testify that Charles's mother believed that 'the stress in the princess's marriage was the result of [this] precondition', dating back to her childhood.[24] Others, like Mary Clarke, who knew her from childhood, insist that Diana became ill 'because of the anger and hurt of finding out she wasn't loved'.[25]

To Diana herself, bulimia was 'a secret disease' she could confess to no-one.

> You inflict it upon yourself because your self-esteem is at a low ebb, and you don't think you're worthy or valuable. You fill your stomach up four or five times a day – some do it more – and it gives you a feeling of comfort. It's like having a pair of arms around you, but it's temporary, temporary. Then you're disgusted at the bloatedness of your stomach, and then you bring it all up again. And it's a repetitive pattern which is very destructive to yourself.[26]

To her, there was no doubt about the cause of her illness: Charles's continuing friendship with Camilla Parker Bowles, with whom she finally had that lunch during his long absence abroad. The conversation reinforced Diana's impression that Camilla felt she owned some special right to Charles. She kept saying, 'Don't push him into this, don't do that,' and she was full of wily female advice as to how to 'handle' the prince. But one recurring refrain above all others lingered in Diana's mind. Was she planning, asked Camilla, to take up fox-hunting when she moved to Highgrove? When Diana said no, that she had disliked riding and horses since an accident in childhood, Camilla failed to hide the relief on her face. It did not take Diana long to work out that hunting would be the key to Camilla's continuing hold over Charles, a way to spend time with him without arousing anyone's suspicions, including hers.

Not for the first time, Diana realized that Camilla saw her primarily as 'a threat'. If she had been a true friend, she would have stayed in touch while Charles was away, soothing her anxieties,

alleviating her loneliness in the vast, unfriendly confines of the
Palace. Said her flatmate Carolyn Bartholomew, 'She went to live
at Buckingham Palace and then the tears started. She wasn't happy,
she was plunged into all this pressure and it was a nightmare for
her. This little thing got so thin. I was so worried about her.'[27] It
hadn't helped when Charles put his arm around her twenty-nine-
inch waist one day and chided her for being 'a bit chubby'. By her
wedding day, it had shrunk to twenty-three inches.

The surface explanation was, of course, her bulimia. But the
bulimia itself was fed by her continuing anxieties about Camilla, in
a vicious circle which would henceforth see each side of the argument blaming the other. In Charles's absence, Diana took the
chance to ask the key members of his staff – Edward Adeane,
Francis Cornish, Michael Colborne – if they thought the prince
would give up Mrs Parker Bowles after the marriage. But they
could offer naught for her comfort. 'If they evaded the question on
principle,' in the words of another Charles apologist, 'they certainly had no answer.'[28]

Charles, for his part, spent his travels wondering quite who this
was with whom he had chosen to spend the rest of his life.
Everywhere he went, especially in Australia, his fellow men con-
gratulated him on his taste, with blokeish nudges and winks that
appalled his royal sense of propriety. To his further distaste, Diana
'lookalikes' were laid on at each of his destinations. The real
Diana's face followed him everywhere, on newspaper front pages,
magazine covers and television news bulletins. To some of those
travelling with him (including the present author), it appeared as if
Charles was curiously content to let his mind be made up for him.
If the rest of the world was falling in love with Diana so fast and
so completely, then perhaps he should, too. If he could.

His return home in early May proved a desperate anticlimax for
his increasingly tense bride-to-be. Clinging to the hope that
her prince would come to her rescue, devote himself to easing her
problems, share his time and his secrets with her, Diana was
brutally disillusioned. When first they were reunited, after six
weeks apart, he gave her a cursory peck on the cheek and disappeared to change for lunch.

If she needed any confirmation that Charles, like his parents,
was not a tactile person, this was a bleak beginning. Occasionally

he would take her hand in an avuncular way, or put his arm round her waist to steer her through a group of people; but even the servants noticed that it was more the way a brother touches a sister than a full-blooded young man embraces his wife-to-be. One night that June, so legend has it, there was a violent thunderstorm which sent a frightened Diana scurrying along the Palace corridors to her fiancé's room in the middle of the night. Although he took her into his bed, it was 'not the momentous night it might have been'. Charles merely offered her his protective arm and told her not to be frightened of the thunder. He treated her, by one cynical account, 'decorously – more decorously than she would have wished.'[29]

Nor was he around as much as she had hoped. Most of Diana's time was still spent alone in her small suite on the Palace's nursery floor, while Charles went about his business in his own suite literally hundreds of yards away. Much of the time he wasn't there at all; as often as not, Diana discovered, he had gone to the country to see Camilla. Gradually she realized how often his staff were covering up for him. 'The lies and the deceit. I was told one thing, but actually another thing was going on.'[30]

Still wondering whether he could bear to give up Camilla for this highly strung young creature who demanded his exclusive attention, Charles hid behind his inborn royal defences. He did not see that it was incumbent on him to inform Diana of his movements. Nor, in the process, did he bother to ensure that she herself was coping with her daunting new life, squaring up to the formidable ordeal of their wedding service, now just two months away.

In truth, he too was racked by doubts. 'She is exquisitely pretty, a perfect poppet,' he told a friend, 'but she is a child. She does not look old enough to be out of school, much less married.'[31] His parents were no use to him: they were uncomfortable discussing personal matters, and anyway were convinced that it was now too late to change his mind. So, too, once the engagement had been announced, was his sister Anne, even though her own marriage had already run into difficulties. 'Just close your eyes and think of England' was her helpful advice. He had no-one else to turn to but Camilla, with whom he soon had an unprecedented row. She had her own private reasons, which Charles half knew, for endorsing Diana as his bride; how could he possibly question her judgement? For a while, in an attempt to stiffen his resolve, Mrs Parker Bowles acted offended and refused to see him or to take his phone calls.

With the wedding less than a week away, a parcel arrived in the small Buckingham Palace office that Diana shared with Michael Colborne, a naval colleague of the prince who had joined his staff as financial controller. Somehow, it had managed to arrive via a separate route from the wedding presents, which were now arriving *en masse*.

Despite Colborne's helpless protests, Diana insisted on opening it herself, to find inside a gold chain bracelet bearing a blue enamel disc, on which the letters G and F were entwined. Charles had christened Camilla his 'Girl Friday', but Diana also knew that their pet nicknames for each other were 'Gladys' and 'Fred'. She had seen a card inscribed 'to Gladys from Fred' when Charles had sent Camilla some flowers while she was ill with meningitis. This was not, as she first thought, a present to her husband-to-be from his long-time lover. Worse, it was the other way round. The prince must be planning to give this keepsake to Camilla.

Diana sought out Charles and demanded an explanation. In a confrontation as uncomfortable as any he had known, the prince stood his ground, explaining that Mrs Parker Bowles had been an intimate friend for years; he felt it 'unnecessary to go into detail'.[32] But now he would be calling an end to the intensity of their friendship, and seeing much less of her. He felt it appropriate to give her a token of his affection, by way of a farewell, and wished Diana could see it the same way. He was sorry that she was so upset, but insisted on going ahead with the gift. In fact, he would be taking it to Camilla personally the following Monday, two days before their wedding. Nothing Diana could say or do, no amount of tears or hysterics, would dissuade him.

It was a defining moment, in which Diana realized for the first time that she might never be rid of the shadow of Camilla Parker Bowles. That weekend, with the wedding only a few days away, she was seen in public to burst into tears while watching Charles play polo. Pleading pre-marital nerves, she fled the scene.

On the Monday morning Charles duly drove himself off, as announced, to give Camilla her bracelet and say his farewells. In a most unusual breach of the royal rules, he did not even take along his protection officer, Chief Inspector John MacLean. When Diana found MacLean in the Palace, but Charles gone, she asked where her fiancé was. 'He's gone out to lunch,' came the reply. At her wits' end, Diana had a tearful lunch with her sisters, and told them that she couldn't go through with it, that she wanted to call the whole thing off. This marriage was going to be a disaster. 'Too late, Duch!' they said light-heartedly, using her childhood nickname to try to cheer her up. 'You can't chicken out now. Your face is already on the tea towels.'[33]

Charles was away all day, as Princess Anne had chosen that afternoon, with remarkably tactless timing, for the christening at Windsor of her second child, a daughter to be rather racily named Zara. One of the godfathers was the princess's former beau, Andrew Parker Bowles, who was naturally there along with his wife. As was Anne's brother Charles, who chose not to bring his fiancée to this family occasion.

At the wedding rehearsal in St Paul's, forty-eight hours before the ceremony, Diana alarmed her fiancé by breaking down and sobbing, 'Absolutely collapsed . . . because of all sorts of things. The Camilla thing rearing its head the whole way through our engagement and I was desperately trying to be mature about the situation but I didn't have the foundations to do it and I couldn't talk to anyone about it.'[34]

Charles put it down to pre-wedding nerves. But that same evening he was relieved to see Diana put on a brave face alongside himself and the Queen in a Palace receiving line for 800 friends and family invited to the eve-of-wedding ball, from Nancy Reagan via Raine Spencer to, of course, Andrew and Camilla Parker Bowles. With a few of her own friends there, Diana was somewhat restored to her usual high spirits, dancing with Rory Scott alongside the prime minister, Margaret Thatcher, to the music of Hot Chocolate. The occasion, by royal standards, went with an unprecedented swing; as royals and commoners alike became the worse for wear, Princess Margaret attached a balloon to her tiara, Prince Andrew tied one to his tuxedo, and Diana's brother, Charles Spencer, found himself bowing to a waiter. 'It was an intoxicatingly happy evening,' recalled one of Diana's friends. 'Everyone horribly drunk and then catching taxis in the early hours . . . It was a blur, a glorious, happy blur.'[35]

As she returned to Clarence House, where decorum required her to spend the eve of her wedding, Diana had no way of knowing whether Camilla Parker Bowles returned home that evening, or, as she later came to believe, spent a few last hours at the Palace in Charles's arms.* Next day, amid her continuing anxieties, she was mollified by the arrival of a gift from her husband-to-be: a signet ring engraved with the Prince of Wales's distinctive three-feather motif, with a card reading, 'I'm so proud of you, and when you come up I'll be there at the altar for you tomorrow. Just look 'em in the eye and knock 'em dead.' During dinner with her sister Jane that evening, nonetheless, Diana gorged herself before leaving the room to be sick. 'The night before the wedding,' in her own words, 'I was very, very calm, deathly calm. I felt I was a lamb to the slaughter. I knew it and I couldn't do anything about it.'[36] Back at the Palace, Charles spent much of the evening staring moodily out of the window, in contemplative mood – showing no signs of joy, according to a companion, but aware that 'a momentous day' was upon him.[37]

Next morning, 29 July 1981, Diana was awoken at 5 a.m. by the noise of the crowds already gathering in the Mall, beneath her bedroom window. Kevin Shanley came to do her hair, Barbara Daly to do her make-up, and the Emanuels to ensure that all was well with her sumptuous wedding gown. When he arrived to offer moral support, even her brother Charles considered it a fairy-tale transformation: 'It was the first time in my life I ever thought of Diana as beautiful. She really did look stunning that day . . . slightly pale, but happy and calm.'[38] Waiting for her at the foot of the Clarence House staircase, her father told her, 'Darling, I'm so proud of you,' before they climbed into the Glass Coach for their stately progress through the crowds to St Paul's – during which, as she affectionately recalled, Earl Spencer 'waved himself stupid'.

With the world watching, Diana's prime concern at the cathedral was 'to get my father up the aisle'. She was well aware that her family was worried the frail old earl might not make it. With Diana's support, in front of 750 million people, he made a slow but steady progress on his daughter's arm to Jeremiah Clarke's *Trumpet Voluntary* – slow enough for Diana to concentrate on her other main preoccupation that morning: trying to spot

* In his book *Diana vs Charles* (1993), James Whitaker testified that the prince's valet, Stephen Barry, told him Camilla slipped away from the party with Charles. 'It was incredibly daring,' he quoted Barry as saying, 'if not incredibly stupid.' Barry died of AIDS in 1984. As a Charles apologist noted with heavy sarcasm, 'He was therefore never able to rebut the charge against either his employer or his own integrity.'[39]

Camilla Parker Bowles. Ten years later, this was still her main memory of what should have been the happiest moment of her life: 'I spotted Camilla, pale grey, veiled pillbox hat, saw it all, her son, Tom, standing on a chair. To this day, you know – vivid memory.'

Camilla was in the third row from the front, on the groom's side, in the midst of his most senior guests, including members of the royal family. Across the aisle was the prime minister, Margaret Thatcher, with her husband, Denis, and members of the Cabinet. As Charles's bride spotted his lover, she thought, 'Well, let's hope *that*'s all over with.'[40]

PART THREE

Three in a Marriage

CHAPTER NINE

'LIKE A LAMB TO THE SLAUGHTER'

EVEN THE ARCHBISHOP OF CANTERBURY, WHO CONDUCTED THE
wedding service and endorsed the media 'fairy tale' from the
pulpit, was in on the secret of Charles and Camilla. 'Oh, yes,'
admitted the Rt Revd Robert Runcie years later, 'I knew about that
already.'

Runcie's friend Ruth, Lady Fermoy, Diana's maternal grandmother, had discreetly discussed Charles's needs with the
Archbishop, confiding her own worries about the prince's craving
for 'a woman to love for and be cared by'. Echoing her evidence
against her own daughter in her custody case with Earl Spencer,
Lady Fermoy did not dissent from Runcie's judgement that her
grand-daughter Diana was 'an actress and a schemer' who would
'never be under control until she fell in love with someone'. The
result, even to the Archbishop who solemnized it, was 'an arranged
marriage'.

When the couple had first come to see Runcie as part of their
preparation for marriage, his chaplain Richard Chartres – 'a very
observant man' in Runcie's view, soon to become Bishop of
London – had said of Charles, 'He's seriously depressed. You can
tell from his voice.' Runcie's own, rather more blasé outlook was,
'They're a very nice couple, and she'll grow into it.' By 1996, the
year of their divorce, the retired Archbishop had to admit he had
been wrong. 'I don't know what will become of her. Sad, really.'[1]

Fifteen years earlier, as he consigned Diana to an uncertain fate,
Runcie was not the only protagonist at the wedding to know the

secret of the married woman in the third pew. The bridegroom's parents, one of whom was Supreme Governor of the Church of England, also knew perfectly well what they were letting Diana in for. 'Here is the stuff of which fairy tales are made,' they heard the Archbishop intone, echoing the famous words of the constitutional historian Walter Bagehot: 'A princely marriage is the brilliant edition of a universal fact, and as such it rivets mankind.'[2] Of no princely marriage in history were Bagehot's words to prove truer, or Runcie's more hollow.

The wedding of Charles Windsor to Diana Spencer on 29 July 1981 was the biggest media event the world had ever seen. Three-quarters of a billion people watched via television as the bride endearingly confused her husband's forenames, while the groom made the not insignificant error of endowing her with her own worldly goods rather than his. As the gloriously sunny day went off without any worse hitches, ending with the first royal kiss ever seen on the balcony of Buckingham Palace, the Prince and Princess of Wales were universally deemed a fairy-tale couple, openly in love.

The innocent young girl in whom a nation reposed its emotional hopes was the first English-born bride of an heir to the throne for more than 300 years. Diana was set to become the first English Queen Consort since the days of King Henry VIII. She also brought to the Windsor line the only royal blood it lacked, that of the Stuarts. Her first-born son would thus be the first potential monarch in British history to be descended from every British king and queen who had issue.

Diana was also on course to become the first British Queen ever to have worked for her living. The last Princess of Wales, later King George V's Queen Mary, never made a speech or used a telephone in her life. Barely a generation after Mary's death, her successor set a new style for the monarchy as a girl-next-door princess, wearing off-the-peg clothes from chain stores. For all her deep-blue blood, Diana was also a thoroughly modern young woman; though no intellectual, she was already savvy, street-wise and smart. Apparently no heart-on-sleeve feminist, either, she showed considerable Spencer pride beneath those demurely lowered eyelashes.

In a long, hot summer disfigured by race riots, the royal wedding was just the shot in the arm Britain needed. The festive street parties toasting the royal couple made a stark contrast with alarming civil disruptions all over the country – rioting and ugly street

violence, looting and arson from Brixton in south London to the
Toxteth area of Liverpool, from the St Paul's district of Bristol to
Handsworth in Birmingham and Moss Side in Manchester. As the
physical damage was counted in scores of millions of pounds, the
social cost was evaluated by a growing coalition of experts anxious
to identify causes and seek solutions. By the time trouble erupted
again four years later, on the Broadwater Farm estate in
Tottenham, north London, Charles would be involved via his
Prince's Trust in attempts to improve the social conditions at the
root of the problem. In that summer of 1981 not only had he at last
found himself, for better or worse, the bride he had so long been
seeking; he had also been offered the sharp focus he so desperately
needed for his public role.

Such thoughts could not have been further from the prince's
mind as he and his bride processed through the streets of London
– lined by a million cheering people, many of whom had slept there
overnight – to the post-wedding 'breakfast' at Buckingham Palace.
Diana, too, had reason to believe that her rival, Camilla, was now
indeed an unhappy memory. Just to make sure, she had struck her
name off the 120-strong guest list, along with that of another rival
for the prince's affections, Dale 'Kanga' Tryon. A defiant Camilla
hosted a lunch party of her own, secure in the knowledge that her
wedding present to Charles had been secreted into the luggage he
would be taking on honeymoon. Few of the excited guests at the
Palace noticed that the bride and groom, though sitting next to
each other, did not exchange a word. Those who did put it down,
quite rightly, to sheer exhaustion. 'We were so shattered,' said
Diana herself, who was 'exhausted at the whole thing'. But she had
'tremendous hopes in my heart'.[3]

At the end of the day, for the new princess, the sight of the
crowds filling the Mall as far as the eye on the balcony could see
was 'overwhelming . . . so humbling, all these thousands and thousands of happy people. It was just wonderful.' Charles said much
the same in a letter to a friend: 'What an unbelievable day it was
. . . I was *totally* overwhelmed'.[4] As they drove away from the
Palace in a horse-drawn carriage, the soldier riding escort right
behind them was the ever loyal Andrew Parker Bowles, no doubt
sharing the 'tremendous hopes' in Diana's heart.

But Diana's disillusion set in immediately, even during the first
three days of the honeymoon, spent with the Romseys at Charles's

old hideaway, Broadlands. 'It was just grim,' she recalled ten years later. All her hopes were dashed as early as 'Day Two, [when] out came the van der Post novels he hadn't read. Seven of them – they came on our honeymoon. He read them and we had to analyse them over lunch every day.'[5] The rest of the time Charles spent fishing. By the time they flew to Gibraltar on 1 August, to board *Britannia* for a Mediterranean cruise, she was already growing ill again.

Aboard the royal yacht, with its crew of 277 to get in the honeymooners' way, Diana was dismayed to find that they were never left alone. Even their evening meals were black-tie affairs in the company of the ship's twenty-one officers, where the day's events were discussed to the accompaniment of a Royal Marines band. Charles, to whom the camaraderie of the mess deck was second nature, felt very much at home; for Diana, the only woman present, it was 'very difficult to accept'. By day, as the yacht cruised down the coast of Italy towards the Greek islands, Charles was still reading van der Post or writing endless letters. 'All I can say is that marriage is very jolly and it's extremely nice being together aboard *Britannia*,' he wrote home. 'Diana dashes about chatting up all the sailors and the cooks in the galley, etc., while I remain hermit-like on the verandah deck, sunk with pure joy into one of Laurens van der Post's books . . .'[6]

Little did Charles realize it was *because* he remained 'hermit-like on the verandah deck' that Diana was 'chatting up the cooks' – and even less *why* she spent so much time in the galley. Its staff were naturally delighted by her constant visits, and amused by her apparently insatiable requests for ice-cream, without themselves realizing what was actually happening. 'Bulimia appalling,' she noted. '[Sick] four times a day on the yacht. Anything I could find I would gobble up and be sick two minutes later.' This, of course, made her very tired, leading to sudden mood swings, so that 'one minute one would be happy, the next blubbing one's eyes out'.[7] The prince professed himself 'perplexed' by all this, but relieved that she was able to hide it from the crew.

The new princess even managed to maintain her public façade when the shadow of Camilla intruded on what should have been an idyllic honeymoon in the sun aboard the world's largest private yacht. In his father's seaborne study, which Charles had hijacked as his private retreat, they were comparing schedules one day when two photographs of Camilla fluttered out of his diary onto the floor.

A few days later, when they entertained Egypt's President Anwar Sadat and his wife to dinner, Diana noticed that her husband was wearing a new pair of gold cufflinks in the shape of two inter-twined 'C's. Under angry questioning, Charles admitted they were a gift from Camilla, but failed to see anything wrong in so charm-ing a gesture from so close a friend. Diana saw things differently. For Charles to attribute her mood swings to 'the transient pres-sures of adapting to her new and exacting role as his consort'[8] was disingenuous, to say the least.

After two weeks at sea, the couple flew from Egypt straight to Scotland, to continue their three-month honeymoon at Balmoral. Looking radiant at a Deeside photocall, Diana told journalists she could 'thoroughly recommend married life'. The reality was already very different. 'I remember crying my eyes out on our honeymoon,' she would say later. Charles could see that something was profoundly wrong, but professed bafflement. For him this was 'a blissful interlude at his favourite home, complete with his books, his fishing rods and his friends', while his new bride was for some reason 'unable to surrender herself to his good humour'.[9] Those friends, of course, were part of the problem, as was the prince's idea of a good time. Where Diana craved his sole attention – more of those moments of intimacy which are the shared memories of most honeymoons – Charles actually seemed to go out of his way to avoid being alone with her.

Already, within weeks, a pattern had begun to emerge. Viewing his bride with dismay as young and empty-headed, Charles sought companionship elsewhere, while consumed with guilt about being unfaithful to Camilla. Diana, for her part, could see that marriage was not going to be the bed of roses she had hoped. Her new husband was not paying her as much attention as fairy-tale brides feel entitled to expect. But she was determined to try to make the marriage work: 'When you've had divorced parents like myself, you'd want to try even harder to make it work. You don't want to fall back into a pattern that you've seen happen in your own family. I desperately wanted it to work, I desperately loved my husband and I wanted to share everything together.'[10]

To her chagrin, however, Diana herself was smart enough to see that Charles really was 'blissfully happy' reading van der Post while leaving her to get on with her tapestries, as women do. The only joint activity he suggested was to go for long walks. His idea of fun was 'to sit on top of the highest hill [and] read Laurens van der Post or Jung to me' even though 'I hadn't a clue about psychic powers or anything'.

For a young bride seeking solitude, to build a relationship with a husband she barely knew, it did not help that the rest of the royal family were never far away. Diana soon perceived that Charles was 'in awe of his mama' and 'intimidated by his father', while it fell to her to be 'always the third person in the room'. In the evenings, as the family gathered for dinner in formal attire, he would ask his mother and grandmother whether they wanted a drink before he asked his bride. 'Fine, no problem,' she reflected. 'But I had to be told that that was normal because I always thought it was the wife first. Stupid thought!'[11]

The princess knew that everyone could see she was getting 'thinner and thinner and sicker and sicker'. In part, as she conceded, this was 'basically [because] they thought I could adapt to being Princess of Wales overnight'. But Charles also began to attribute her unpredictability – laughing one minute, weeping the next – to a growing 'obsession' with Camilla Parker Bowles. Diana's insecurity about his feelings for Camilla, he told friends, was 'fed by the canker of jealousy'. She simply refused to believe that her husband had, as he faithfully promised, given up his lover for good. What about those photographs, that exchange of expensive gifts? How could he wear those cufflinks during their honeymoon? As the rows escalated, Charles drew back from his bride 'in bewilderment and despondency'.[12]

The prince was right: Diana was 'obsessed' with Camilla. During their extended honeymoon at Balmoral, by her own confession, she had recurring bad dreams about the other woman in her husband's life. She was, in her own words, 'obsessed by Camilla totally'. She did not trust Charles. She persuaded herself that he was 'ringing her up every five minutes asking how to handle his marriage'.[13]

By October he was – breaking his vow of self-denial after barely three months. Diana's behaviour so baffled and alarmed Charles that he also asked his friend Michael Colborne, then his mentor van der Post, to come to Balmoral to talk to her. He could scarcely, of course, have made a worse choice of confidants for Diana. Here was one man who had tried to hide Camilla's secret gift from her, and another who had already haunted her honeymoon via his books, with which Charles had spent more time than with her. Now she was required to confide her problems to the elderly sage, who was hardly likely to take her side against his protégé. As it was, the princess proved beyond van der Post's Jungian ken. 'Laurens', she said, 'didn't understand me.'[14]

Soon, while still technically on her honeymoon, Diana had travelled secretly to London for counselling. After clandestine meetings with psychiatrists at Buckingham Palace, she was prescribed a tranquillizer, Prozac, which she took most reluctantly. Charles was appalled, being a strong, and public, opponent of such drugs, and a firm believer in hiding your emotions, gritting your teeth and getting on with things. To Diana, who had not been able to share her true worries with them, the doctors did not understand her real problem: that she craved sympathy, attention and under-standing from her husband. In its absence, there was no-one else to whom she could turn for solace. The royal family and its advisers expected her to adapt to the stresses and strains of life as a princess, including overnight global adulation, as if it were second nature.

As yet the Windsors were probably unaware of Diana's other preoccupation: Camilla. Nor did they know that her thoughts were already turning to suicide – not because she genuinely wished to die, but as one way of showing her husband and his family quite how desperate she was feeling.

At first the Prozac saw her through to the end of a honeymoon that had turned into a protracted nightmare. Her demons, thought the doctors, had been caged. 'They could go to bed at night and sleep,' as she put it, 'knowing the Princess of Wales wasn't going to stab anyone.'[15]

But when the three-month honeymoon came to an end, she returned to her downward spiral. As she and Charles set off on their first official engagement together – a three-day tour of Wales at the end of October, for the prince formally to present his bride to his principality – she was the radiant and graceful Diana whom the world was fast taking to its heart, with a natural touch un-familiar from the Windsors that would soon become her trademark. Already there were ominous signs that the crowds were far more interested in her than in Charles. 'I know my place,' he joked to crowds who groaned when they found themselves on his side rather than hers. 'If only I had two wives!'

But the crowds also noticed, close up, how pathetically thin the princess was looking, and in private she gave up trying to hide the strain from outsiders. Back in the privacy of the royal train Diana constantly broke down in tears, drained of all energy, pleading that she could not face another crowd. 'Stay close to her,' Charles told her lady-in-waiting, 'she needs your support' – still not realizing, apparently, that the support she actually needed was his. When she made it safely through the first public speech of her life – partly in Welsh – on receiving the freedom of the City of Cardiff, Diana was so upset at the lack of congratulations from Charles that she no longer troubled to conceal her unhappiness from their staff.

On the second day of the Welsh tour, however, another reason for Diana's malaise emerged with confirmation from London that she was pregnant. Charles decided that this must be reason enough for her constant sickness and tantrums, and Diana, too, cheered up for a while. 'A godsend,' she called it. 'Marvellous news, occupied my mind.'[16] It was also an excuse to give up the Prozac, for fear it might harm the baby. Maybe now, with Charles sharing her delight in the prospect of their first child, he might at last begin to take more interest in her.

On 2 November, three days before Buckingham Palace announced Diana's pregnancy, Charles went out hunting in the Gloucestershire countryside near Cirencester. At one point, as the fox went to ground beside a main road, the prince found himself riding towards a crowd of spectators, including some journalists, at whom he yelled, 'When are you going to stop making my life a misery?' As they watched him turn away to rejoin the main group, shaken by the vehemence of his outburst, they saw him ride back out of range beside a woman who 'looked suspiciously like Camilla Parker Bowles'.[17] Such was Fleet Street's euphoria about the news of a forthcoming royal birth that the incident went unreported.

So Diana, too, knew nothing about it. But her pregnancy was not proving easy. With acute morning sickness complicating her bulimia, the princess grew ever thinner and weaker. Each public appearance still won her unqualified adulation, but seemed to do little to improve her spirits. Towards the end of the year, it was all she could do to avoid being sick in public as she formally switched on the Christmas lights in London's Regent Street. Over the autumn she had embarked on a series of long, candid conversations with her husband's friends and advisers about the reasons for her unhappiness, harping on themes which they summarized as 'the loss of freedom, the absence of a role, the boredom, the emptiness in her life, the heartlessness of her husband'. Surprised by her candour, they patiently tried to explain those aspects of her new role with which she was having trouble coming to terms: her husband's frequent absences, the complex interplay between the private and the public man, the need for her to find her own separate identity in the shape of royal patronages – 'something in Wales', perhaps, or 'something with children'.[18]

Some of their staff, such as the private secretary assigned to Diana, Oliver Everett, were understandably bemused by her continuing volatility – one moment offering profuse thanks for his help, the next coldly ignoring him. Charles's own private secretary, Edward Adeane, was already losing patience with some aspects of the prince's conduct of his public life, and had even less patience for his wife. A lofty courtier of the old school, whose father and grandfather before him had been private secretaries to Windsor monarchs, Adeane and his crusty bachelor outlook had little time for the naïve young ingenue his boss had chosen to impose on the royal household. Adeane's 'stuffy' ways brought out Diana's natural playfulness, wagging her finger at him as she picked up his cigar butts, which Adeane found unbecoming. More than once, Charles confided, he had to intervene to 'soothe his private secretary's feelings'.[19]

Diana's pregnancy was at least an excuse for her to take things a little easier and cut back on public appearances; but that, of course, merely left her more time to feel lonely and to brood. Though thrilled by the prospect of becoming a mother, she became increasingly distraught at what she saw as Charles's neglect, which climaxed that Christmas at Sandringham. She had hoped that the long annual break in his public duties might at last afford them some time alone together, like most young newlyweds excitedly looking forward to the birth of their first child. Instead, predictably enough, it was offstage royal business as usual: Charles enjoying the great outdoors most of the time, walking or shooting, leaving his edgy, unhappy wife on her best behaviour, without his moral support, amid his daunting and cheerless extended family. After enduring two weeks of this apparent indifference, through Christmas and New Year, Diana finally cracked and confronted

Charles noisily with her feelings. The ensuing row could be heard all over Sandringham House. At the point of real despair, Diana threatened suicide; Charles accused her of being melodramatic, and coolly laid plans to go out riding. She had little alternative, as she saw it, but to carry out her threat.

Standing at the top of Sandringham's main staircase that day in January 1982, three months pregnant, Diana hurled herself down the stairs, landing at the feet of her horrified mother-in-law. Visibly shaking with shock, the Queen could not believe what she had seen; Charles, on hearing what had happened, went out riding as planned. As a local doctor tended Diana, pending the arrival from London of her gynaecologist, Dr George Pinker, it was clear that she had suffered severe bruising around her stomach. Mercifully, Pinker was later able to confirm that the baby had not been harmed.

Over the coming months, the princess persisted in further dramatic acts of self-mutilation: slashing at her wrists with a razor blade, throwing herself at a glass cabinet in Kensington Palace, cutting herself with the serrated edge of a lemon slicer and stabbing her chest and thighs with a penknife. She later acknowledged that these were not genuine suicide attempts, but 'cries for help'.

> When no-one listens to you, or you feel no-one's listening to you, all sorts of things start to happen . . . You have so much pain inside yourself that you try and hurt yourself on the outside because you want help, but it's the wrong help you're asking for. People see it as crying wolf or attention-seeking, and they think because you're in the media all the time you've got enough 'attention' . . . But I was actually crying out because I wanted to get better in order to go forward and continue my duty and my role as wife, mother, Princess of Wales. So yes, I did inflict [injuries] upon myself. I didn't like myself, I was ashamed because I couldn't cope with the pressures.[20]

These 'cries for help' were also the point of no return, after barely six months, for the marriage. Charles's failure to heed them was, to Diana, the ultimate rejection. As one eyewitness of her miseries put it to Andrew Morton, the journalist through whom she eventually revealed them to the world, 'His indifference pushed her to the edge, whereas he could have romanced her to the end of the

world. They could have set the world alight. Through no fault of
his own, because of his own ignorance, upbringing and lack of a
whole relationship with anyone in his life, he instilled this hatred
of himself.'[21]

That Charles could ignore these alarming acts of desperation,
dismissing them as 'fake' while going blithely about his business,
may seem extraordinary. Even he has confessed that he was 'not
always solicitous' and 'did sometimes rebuff her'. For his part, he
too was feeling deprived of 'the emotional support at home to
which, in his romantic way, he had for so long aspired'. As he saw
it, though 'drained by the persistence of his wife's reproaches', he
usually 'tried to console her and rarely offered any rebuke for what
his friends judged to be her waywardness. If his ministrations were
inadequate and – given his public duties – intermittent, they lacked
neither sincerity nor compassion'. Besides, his attempts to console
her were all too often rejected.

Charles's reaction to his wife's sudden spate of assaults upon
herself – 'they drew blood but a sticking plaster invariably sufficed
to stem the bleeding' – was as 'shocked and uncompre-
hending' as all those privy to them. However 'incompetent' his
attempts to comfort her, he felt 'tenderness and pity for his
wife when she was stricken by these apparently inexplicable
moods'.[22]

Amid it all, the lower reaches of the British press did not regard
the princess's pregnancy as any reason to diminish the pressures on
her. In February 1982, when she and Charles were taking a break
with the Romseys on Eleuthera, a group of tabloid reporters and
photographers crawled hundreds of yards on their bellies through
tropical undergrowth to secure a photograph of the pregnant
princess in a bikini. Next day, amid uproar, Rupert Murdoch's *Sun*
even had the gall to apologize for taking the photograph alongside
a lavish front-page reproduction of it.

Though the vacation otherwise passed uneventfully, Norton and
Penny Romsey still noticed Diana's impatience with Charles's
penchant for spending his leisure time reading and painting; and,
as they feared, the remaining months of her pregnancy saw little
improvement in her spirits. To Charles, preoccupied with the
Falklands conflict, Diana seemed to resent the fact that the press
was giving a distant war priority over her. Some of his friends,
meanwhile, did not help by persuading him of the bizarre

conclusion that his wife 'sought to possess him, but only in order to be able to reject him'.[23]

On the evening of 21 June 1982, the gulf between husband and wife was briefly forgotten when Diana gave birth to a son in St Mary's Hospital, Paddington. At her most bitter, Diana would later say they had to find a date for William's birth 'that suited Charles and his polo'; the child was induced, at her request, in truth partly because her bulimia had left her so weak, partly because the media anticipation had become so intense that she could bear it no longer. 'I felt the whole country was in labour with me,' she said years later.[24] At the time, Charles chalked up another Windsor first by staying at his wife's bedside throughout the birth; and Diana could enjoy a joke at his expense when the Queen's first comment on seeing her new grandchild was, 'Thank heavens he hasn't got his father's ears.'

It took two days for them to negotiate the names of William Arthur Philip Louis – the three royal names were a quid pro quo for Diana's choice of William – before embarking on the first few months of uncomplicated happiness in their married life. Diana had fulfilled her side of the unspoken bargain that is an arranged marriage: she had delivered her husband a male heir, as was his constitutional duty, to ensure the royal succession. But still it seemed to her that she got little thanks for it.

The previous month, with the help of the interior designer Dudley Poplak, a friend of her mother, Diana had completed the redecoration of the apartment at Kensington Palace that was to be their home. Five weeks before William's birth, she and Charles had finally moved into the 'royal ghetto' they were to share with Princess Margaret, the Duke and Duchess of Gloucester, and Prince and Princess Michael of Kent.

All too soon, however, Diana's initial euphoria became clouded by a chronic case of post-natal depression. With it returned the sickness, the bulimia, the tantrums and the obsession with Camilla. This last was not entirely unjustified; one day she overheard Charles speaking to Mrs Parker Bowles by phone from his bath, saying, 'Whatever happens, I will always love you.'[25] There ensued 'a filthy row', and a period when Diana would become highly distressed whenever she did not know where Charles was, if he did not tell her where he was going, or if he was late home from an engagement. Soon both of them were plunged back into a corrosive cycle of mutual hostility and suspicion, abuse and recrimination. They moved into separate bedrooms.

As Diana devoted all her emotional energies to her baby, fortunate that she had chosen an extremely patient nanny in Barbara Barnes, Charles chose very different forms of consolation for his lack of emotional fulfilment. It was during this period that he first began to alarm his parents with what they saw as eccentricities: giving up shooting, and turning vegetarian ('Oh, Charles, don't be so silly,' said the Queen). While the Windsors naturally blamed Diana, they might more logically have looked into their own hearts. Their neglect during his own childhood had surely launched Charles on the long quest of self-discovery which saw him seeking consolation in religions other than his own, of which he was one day destined to become Supreme Governor. His aversion to killing, albeit short-lived, was in part a return to the Buddhist beliefs he had once shared with Zoe Sallis, as was his natural aversion to eating meat, accentuated at this time by intense conversations with his vegetarian bodyguard, Paul Officer.

The logical culmination of these thought processes was to come a few months later, that December, when the prince made his first public speech advocating 'alternative' medicine. Like their colleagues in architecture, the leading lights of Britain's medical profession were not entirely pleased to be told how to do their jobs by an unelected princeling with no medical experience or qualifications. A good doctor, Charles told them, 'should be intimate with nature . . . He must have the "feel" and "touch" which makes it possible for him to be in sympathetic communication with the patient's spirits.'[26]

It was not only the doctors who were mildly offended by this speech. So was Charles's wife, a mistress of the arts of 'feel' and 'touch', woefully deprived of any such thing from her husband. At the time, moreover, she was still afflicted by post-natal depression. Denial from her husband was the last thing she needed.

In her heart, Diana knew that Charles was ill-equipped by his upbringing to deal with a psychological disorder in anyone, let alone someone close to him. But she could not help feeling 'misunderstood' and 'very, very low'. It was quite out of character. 'I'd never had a depression in my life. But then when I analysed it I could see that the changes I'd made in the last year had all caught up with me, and my body had said: "We want a rest." ' But Diana's sufferings gave her an even deeper, more lasting cause for concern. As far as she could tell, no-one in the royal family, including Charles, had any personal experience of dealing with depression. 'Maybe I was the first person in this family who ever had a depression or was ever openly tearful.' The consequences were ominous. 'It gave everybody [in the royal family] a wonderful new label: Diana's unstable, Diana's mentally unbalanced.' Unfortunately, as she soon realized, that label 'seemed to stick'.[27]

At William's christening in early August 1982, she complained of feeling 'totally excluded' amid 'endless pictures of the Queen, Queen Mother, Charles and William'. The family then repaired, as usual, to Balmoral, where she grew steadily worse. At a total loss, Charles arranged for her to return to London to see another round of counsellors and psychiatrists.

Misinterpreting her motives, the press decided that Diana had become 'bored' at the royal family's rain-soaked Scottish retreat, where there was no nightlife to suit the mythical 'Disco Di', who had fled to go shopping in Knightsbridge. For the first time, barely a year after the marriage, the tribunes of the people turned against her; the gossip columnist Nigel Dempster labelled her 'a monster and a fiend' for supposedly destabilizing the prince's staff and driving away his friends.

Later, there might have been some substance to this charge; but not yet. In letters to friends, Charles still nursed some hope that things might improve. But progress was patchy; every apparent step forward was always followed by some frustrating setback. That very day, for instance, after a 'hopeful' morning, the afternoon had seen a 'heavy feeling' descend.[28] Behind the façade, in private as in public, he too was close to despair.

There was a hopeful sign that September, when Diana volunteered to represent the Queen at the funeral of her soulmate, Princess Grace of Monaco, killed that month in a car crash. Charles disapproved; in an exchange of memos with his wife – the only way the royals see fit to discuss such matters – he argued that she was not yet ready to undertake her first solo engagement abroad on behalf of the monarchy. But Diana felt a kinship with Grace, another outsider who had endured difficulties in becoming royal, and a debt of honour for her kindness on her public début eighteen months before. She dug in her heels, and went over Charles's head direct to his mother, again by memo. No doubt taking it as a healthy sign of Diana's intent to prove herself, and relieved to find someone willing to pay the Windsors' respects to a woman she had always regarded as 'vulgar', the Queen agreed. To Charles's chagrin, Diana won universal praise for the dignity with which she graced an occasion as Hollywood as it was Monégasque.

But Diana's apparent revival did not last long. Palace staff were privy to another domestic row the following month, when Charles loudly berated his wife for her last-minute refusal to accompany him to the British Legion remembrance service at the Royal Albert Hall. On the eve of the annual ceremony at the Cenotaph, when the royal family leads the nation's homage to the dead of two world wars, the occasion is regarded as one of the most important fixed points in the royal calendar. After a seething Charles had left without her, Diana evidently underwent a change of heart; she was seen by astonished spectators to arrive in the royal box fifteen minutes late, after the ceremony had begun, looking 'grumpy and fed-up'. To arrive after the Queen was a gross breach of protocol, for which she would not swiftly be forgiven.

The incident was but the latest climax in Diana's continuing concerns: Charles's apparent indifference to her, the loneliness and boredom of royal life, her unshakeable obsession with Camilla. But the princess also felt resentful that her husband and his staff had offered her no help in coping with her new status. 'No-one sat me down with a piece of paper and said: "This is what is expected of you."' So she did what came naturally, which only exacerbated the problem. When Diana was photographed sitting on hospital beds and holding patients' hands, Charles and his staff were 'shocked . . . They said they had never seen this before, while to me it was quite a normal thing to do.'

But there had never been a royal quite like Diana before, as she herself was well aware: 'Here was a situation which hadn't ever happened before in history, in the sense that the media were everywhere, and here was a fairy story that everybody wanted to work.' It was 'isolating', yes, 'but it was also a situation where you couldn't indulge in feeling sorry for yourself. You had to learn very fast. You either had to sink or swim.'[29] Diana became determined to swim.

She had to fight to stay afloat when some indiscreet remarks by the couple's then press secretary, the Canadian Vic Chapman, suggested that she had developed other obsessions, such as demanding that her shoes be polished daily and arranged in immaculately neat straight lines. Leaks of this kind of irrational behaviour, amid further comments on her thinness, prompted the first public rumours that Diana might be suffering from an eating disorder – perhaps, like her sister Sarah, anorexia nervosa.

As an informed guess, it was only half wrong. Diana's bulimia was growing steadily worse. If she had been on an official visit around the country – what she called an 'awayday' – she would return home feeling 'pretty empty, because my engagements at that time would be to do with people dying, people very sick, people's marriage problems'. She found it 'very difficult to know how to comfort myself, having been comforting lots of other people, so it would be a regular pattern to jump into the fridge'.

Where Charles saw her illness as the source of their problems, Diana still insisted that it was the product of his dismissive attitude towards her. 'I was crying out for help,' she said, 'but giving the wrong signals.' To her, Charles was 'using' her bulimia as 'a coat on a hanger . . . [He] decided that was the problem: Diana was unstable.' At mealtimes together, far from expressing sympathy, he would accuse her of 'wasting' food. Remarks like these, of course, only added to the pressure on her. 'So of course I would, because it was my release valve.'[30]

From his viewpoint, Charles could only watch with mounting dismay as Diana thrashed around in her own private agonies, now compounded by the withdrawal of the media's unqualified support. As they prepared to embark on a year of major foreign tours together, he could only grit his teeth and hope.

When they flew to Australia the following March, for their first official foreign tour together, amounting to six weeks away, Charles and Diana took nine-month-old William with them. Seeking controversy where there was none, the press was wrong to suggest that the Queen disapproved; in fact, she had not even been consulted. Mindful of his parents' long absences during his own infancy and childhood, Charles was only too pleased to accept the thoughtful suggestion of the Australian prime minister, Malcolm Fraser, that they might enjoy the trip more if they brought their son along. Diana, of course, was thrilled.

They based themselves at Woomargama, a sheep station in New South Wales, where William was left with his nanny, Barbara

Barnes, while the prince and princess undertook an arduous schedule of public engagements. The scale of the adulation – with
millions materializing to see them from a population of only
17 million – was like nothing Charles had ever known; the clamour
and crush, apart from being dangerous, offended his sense of
decorum and stretched his nerves. To the prince, by now, these
overseas visits were more of a duty than a pleasure; in his thirty-
fifth year, he had already 'endured' more than fifty of them. For
Diana, of course, it was a whole new experience – and a daunting
one, despite her husband's supposedly reassuring presence. Thanks
to her, the crowds were bigger than Charles had ever known; in
Brisbane alone, more than a quarter of a million turned out for a
glimpse of the world's most glamorous couple. But it was 'Lady Di'
who dominated the headlines, and the pictorial coverage. It was
another forceful reminder for Charles that his future subjects,
while warm towards him, were 'besotted' with his wife.

He did not take kindly to this. Back at Woomargama, Charles
immersed himself in Turgenev and Jung while Diana relaxed with
William. But both agreed, for once, that they worked as a mutual
support system during the unusual ardours of their antipodean
journey, which took them to New Zealand for two weeks after four
in Australia. The whole thing, for Charles, had become too much
of a circus, with Diana's every twitch being photographed for
posterity. 'It frightens me,' he wrote to friends, 'and I know for a
fact it petrifies Diana.' She was 'marvellous', he reported, and
helped keep him going; for her part, the princess acknowledged
that Charles had 'pulled her out of her shell and helped her cope
with the pressure . . . We were a very good team in public, albeit
what was going on in private . . . We had unique pressures put
upon us, but we both tried our hardest to cover them up.'[31]

It was during this trip, however, that another source of tension
between them began to surface: Charles's natural resentment, as he
was candid enough to admit to friends, at being 'upstaged and out-
shone' by his wife. To a proud man, accustomed all his life to being
the centre of attention, it had at first been a relief when Diana took
some of the pressure off him; but when the spotlight showed no
sign of swinging back his way, Charles's *amour propre* began to
suffer. As she herself realized, he felt 'low about it, instead of feeling happy and sharing it'.[32] But Diana did not entirely understand
his priorities. To Charles, this was not just a matter of personal

jealousy, but of royal protocol; Diana was there as his wife and consort, not as his superior.

The same proved true on a tour of Canada a few weeks later. Though the crowds were neither as large nor as manic as in Australia, they were all there to see Diana rather than Charles. In strict terms of status, he should have been the star of the travelling roadshow; but in terms of public esteem, it was clear that the pulling power was all hers. If it was Diana's obsessions and pre-occupations that had so far undermined their chance of marital happiness, whether justified or not, Charles now had one of his own to eat away at what little hope they had left.

Back in London, they basked in universal adulation, summed up in a typically effusive tribute from the speaker of the House of Commons, George Thomas, that same devout Welshman who had fluttered around Charles during his investiture. 'Not only the royal family have gained by their success,' trilled Thomas, 'but the whole nation and the Commonwealth have received a blessing beyond measure . . . In the rapidly changing world that we have, I believe that the Prince and Princess of Wales and their son will give us the continuity that assures us stability.'[33]

Speaker Thomas could not be expected to discern the deep irony behind his rhetorical flourish. Stability, the quality the Wales marriage was supposedly going to supply to the nation, was the one thing the union itself sorely lacked. Continuity, as a result, was already in long-term doubt. The causes of their unhappiness did not vary; Diana's complaints remained the same, Charles refused to mend his ways, and they had found no way of communicating; by mutual agreement, they had failed to build 'the intimacy and mutual understanding without which the relationship could not grow'.[34]

That autumn was the worst they had yet known. While at Highgrove, Charles took to joining Camilla with the Beaufort Hunt as soon as his wife left for London. It did not take Diana long to work out what was going on; all her worst fears, still written off as her irrational 'obsession', were being realized. That November, when she joined her husband for a weekend at Highgrove, a suspicious Diana pressed the 'recall' button on the phone in his study, to find it ringing Camilla's number. There was a 'monumental row' in front of the domestic staff as Charles nevertheless insisted on going out hunting with Camilla, even with Diana in residence. The servants watched in horror as the princess broke down in hysterical tears; Charles, by now past caring, rode off regardless.

Both still wanted more children; and they must have called a truce over Christmas and New Year at Sandringham long enough for the princess to become pregnant again. As she relaxed her timetable accordingly, Charles had an unusually busy year ahead, with trips to Brunei in February, East Africa in March, Papua New Guinea in August, France, Monaco and Holland in the autumn. To his mind, Diana now took advantage of these absences to 'banish' some of his closest friends, including the Romseys, the Palmer-Tomkinsons, the Brabournes and Nicholas Soames.

Convinced that these pre-marital loyalists were conspiring with Charles against her, and facilitating his secret meetings with Camilla, Diana ensured that they were no longer invited to Highgrove or Kensington Palace. For all his subsequent protests, Charles chose at the time to go along with this considerable sacrifice. These friends testify that, for a period, his phone calls and letters ceased to come. Understandably hurt, but suspecting what was really happening, they did not take the matter up with the prince for fear of placing him in a difficult position.

Charles would later deny it, but Diana believed that her husband had already 'gone back to his lady'. She also knew from a scan that the child in her womb was a boy, while he was desperately hoping for a girl. For the moment, she decided not to tell him, as her pregnancy again occasioned sporadic oases of calm amid all the turbulence. Already Diana wanted out, as she confided to her friend Sarah Ferguson. But the princess knew that that was impossible then, if ever, and during that summer of her second pregnancy she managed to appear calmer and more content than at any other time in the marriage.

Charles responded wholeheartedly to Diana's welcome transformation, giving her no cause for suspicion of Camilla, and treating his heavily pregnant wife with unusual solicitude at Balmoral. 'We were very, very close to each other the six weeks before Harry was born,' she recalled, 'the closest we've ever, ever been.'[35] But it was to prove the calm before a climactic storm.

At 4.20 p.m. on Saturday, 15 September, Diana gave birth to a second son in the Lindo wing of St Mary's Hospital. She had still failed to summon the nerve to let Charles in on the secret of their child's gender. 'Oh, God,' he exclaimed, 'it's a boy.' And, he added, in a biting reference to his son's Spencer genes, 'He's even got red hair.'

With this, the prince left for Windsor to play polo. 'Something inside me closed off,' said Diana. 'It just went bang, our marriage, the whole thing went down the drain.'[36]

Charles and Diana had been married barely three years. Henceforth, as well as occupying separate beds, they would start to lead separate lives.

CHAPTER TEN

'WHY CAN'T YOU BE MORE LIKE FERGIE?'

IT WAS NOT ONLY ON THE DOMESTIC FRONT THAT CHARLES'S LIFE WAS disintegrating. Now, early in 1985, Edward Adeane chose to resign as the Prince of Wales's private secretary. Only within the Palace was the huge significance of Adeane's departure appreciated. His father, Lord Adeane, had been private secretary to Charles's mother and grandfather, Elizabeth II and George VI; his grand-father, Viscount Stamfordham, had been private secretary to Queen Victoria and her grandson, George V. It was Adeane's grandfather, indeed, who had given the royal dynasty its name of Windsor; at the height of the First World War, when George V was reluctantly persuaded to drop the German name of Saxe-Coburg-Gotha, Stamfordham suggested instead the name of the historic Berkshire town where the king spent his weekends. In 1980, a year after becoming Charles's private secretary, Edward Adeane fulfilled a cherished personal ambition by completing a century of un-broken royal service by his family.

It had thus been taken for granted, a *fait accompli*, that the bachelor Adeane would in turn devote his life to the royal family, like his father and grandfather before him, staying at his master's side for as long as it took to maintain his family's proud tradition by becoming private secretary to King Charles III. His abrupt departure signalled that something really was rotten in the House of Windsor.

Not long before, Charles had also lost the services of his long-standing naval friend, Michael Colborne, who had been supervising his personal finances, with the title of secretary to the prince's office. Three years earlier his long-serving valet Stephen Barry had been among the first of his staff to leave, within six months of the marriage. By the end of 1985, no fewer than forty members of the royal household had chosen to quit: apart from Adeane, Colborne and Barry, there was Alan Fisher, the butler the Waleses inherited from Bing Crosby; Lieutenant-Colonel Philip Creasy, comptroller (financial controller) of the prince's household; and the hapless Oliver Everett, who had given up a promising Foreign Office career for temporary secondment to the prince's office, only to wind up becoming his wife's reluctant private secretary and now the Queen's librarian. Even Charles's loyal, long-time detectives, Paul Officer and John MacLean, eventually bade their prince farewell as, in the words of her brother Charles, Diana 'got rid of all the hangers-on who surrounded Charles'.[1]

Remarks like that bolstered the public perception that the princess was systematically cleansing the Wales stables, purging first friends and now staff, while a browbeaten Charles surrendered purse strings as much as apron strings. Loyal retainers who felt obliged to quit were quoted blaming the princess and her petulant ways. 'The debonair prince is pussy-whipped from here to eternity,' an American magazine stated that year, before the couple's visit to the Reagan White House.[2] The truth was subtly different. To some extent, as her self-confidence grew, Diana did make attempts to change the climate of the alien world in which she found herself, and to construct a personal landscape in which she had a chance of taking more control. From the moment she struck the names of Parker Bowles and Tryon off the guest list for the wedding breakfast, she had made the understandable effort of many a young bride to persuade her husband to leave his bachelor world behind. She had not, of course, entirely succeeded; so the process naturally continued with the staff, many of whom anyway felt uncomfortable being privy to the couple's perpetual squabbles.

But the cases of those closest to Charles belie the suggestion that Diana's behaviour was primarily to blame. Stephen Barry, his valet for twelve years before the wedding, may not have been personally close to the prince in terms of anything like friendship, but he was the man who had woken him up every day for twelve years, taken him breakfast in bed, shared many of his most private secrets, and had thus become close to Charles in quite another sense.

'I did not have a row with Princess Diana,' Barry testified. 'Nothing of the kind happened.' He decided to quit because the prince's centre of gravity was shifting to Highgrove, and his own life was in London. After covering most of the globe with Charles, he had also lost his appetite for travel. And, as he sensibly put it at the time, 'It's quite reasonable and not surprising that anyone as young as Princess Diana would want to be surrounded by people of her own choice.'

When Barry informed her of his decision to go, Diana immediately joked, 'People will say we've had a terrible row!'

'As long as we know we haven't,' he replied, 'that's all right, isn't it?' The bulimic Diana nodded, and 'took another spoonful of yogurt'.[3]

Colborne's departure also had little, if nothing, to do with Diana. In fact, it was more Charles's fault for failing to cut through the Palace protocol that denied the title of comptroller to one of his navy chum's humble status. A key player in the administrative side of the prince's life, and a trusted friend, Colborne was a grievous, and unnecessary, loss. Like all the others who left in this lemming-like parade, he was glad to be spared the constant rows and tension between the prince and princess; but he would have stayed on, lending Charles valuable moral support, had he been promoted to a rank and salary befitting his contribution to the smooth running of Charles's life.

Adeane, too, had become weary of the marital spats; but it was not, as bruited about at the time, Diana's waywardness that drove him out of royal life. It was Charles's.

'Edward', said Diana, perhaps diplomatically, 'was wonderful. We got on so well.' She especially appreciated the candidates he proposed for her ladies-in-waiting: 'One or two [fell] by the wayside but the others remained very strong.'[4] For all the petty irritations, the princess genuinely endeared herself to this punctilious courtier of the old school by the efficiency and dispatch with which she dealt with paperwork, especially letters – a dutiful habit drummed into her in childhood. Her husband, by contrast, was notoriously slapdash about paperwork, which he had always hated.

As the prince began to assemble his portfolio of causes to champion, Adeane had made it clear that he thought some of them inappropriate, also taking a dim view of the growing army of informal advisers recruited by the prince. Even Charles's admirers concede that '[his] enthusiasms too often bore the imprint of the last conversation he had held or the latest article to have caught his eye', as well as 'his tendency to reach instant conclusions on the basis of insufficient thought'.[5]

Under the pressure of countless new initiatives, many turning out to be mere dalliances that were soon forgotten, the Prince of Wales's private office – inadequately staffed to meet the mounting flow of business – began to spin increasingly out of control, with piles of paper accumulating at random, and heaps of letters lying around unanswered. Uncomfortable with such carelessness, Adeane was even less pleased to note that his advice was increasingly being ignored. The climax came on 30 May 1984, with the prince's infamous 'carbuncle speech' at Hampton Court Palace.

When Charles criticized Peter Ahrends's design for the National Gallery extension in Trafalgar Square as 'a monstrous carbuncle on the face of a much-loved friend', and launched into a wholesale assault on modern architecture, he was not just abusing the hospitality of the Royal Institute of British Architects at a cele-bratory dinner on the occasion of their 150th anniversary. He was insulting the eminent Indian architect Charles Correa, whom he ignored throughout the evening, although the prime reason for the prince's presence was to present Correa with the RIBA's Gold Medal for his outstanding work for the Third World homeless – precisely the kind of work that Charles has otherwise claimed as his own. He was also causing commercial damage to a British com-pany, and subverting statutory planning procedures. Above all, he was committing a damaging, and unjustified, slander – the kind of slur which, had it come from anyone else in public life, might well have earned them an expensive lawsuit.

His private secretary, for once, was on the side of the prince's opponents. The speech, to Adeane as to its audience, was symptomatic of Charles's failure to grasp the complexities of the architectural process, which is not merely about style, but about the handling of space and scale, interminable negotiations with planners and developers, and the immense complexities of design-ing modern, high-technology buildings to last centuries. Had the prince done a modicum of research before launching so vicious a public assault on a distinguished man's reputation, he would have known that the design he criticized was in fact a compromise between the gallery's trustees and the architect, then at an interim stage about which Ahrends himself was less than happy. At the request of the trustees, the architect had already made certain revisions to his original design. So when the prince questioned, for instance, the sacrifice of gallery space to office space, he was in fact attacking the brief given Ahrends by his client, the gallery's trustees (of which Charles himself would soon be one).[6]

At the time of the prince's speech a public planning inquiry was under way, at the end of which the secretary of state for the environment, Patrick Jenkin, was due to make a final ruling. But the views of the public became irrelevant from the moment Charles stood up to speak. Jenkin happened to be in the audience at Hampton Court; while the prince was still on his feet, he whispered to his neighbour, 'Well, that's one decision I don't have to make!'[7]

Peter Ahrends's distinguished career was blighted that evening. Soon his practice, one of Britain's leading architectural partnerships, was losing millions of pounds in potential commissions. Developers who feared the prince's veto no longer invited the 'carbuncle architects' to enter competitions, the meat and drink of the their profession. That night, in the heat of the moment, Ahrends gave vent to his feelings; the prince's remarks, he told journalists, were 'offensive, reactionary, ill-considered . . . if he holds such strong views, I'm surprised he did not take the opportunity offered by the public inquiry to express them'. Ever since, he has shown dignified restraint by holding his peace, though described by colleagues as 'a broken man' – 'a tragic figure' who had 'every right to feel aggrieved'.*

For days Adeane had been trying to talk Charles out of the speech. Its passionate partiality, apart from constituting an abuse of hospitality, would incur the enmity of a British professional institute under royal patronage; and it would involve him in a heated public debate in an area which was wholly new ground to him. Charles listened testily, unaccustomed to internal opposition of such force. But his stubborn streak won the day; unknown to Adeane, who was still trying to talk him out of the speech in the

---

* Seven years later, in July 1991, the Prince of Wales watched his mother open the building hastily commissioned to replace the British architect's design: the new Sainsbury Wing of the National Gallery, designed by an American architect, Robert Venturi. Could Charles *really*, asked one architectural critic, admire this 'limp, sub-classical' result of his intervention? 'For those committed Classicists whose work the prince has endorsed, this building is not so much a joke as a crime – an insult to the hallowed tradition of Vitruvius and Palladio.'[8]

car *en route* to Hampton Court, he had already leaked the text to
The Times and the *Guardian*. Telephoned for a response, the
RIBA's president, Michael Manser, had been so horrified as to
threaten to boycott the evening. As it was, he contented himself
with a measured slap of the royal wrist. It was 'deeply unsatis-
factory', said Manser, 'that the debate should become locked into
the arguments of new versus old. What we need to discuss is good
or bad.'9

For Adeane, all this fuss, in the teeth of his advice, was the last
straw; he was gone within six months. For Charles, it was the start
of a campaign that would earn him vigorous opposition, at times
obloquy, symbolizing his painfully swift transition, in the eyes of
the press and many of its readers, from caped crusader to comic
crank.

Diana, meanwhile, was visibly growing in self-confidence. Her
unexpected staying power as a world superstar was bolstering her
self-esteem and giving her the upper hand in the relationship,
publicly if not privately. As she mastered the art of the royal
appearance, the princess began to take an almost sadistic pleasure
in upstaging her husband. For every new speech he made, she
would wear a different hairstyle or hat; the photographers, she well
knew, were much more interested in her than in him – as, still, were
the crowds, who continued to groan if Charles rather than Di
headed in their direction. But Charles's increasing distress sprang
from more than merely a bruised royal ego. The public's insatiable
appetite for details of the Princess of Wales's clothes, her hair, her
hats, her tiniest asides, drowned out anything he might do or say.
For a man desperate to be taken seriously, the tidal wave of trivia
became unbearably irritating.

As his preoccupations grew more earnest, so hers seemed to
grow more frivolous. While Charles denounced the ways of the
modern world, Diana frequented fashion shows and a social milieu
not normally visited by royalty. Whenever Charles toured Britain's
inner cities, on a social campaign that became a crusade, his wife
was now rarely at his side. He did not want her there, to steal his
column-inches, and she herself had no wish to be.

If Diana was exacting her revenge for what she saw as Charles's
betrayals, it was also the first sign of the intuitive knack for public
relations that would later prove the making of her. At this stage of

her development, as well she knew, hers was a passive power, both over her public and her husband. It was best preserved by opening her mouth as little as possible, and best explained by telling delighted bystanders, 'I'm as thick as a plank.' This remark (which became a regular one-liner) suggested just how savvy Diana really was, while reinforcing the empty-headedness of which her reflective husband increasingly despaired. Inspecting the sumptuous garden of a friend's country home, he complimented his foreign hostess on her excellent English. 'My father believed in educating girls,' she explained. 'I wish', muttered Charles ruefully, 'that had been the philosophy in my wife's family.'[10]

Only now, when increasingly on her own at public functions, did Diana feel free to let her true self show through. It was during this 'cold war' of 1985 that the guests of her favourite fashion designer, Bruce Oldfield, were astonished by her extravagant behaviour at a fundraising ball, one of the first of such events that she attended conspicuously alone, leaving a moody Charles behind at Highgrove. Any doubts about recent rumours that she had been out partying alone, dancing the night away without her husband, were staunched when the princess stayed on after the appointed witching hour of midnight – on and on, until the French musician, Jean-Michel Jarre, husband of Charlotte Rampling, asked her to dance. Diana, said one witness, 'positively lit up . . . Everyone within twenty yards got the fallout from Diana's mood that night. She was suddenly aware of everything she had been missing.'[11]

As they began to go their separate ways – with the public, as yet, only barely aware of what was happening – Charles found himself unable to compete with Diana's instinctive skills as a public performer. It was now, with two pregnancies behind her and another highly unlikely, that she began to emerge as a global fashion icon, the world's most popular cover girl, besieged by designers wanting her to be seen in their wares. Charles watched helplessly, and not altogether approvingly, as the charmingly informal touches she brought to formal public occasions began to build her a huge army of followers. To him, this style of 'showbiz' monarchy was anathema, and would not last. The ancient institution to which he was heir could not survive, he believed, as a branch of the entertainment industry. Doggedly, he pursued his own more serious agenda, launching the inner-city campaign that was to bring him into conflict with the Thatcher government.

In a speech to the cream of British management, the Institute of Directors, the prince startled his audience with a *cri de cœur* about the 'inhuman conditions' endured by so many urban Britons: 'The hopelessness left in such communities is compounded by decay all around, the vandalism and the inability to control their own lives in any way beyond the basic requirements of day-to-day survival in a hostile environment.'[12] This mild flirtation with political controversy was as nothing to the explosion eight months later, in October 1985, when Charles was quoted as fearing that he would inherit a 'divided' Britain. Under the headline PRINCE CHARLES: MY FEARS FOR THE FUTURE, a Manchester paper reported that the prince was 'prepared to force his way through parliamentary red tape to ensure that his country is not split into factions of the haves and have-nots'. Charles was said to be worried that 'when he becomes king there will be no-go areas in the inner cities, and that the minorities will be alienated from the rest of the country'.[13]

From New York, where she was addressing the United Nations, an incensed Margaret Thatcher telephoned Buckingham Palace to demand an explanation. The prime minister was less than convinced by the protests of courtiers that Charles had intended no criticism of her government. But the provenance of the royal remarks was murky. They had been leaked by Rod Hackney, one of his more personally ambitious architectural advisers, after a private conversation on the royal train. Hackney, whose brand of 'community architecture' had seen him forge a post-Hampton Court alliance with the prince, was swift to apologize for the trouble he had caused. But there could be no forgiveness for so damaging an indiscretion. He received a strongly worded letter of rebuke, and was banished from the charmed circle of Charles's advisers.

The British constitution defines no role for the heir to the throne. Its unwritten rules are eloquent as to what the Prince of Wales should not do, unhelpfully silent as to what he should. Beyond staying out of party politics, the job description is a *tabula rasa*. History has thus seen some monarchs-in-waiting set themselves up as rivals to their royal parents, acting as unofficial leaders of the opposition, barely disguising their eagerness to take over; others have taken the chance to make themselves useful, as patrons of the arts or activists in other non-controversial fields. Rather more, denied any role in affairs of state, have used the position and its perks to enjoy lives of self-indulgent dissipation.

The history of the office is not, as a result, a particularly distinguished one. Charles, the twenty-first English Prince of Wales in 700 years, entered his thirties intent on changing all that. One of the better-educated heirs to the throne, endowed with a strong sense of history, he seemed by disposition more earnest, reflective and well meaning than the majority of his predecessors, if equally aloof from the daily lifestyles and concerns of his future subjects. In early adulthood, his modest intelligence appeared to belie genetic theory. Heir to the throne since the age of three, but unlikely to inherit it until he was a septuagenarian grandfather, he had spent most of his youth frustrated by the prospect of so long and tiresome a wait in the wings, and increasingly irritated by continual taunts that he should get 'a proper job' – not least from Cabinet ministers such as Norman Tebbit. In the mid-1980s Charles made a conscious decision to turn necessity to advantage by earning himself a niche as a crusader Prince of Wales, riding a populist white charger to the rescue of disadvantaged minorities around his future realm.

From architecture to conservation, employment to the inner cities, race relations to other urgent social concerns of the day, the prince boldly used his office to launch initiatives like grapeshot, and won a positive public response. The mid-1980s saw him ready to ride to the rescue of any underprivileged minority with whom he could sympathize without incurring the wrath of Thatcher, midway through her eleven years in power. Under pressure from her right-wing backbenchers, the then prime minister steered him away from tacit criticism of the government, deleting urban deprivation and inner-city blight from his agenda; but a philosophical jigsaw nevertheless appeared to be falling into place, its disparate pieces fusing the wild profusion of causes he had espoused.

While still in the navy, in the mid-1970s, Charles had founded the Prince's Trust, designed to make small financial grants to unemployed youths intent on community service. The Trust's work was worthy but dull stuff to a tabloid press then intent on chronicling the 'macho' lifestyle of the playboy prince, playing the field as he open-endedly postponed his choice of bride. Having entered his thirties a frustrated and somewhat embittered figure, he was finally liberated by his eventual marriage from the long and

Angela, packing her suitcase while she slept, and telephoning her husband in France to inform him of her travel plans.

When Diana returned to Scotland the atmosphere was frostier than ever. Charles took his family's side in suggesting she had made an unnecessary drama of one man's death from AIDS. At Ward-Jackson's memorial service a few weeks later, Diana was forbidden to sit with his family and friends, including Angela, on the left-hand side of St Paul's Church, Knightsbridge. Charles's staff insisted that, as a member of the royal family, she sit in their traditional place at the front of the church, on the right-hand side. Such absurdities only reinforced the change in Diana wrought by the whole experience. 'I reached a depth inside which I never imagined,' she wrote to Angela Serota. 'My outlook on life has changed its course and become more positive and balanced.'[9]

That September saw Harry join his brother William at boarding school, Ludgrove in Berkshire, leaving Diana alone in the 'empty nest' she now called her apartment in Kensington Palace. But the princess was fast developing her own circle of supporters, privy to the secrets of her marriage, who offered a wide range of positive advice. In Lucia Flecha da Lima, wife of the Brazilian ambassador to London, she had found a wise and forceful counsellor, as much a substitute mother as Mara Berni, while surrogate sisters included Angela Serota, her former flatmate Carolyn Bartholomew and the Hon. Rosa Monckton, managing director of the London branch of Tiffany's. Girlfriends on whom she relied less for wise counsel than light relief included Kate Menzies, Julia Samuel, Julia Dodd-Noble and Catherine Soames, ex-wife of Charles's friend Nicholas.

Like the royal staff, however, most of Diana's friends were to find themselves dropped and taken up again on the most baffling whims. 'She found it difficult to accept criticism,' conceded Rosa Monckton, whose friendship with Diana once ceased abruptly for four months after she had offered some constructive criticism. 'Then, as usually happened, she just picked up the telephone one day, said, "Rosa, how are you?" and off we went again.'[10] Rosa remained her firm friend to the very end, spending a week alone in Greece with the princess just a fortnight before her death.

Charles, too, had a loyal, tight-knit circle of friends to see him through this darkest year of his failing marriage. Nicholas Soames, now a rising Conservative MP, remained his oldest and most devoted ally, predating even Andrew Parker Bowles and Camilla – who was now chatelaine of Highgrove in all but name, hosting gatherings of the select coterie who visited in Diana's absence. Besides the Palmer-Tomkinsons and the Tryons, there was Camilla's sister Annabel and Norfolk neighbours Hugh and Emilie van Cutsem. Older figures like van der Post and Lady Susan Hussey, his mother's favourite lady-in-waiting, were also frequent visitors to Highgrove. When their presence coincided with hers, Diana tried to treat them with civility, but found them 'stuffy' and 'dull'. She was also aware that they considered her beneath them, tolerated as Charles's wife but not up to their level of smart sophistication.

They certainly found it highly amusing when Charles celebrated his forty-third birthday that November by taking his wife to see Oscar Wilde's play *A Woman of No Importance*. The other woman in his life at the time – apart, of course, from Camilla – was the *Mary Rose*, a warship sunk off Portsmouth Harbour in 1545, which had recently been recovered. Knowing the project to have been close to Mountbatten's heart, Charles became involved in the restoration work, and assumed the leadership of ambitious plans to build an appropriate museum.

But they ended in failure after he rejected the original design, then fell out with the architect whom he commissioned to produce an alternative, Professor Christopher Alexander of University of Berkeley, California. Charles had more success with his continuing campaign to defend Shakespeare's place on the national curriculum. With one of his lesser-known mentors, his former schoolteacher Eric Anderson (by now headmaster of Eton), he hosted a lunch for educationalists which led to the foundation of Shakespeare summer schools at Stratford-on-Avon, and which have since become an annual fixture under the auspices of the Royal Shakespeare Company.

Still, however, he would not give an inch on the domestic front. Later that month, December 1991, Diana was photographed in public tears as she left St James's Palace after a memorial service for the Romseys' daughter, Leonora Knatchbull, who had died of cancer at the age of only six. Six months earlier, Diana had held Leonora's hand on the balcony of Buckingham Palace, as together they watched the Trooping the Colour ceremony. But her tears that day were not just for a tragic little child prematurely taken from her parents. They were tears of rage because of the unexpected presence of Camilla Parker Bowles – who, as far as Diana knew, had only recently got to know the Romseys – at the intimate family occasion. In fact, Camilla was closer to the Romseys than Diana realized: Broadlands, where Mountbatten had once hosted clandestine meetings between the prince and his paramour, was now the Romseys' home, and so continued to be a 'safe house' for their secret trysts.

To Charles's intimate circle, Camilla's presence alongside his wife was another sign that he was no longer bothered about keeping their relationship secret. Diana knew all about it, after all; if she could not maintain her public dignity, that was her problem. The Princess of Wales alternated between rage and hysteria as she imagined the two of them laughing behind her back at her distress. Charles remained oblivious, strengthening his wife's resolve to continue her public work, while finding a way out of the marriage. She saw it as a domestic triumph that Christmas when the Queen went out of her way in her Christmas broadcast to remind her subjects that she had no intention of abdicating in Charles's favour. Though he knew in his heart that this would always be the case, the prince was distressed at this coded signal of his mother's displeasure, milked by the media as a public humiliation.

Only one more unscripted, impromptu scene remained before the drama that was the Wales marriage entered its final act. It came out of the blue three months later, when Charles and Diana were on a skiing holiday with their sons – not, at Diana's insistence, in Klosters, but in the Austrian resort of Lech. Here, on 29 March 1992, the princess received the news that her father had died. As she made immediate plans to return home, leaving her children in their father's care, Charles insisted on returning with her. Sensing the public-relations ploy implicit in his offer, Diana told him bitterly that it was 'a bit late to start playing the caring husband'.[11]

Charles had not originally intended to join his wife and children in Lech, having laid alternative plans to visit Milan that week. When he decided to fly in for the weekend, his staff ensured that photographers were alerted to his arrival at the Arlberg Hotel, via a radio-co-ordinated operation ensuring that his sons were waiting on the hotel doorstep, ready to fly into his arms for the cameras. There were more 'happy family' photocalls the next morning. The whole episode – part of Aylard's new 'charm offensive' to paint Charles as a caring father – thoroughly sickened Diana, who was now in no mood to let him in on her grief for her father. Even as she mourned, an untimely row ensued in the royal hotel suite, as Aylard and other members of Charles's staff took his part, insisting that Diana must let him accompany her home. But the princess would not be moved. Charles, she said, had made no effort in life to befriend his father-in-law, so she saw no reason why he should now be allowed to intrude on her family's private grief.

To the prince, this was not the point. He could not risk the negative publicity that would inevitably attend his bereaved wife's return home without him. Eventually Aylard prevailed upon the princess to let the Queen act as referee, extracting an agreement that she would abide by her mother-in-law's decision. Un-surprisingly, a phone call to Windsor resulted in a royal command that the couple fly home together. On their arrival at RAF Northolt, in a BAe 146 of the Queen's Flight, the media pack waiting on the tarmac noted that Charles came down the steps first, stopping at the bottom to chat with Aylard, while a gaunt-faced Diana struggled after him, carrying her own hand luggage. Sycophantic to the last, they duly reported next morning that Charles had loyally abandoned his holiday to support his wife in her moment of need.

In truth he drove straight off to Highgrove and Camilla, leaving Diana to mourn her father alone at Kensington Palace. Two days later, the prince could not even bring himself to drive up to Northamptonshire with his wife for her father's funeral. He took a helicopter from Highgrove to Althorp, the Spencer family seat, leaving Diana to travel from London without him. After the service he returned briefly to Althorp before returning to his heli-copter, pleading a prior engagement in London. That night, as Diana stayed with her grieving family, Charles was back at Highgrove.

Even during the few minutes he took to offer his condolences to Diana's family, Charles managed to leave a remarkably clumsy calling card. It is unclear whether he knew of the conflict of emotions assailing the new Earl Spencer, his brother-in-law Charles, who, unlike Diana, had remained estranged from his father at the time of his death. Either way, Charles Spencer was surprised at the style in which his sister's husband chose to couch his message of sympathy. 'You lucky man,' were the Prince of Wales's words of consolation. 'I wish I had inherited so young!'[12]

CHAPTER FOURTEEN

'WHY DON'T YOU GO OFF WITH YOUR LADY?'

FEBRUARY 1992 MARKED THE FORTIETH ANNIVERSARY OF ELIZABETH II'S accession to the throne, seen by Buckingham Palace as the perfect springboard for year-long celebrations, echoing the national euphoria that had greeted the Queen's silver jubilee fifteen years earlier, and deflecting national attention from the marital problems of her children. Helpfully, as he thought, her son and heir suggested a neo-classical fountain in his mother's honour in Parliament Square, to be funded by public subscription.

Amid the depths of a recession, with hard-pressed British tax-payers protesting about subsidizing the world's wealthiest woman, the Queen herself was quick to veto her loving son's idea. It proved a sound judgement on the monarch's part, as her personal mile-stone that February was obscured by the visible deterioration of Charles's marriage during a disastrous six-day visit to India. Beside the Taj Mahal, built by a seventeenth-century Mogul emperor for his wife, who had died in childbirth, the Princess of Wales posed poignantly alone, sending a deliberate 'postcard home', bearing the clear message that she now saw herself as an abandoned woman. Despite a longstanding public promise to take his bride to the Taj Mahal, made during his bachelor days, the prince had opted to remain behind in Delhi.

In vain did Charles's office plead that there was no room in his busy schedule to permit 'sightseeing' at the Taj Mahal. Neither press nor public could be convinced that a meeting with trainee Indian journalists was more important than a photo opportunity with his wife at one of the world's most celebrated symbols of marital love. And the price he paid for his wife's superior sense of public relations grew heavier two days later, on St Valentine's eve, when Diana agreed to present the prizes after a polo match in Jaipur – for which, as it was drily observed, the prince had somehow found time in his busy public schedule.

Among those due to receive a prize was her husband, who stood meekly in line with his victorious team-mates, awaiting his chance to be photographed with the world's most famous woman. When it came, with a hundred lenses poised, Charles naturally leant forward to kiss his wife on the cheek – strictly for public consumption. Diana waited until he was committed to the move, then withdrew her head at the last minute, leaving her husband kissing her earring. It was, in the words of one of those present, 'one of the cruellest, most public put-downs of any man by his wife, executed in front of a hundred professional cameramen and five thousand laughing Indians'. Diana had 'triumph in her eyes'.[1] The resulting photo made a powerfully negative image, prompting fevered discussions in Palace circles as to how much longer this public humiliation of the prince could be allowed to go on.

Diana's tricks were in part Charles's come-uppance for some machiavellian scheming of his own before the trip. On hearing that the Foreign Office was organizing his wife's public schedule around the issue of family planning, the prince had protested that he had himself wanted to 'spearhead' that particular issue. The FO planners did not dissent from Diana's pained comment that they should 'disregard the spoiled boy'. As one of those involved put it at the time, 'It's time he started seeing her as an asset, not as a threat, and accepted her as an equal partner. At the moment her position within the organization is a very loose one.'[2]

They were not to know that Charles was long since past that point. Instead, he consulted the eminent lawyer Lord Goodman about the woeful state of his marriage – purely, at this stage, to explore the legal options open to him. Lobbied by his closest friends, notably the Romseys and the van Cutsems, the Queen and Prince Philip rallied to their son's support, registering sympathy rather than disapproval for the first time in the long course of his marital woes. But soon these woebegone parents were distracted by domestic disarray on three simultaneous fronts.

The following month, to its own mortification, the House of

Windsor swept the first week of a general election campaign off the
front pages by announcing the formal separation of the Duke and
Duchess of York. The politicians had barely managed to complete
their election before their headlines were again stolen by the Prince
of Wales's failure to support his wife through her father's funeral.
But the woes of the Waleses were, for once, themselves being
upstaged. On the day that the Duchess of York left Britain for a
five-week holiday to the Far East with her so-called financial
adviser, taking her children out of school for the duration,
Buckingham Palace was obliged to announce that the Princess
Royal's divorce from Captain Mark Phillips had finally become
absolute.

As is his wont at moments of crisis, Charles felt overwhelmed.
His birthright was being rapidly devalued, perhaps even en-
dangered, yet he could see nothing that he could do to help. His
marriage, to him, was beyond salvation; besides, events in India
had proved that Diana could not now be trusted even to smile her
way through joint public appearances. Any other intervention
would have to be approved by his mother, whose oft-stated prefer-
ence was that he try to stay out of the newspapers for a while.

Opting to keep a low profile, Charles escaped from it all by tour-
ing Britain's stately homes to gather material for a book on
Highgrove and its garden. He himself was only too glad to see the
back of Fergie, Duchess of York, who to his mind, as to his father's,
had besmirched the monarchy's dignity beyond the point of any
forgiveness. His wife, he knew, was more distressed at losing a
close friend from the family circle – her only fellow outsider, with
a uniquely shared perspective on the difficulties they faced.

Of late, however, Diana had carefully distanced herself from the
fellow 'Sloane Ranger' with whom she had once relished public
horseplay; the Gulf War episode had shown her that the public preferred its princesses statuesque, dignified and reticent. Once, the
two unhappy Windsor wives had plotted simultaneous exits from
the royal scene; now Diana, recognizing her loftier obligations as
mother of a future king, had let her friend 'go it alone'. If Fergie
was resentful, the bond between the two would soon be renewed
by Diana's own separation. In the meantime, Charles saw little
reason to offer his wife much sympathy over the fate of her some-
time friend.

At the time, he was more concerned about what he saw as wilful intrusion by Diana into a relationship he had hoped to develop with Mother Teresa of Calcutta. Earlier that year, when she had been hospitalized with a heart condition, Charles had instructed Aylard to send flowers, ensuring that the card was signed by him alone, rather than himself and his wife. Now Diana had avenged herself by taking a trip to Rome to meet Mother Teresa. As he berated his wife for what he saw as a spiteful intervention, their voices grew so loud that they could be heard in the adjacent office, where the inadvertent eavesdroppers thought they detected a chilling note of finality in this latest domestic spat. 'It was', in the words of one member of their staff, 'like a slowly spreading pool of blood seeping out from under a locked door.'[3]

Even those of their staff naturally loyal to the status quo, and thus to the prince, felt some sympathy as a tearful Diana begged him to soften his attitude towards her, or else she would have to 'reconsider her position'. She fled from the room and ran upstairs, sobbing, heading for the bathroom in the hope that the children would not see her upset. By her account, however, Prince William pushed some tissues beneath the door, saying, 'Mummy, I hate to see you sad.'[4]

At the lowest ebb of their forlorn, fractious marriage, Charles and Diana were both intent on trying to hide their difficulties from their children, as keen as any other parents to spare them undue suffering. Like all such couples, however, they deluded themselves about the extent to which they could succeed. At the ages of nine and seven, William and Harry were as sensitive as any other youngsters to problems between their parents, which is, of course, invariably more than the parents think. Charles's sense of a proper distance between father and son, inbred by his own childhood, proved useful for once in hiding his own unhappiness from his children, with whom his dealings proceeded on a perfectly normal basis. Diana, however, could not help letting her suffering show, taking them into her bed and smothering them in angst-ridden mother-love. Charles, of course, was not to know this, until she herself chose to reveal it to the world; nor can he be expected, like any other father, to have considered it fair play. For the present, however, both tried to maintain a façade of business as usual, which meant putting a bold private face on increasingly acrimonious public warfare.

It was now that Diana embarked in earnest on establishing her

own separate public identity, constructing the private agenda that
would earn her such goodwill, to offset what she saw as the crash-
ingly dull public schedule that reflected Charles's priorities. That
month, for instance, she delivered a passionate speech about AIDS,
to a private gathering of media executives, within hours of doing
her Palace duty by charming all comers as guest of honour at the
Ideal Home Exhibition (to mark 'National Bed Week'). As he
toured the Duchy of Cornwall, paying his annual round of
landlord–tenant visits with few journalists in sight, Charles was
effectively being sidelined – not just by his vengeful wife, but by the
antics of his increasingly dysfunctional family.

That April, the Princess Royal was seen in public for the first
time with her new beau, Captain Tim Laurence, while rumours
abounded that the royals were negotiating the Duchess of York's
silence. Into this bleak family album the Princess of Wales now
pasted another forlorn 'postcard home', as she again allowed herself to be photographed travelling poignantly alone, this time at the
Pyramids. Although she and Charles had flown out on the same
aircraft, the princess disembarked in Egypt for an official visit
while her husband proceeded to Turkey to see the Sufi whirling
dervishes at Konya. Staff at a nearby luxury villa, lent to the prince
by a wealthy Turkish friend, later revealed that he had been joined
there by Camilla Parker Bowles.

It did not go unnoticed that the Prince and Princess of Wales
returned from the same part of the world in separate aircraft of the
Queen's Flight. When they then flew on to Spain, to represent
Britain at the World Expo trade fair in Seville, their half-hearted
show of togetherness fooled few. That weekend, in some ways
mercifully, the years of pretence were at last ended, and the Wales
marriage undone beyond the remotest chance of recovery, by the
first of five torrid newspaper extracts from Andrew Morton's
book, *Diana, Her True Story*. Because of Charles's affair with
Camilla, the public now knew beyond any doubt, their future
queen's marital miseries had been acute enough to make her ill,
even to drive her to five desperate half-attempts at suicide.

For the prince, Morton's revelations were 'a humiliation of almost
unendurable proportions'.[5] That June weekend, sensing what was
coming, Charles had taken the precaution of inviting wise and
loyal friends, Eric and Poppy Anderson, to join him at Highgrove.

He was astounded by Diana's apparent complicity in a book that paraded their marital miseries in such detail, giving so partial an account of their differences, exposing himself and Camilla Parker Bowles to public scorn and contempt.

His parents, for once, were in complete agreement with Charles that his wife's behaviour was inexcusable. That Sunday afternoon, as the public lapped up Morton's revelations, the prince boldly went to play polo, as usual, at Windsor Great Park, where his mother offered him significant public support by inviting the Parker Bowleses to take tea with her in the royal enclosure. Camilla was wearing a suit in Prince of Wales check.

At Windsor that evening, for the first time, the prince broached with his parents the once 'unthinkable' prospect of divorce. It was not a notion to which the Queen warmed. The following morning Charles met Diana at Kensington Palace to explore whether their marriage could now have any future at all. After a brief and very bitter exchange, both agreed it was quite beyond redemption. Although it would take six more painful months to come about, their formal separation was agreed in principle that morning.

That week, as fate would have it, also saw the beginning of Royal Ascot, traditionally a time for 'happy family' public appearances. At lunchtime Charles and Diana were obliged to ride side by side, grim-faced, in an open carriage to the annual ceremony of the Order of the Garter in St George's Chapel, Windsor. The next day, as the race meeting got under way, the royal family tried its usual tactic of 'business as usual', processing down the racecourse and waving to the crowds as if their world were as serene as ever. What was always in danger of becoming a surreal occasion got off to a distinctly unorthodox start, with the estranged Yorks and their daughters among the crowd waving to the surprised-looking royal cortège.

That afternoon, Charles's parents again offered him moral support by publicly rubbing salt in Diana's private wounds. Camilla, unsurprisingly, was nowhere to be seen; but the Queen saw fit to invite her husband, Andrew Parker Bowles, to join the royal family – including Diana – in the royal box. In full view of journalists, Prince Philip then ignored the princess as she walked past him, trying to hide her distress. The war of the Waleses, it seemed, had now been extended to include the rest of the Windsors.

At the end of the day, for the benefit of the cameras, Charles and Diana left Ascot together, only for the royal limousine to stop a mile down the road, in full view of the astonished royal press corps, so the couple could switch cars and go their separate ways. This procedure was repeated daily, as the nation debated the truth or otherwise of Morton's revelations. After three days of public torture, Diana herself resolved the issue by visiting her friend Carolyn Bartholomew, known to be one of his informants, and kissing her in front of photographers. It was her way of saying, 'Yes, it's all true.'

Two days later, moved by the warmth of her reception at an engagement in Southport, Lancashire, the princess could not stop herself dissolving into public tears. There followed a Windsor summit, at which Charles's parents would not hear any talk of separation. Instead, they demanded a 'cooling-off period' of at least three months, preferably six, during which the couple should 'try to resolve their differences'.

Besieged by hate mail, Camilla Parker Bowles fled to Venice with her sister. Asked about Morton's book, Camilla said, 'I haven't read it, but I will with interest when the time comes.' Her husband, meanwhile, denounced it as 'fiction, fiction'.

As the establishment closed ranks around the royals, the Archbishop of Canterbury fretted that 'the current speculation about intimate personal matters has exceeded the boundaries which should be observed in a society claiming to respect basic human values'. The chairman of the Press Complaints Commission, Lord McGregor of Durris, felt moved to borrow a phrase from Virginia Woolf, accusing journalists of an 'odious exhibition' of 'dabbling their fingers in the stuff of other people's souls'.

The very next day, McGregor was privately disabused by evidence from senior newspaper executives to the effect that the royals in question were orchestrating the dabbling themselves. He also received an apology from the Queen's private secretary, Sir Robert Fellowes, for misleading him 'in good faith' about his sister-in-law's involvement in the Morton book. (Fellowes also offered his resignation to the Queen, who declined to accept it.)

None of this emerged for six months, and might never have become public at all, were it not for leaks in January 1993 from Sir David Calcutt's report advocating legislation to curb press excesses. McGregor was forced to come clean – and John Major's government was sorely embarrassed – by evidence that Major and his Cabinet colleagues had been informed that the Prince and Princess of Wales had both been feeding information to the press throughout the period when both Palace and government had been blaming the media for invading the couple's privacy.

As long ago as May 1991, it emerged, McGregor had been told at a private dinner in Luxembourg by Lord Rothermere, owner of the *Daily Mail* and the *Mail on Sunday*, that the prince and princess had each 'recruited national newspapers to carry their own accounts of their marital rifts'. Later he had been told by Andrew Knight, executive chairman of Rupert Murdoch's News International (owners of the *Sun*, the *News of the World, The Times* and the *Sunday Times*), that Diana was personally 'participating in the provision of information for tabloid editors about the state of her marriage'.

'I took further soundings,' McGregor eventually revealed, 'and was satisfied that what Mr Knight told me was true.' Knight also told McGregor that it was Diana who had tipped off photographers about her visit to Carolyn Bartholomew, legitimizing the contents of Morton's book.

At first, McGregor accused both the Prince and Princess of Wales of 'using' newspapers to reveal details of their marital problems in what amounted to open warfare. Eventually he was prevailed upon to withdraw his charge against the prince, maintaining it solely against the princess, about whom he did not mince his words. Her actions, said his lordship, had 'seriously embarrassed' the Commission and undermined the purpose of his 'carefully timed' and 'emotively phrased statement'.

But his revised position, based on briefings from the Palace, did not ring entirely true with newspaper readers, to whom the princess had been declared guilty without evidence or trial. Lord Rothermere had asked for his evidence of press recruitment to remain confidential; it would never have become public but for leaks to the *Guardian*. To what, however, could Rothermere have been referring, beyond the leak from Prince Charles's friends to Rothermere's own employee, Nigel Dempster of the *Daily Mail*, about Charles's spurned offer to throw his wife a thirtieth-birthday party?[26]

Charles, unlike Diana, had lost control of his friends. Hers, so the argument went, had demanded her permission to tell all to Morton because they were seriously concerned about her mental and physical health. His, outraged at so one-sided an account of the marriage, defied his instructions to keep silent. McGregor's dutiful service to the Palace again rebounded on him as those unnamed 'friends of the prince' got back to work, adopting a new and ugly *ad feminam* line. To the London *Evening Standard*, 'one of Charles's circle' revealed that Diana was in 'a familiar state of nervous excitement'. This made her 'very dangerous'. The prince's camp could not 'carry on indulging her neurotic tyranny'. In the heat of the moment the *Standard*'s reporter, Rory Knight-Bruce, himself felt moved to abandon any pretence at impartiality: 'It is time for the Establishment to see off the woman who thought that she was more powerful than the royal family.' He then wheeled on another 'senior source in the Church of England' to call the princess 'a little girl lost'. But the anonymous cleric proceeded to let the side down with an apparent pang of guilt: 'She may be flirtatious – and she is, I've met her several times – but she is surely incapable of adultery.'[7]

The Morton furore showed Charles at his most remarkably phlegmatic, calmly carrying on business as usual while his world imploded on him. On 5 July, for instance, he found time to write to the colonel commandant of the Parachute Regiment, indignant that the troops who processed past him the previous day had been wearing T-shirts or 'scruffy' anoraks. 'At the risk of being a dreadful bore, and a frightful fusspot,' he expressed shock and amazement that any soldier from such a regiment could appear on parade so badly turned out.[8]

Perhaps the prince thought he could afford to relax. He had taken the precaution of hiring his own version of Andrew Morton, whose revelations were to start appearing the following day. After an approach from his private office, Charles's version of events was to be told in the *Today* newspaper – a mid-market rival of the *Mail* – under the byline of Penny Junor, a writer so doggedly loyal as to be unafraid of risking her own reputation to save that of the prince. In a tenth-wedding-anniversary book in 1991, as Diana poured her woes into Andrew Morton's tape-recorder, Junor had written that the marriage was 'actually very healthy'.[9]

Now, under the headline, CHARLES: HIS TRUE STORY, Junor told the world that Diana was 'a sick woman', whose conduct had been 'irrational, unreasonable and hysterical'. The marriage had deteriorated entirely because of her bulimia, which had 'caused her to distort the truth and to seek someone to blame for her misery, the prince himself', while also subverting their children against him. Charles had 'encouraged his wife to get treatment, to try to accommodate her whims and to cope with her jealousy, only to be met with tears and shouting'.

There was nothing, of course, for Diana to be jealous about. 'There is no doubt that Charles loves Camilla very dearly, but as a friend, and a friend he has had to rely on increasingly over the years to maintain his sanity.' That, insisted Junor, was the full extent of their relationship. 'The Prince of Wales was "not the adulterous kind".'[10]

'Why don't you save yourself a phone call and ring the papers direct?' Diana raged at Charles as the falsehoods peddled in his name continued to blacken hers.[11] For once, however, it looked as if the might of the British Establishment might not prevail. The British people were not going to surrender their beloved Diana without a struggle. When she visited the city of Liverpool in mid-1992, thousands of people turned out for a glimpse of her. In the same city, in December of the same year, just eight of his future subjects turned up to greet the Prince of Wales.

Refusing to give up, however hopelessly, the Queen's staff insisted that the couple go ahead, as planned, with their annual vacation on John Latsis's yacht, the *Alexander*. The Palace billed it as a 'second honeymoon', which Fleet Street graciously translated into a 'reconciliation' cruise. Charles invited the Romseys along, with his cousin Princess Alexandra and her husband, Sir Angus Ogilvy, to share the strain. For Diana this was 'the holiday from hell'; she had 'too many painful memories' of previous holidays aboard the same yacht. Again she insisted on separate quarters, taking her meals alone with the children, and again she picked up the ship-to-shore phone to hear Charles talking to Camilla.

Another inevitable row ensued. 'Why don't you go off with your lady and have an end to it?' she stormed. Charles walked out of the room in despair. The marriage, observed one of their fellow travellers, was 'all over bar the statement'.[12]

'We must not let in daylight upon magic.' It was 125 years since the journalist Walter Bagehot, in his classic work *The English Constitution*,[13] had warned of the dangers for the mystical institution of monarchy in becoming too familiar with its people. In recent years, largely thanks to the Waleses, that daylight had become a hole in the royal ozone layer.

As Charles and Diana went their separate ways for the summer, August 1992 saw the Duchess of York's topless frolics with her financial adviser beside a French swimming-pool, *devant les enfants*, earn her final banishment from Balmoral. Even a government minister, Alan Clark, felt moved to despair of the whole royal spectacle as 'vulgar and brutish'. The House of Windsor was in a turmoil widely seen as terminal. Comparing the duchess with Woody Allen, whose marital troubles surfaced that same week, even the super-sober *Sunday Telegraph* felt moved to conclude: 'There is no such thing as a free bonk.'[14]

These were dark days in Elizabeth II's forty-year reign. Charles's mother was far from amused by the extent to which her children were undermining all her work in maintaining the dignity of the institution in her care. Had the Queen been over-indulgent towards her offspring? How could she have allowed matters to reach the point where one daughter-in-law was revealed to have made five apparent suicide attempts while the other paraded topless on front pages the world over? With her only sister and her only daughter divorced, two sons *en route* and the third conspicuously unmarried, the Queen was presiding over a domestic shambles fast curdling to a constitutional crisis. 'If this were an ordinary family visited by the local social services,' wrote one columnist in *The Times*, 'the lot of them would by now have been taken into care.' Perhaps, he suggested, it was time to institute a formal ceremony called 'The Severing of the Ties', at which the royal family would also repay the public money lavished on all those weddings.[15]

On the surface, the House of Windsor's woes had been brought about by the failure of its younger male members to marry the right sort of women – or, perhaps, to treat them as the equal partners generally assumed to share most modern middle-class marriages. Buckingham Palace maintained its traditional, supposedly dignified silence on the subject, adopting its familiar if increasingly desperate optimism that this was just another storm which would blow over. The Crown's more vocal supporters meanwhile downplayed the crisis by invoking British history: many a reign had seen

more scandalous royal conduct; the monarchy had survived far
worse than this. Both camps, however, were overlooking funda-
mental shifts in British society during the present Queen's reign. If
not yet a more genuinely democratic, egalitarian society, post-war
Britain at least nourished such aspirations.

By 1992, a three-year recession declining into slump had sharpened class distinctions, bringing with it resentment against the
Windsors' heedless pursuit of pleasure; and as Britain hesitantly
progressed towards the heart of a federalist Europe, the Crown's
constitutional role was in danger of erosion, if not extinction. Since
the Gulf War antics of the junior royals, the pomp and circum-
stance of monarchy, in which Britons had traditionally taken such
pride, had come to look like an incongruous symbol of Britain's
imperial past – and currently the perquisite of a pampered, un-
deserving élite, oblivious to the hard times being endured by their
fellow countrymen. The generation advancing towards the seats of
power no longer shared the unthinking, tribal loyalty to the Crown
engendered in its parents.

'Above all things,' Bagehot also wrote, 'our royalty needs to be
reverenced . . . We have come to regard the Crown as the head of
our *morality*.' With the ancient institution of monarchy buckling
beneath the strain, July was to prove the cruellest month, beginning and ending with the Prince and Princess of Wales
conspicuously apart on her thirty-first birthday and their eleventh
wedding anniversary.

To counter the public perception that he was an absentee parent,
Charles unprecedentedly took his younger son to school – an event
considered momentous enough to lead the front page of the
London *Evening Standard*. The most celebrated marital feud since
Samson and Delilah was being conducted almost entirely in public,
through the columns of the very tabloid press which the pro-
tagonists affected to despise. But the media blitz of Charles's
friends did him little good. A *Daily Express* poll showed that
the public squarely blamed the prince for his marital problems,
still favouring Diana as far and away the most popular royal,
23 per cent ahead of Princess Anne, with the Queen herself in
third place on 11 per cent and Charles a distant fifth on 9 per
cent.[16]

To Diana, there was something sinister about the timing of the
sudden release of the so-called 'Squidgygate' tape – the transcript

of her conversation with James Gilbey on New Year's Eve, 1989. Under the auspices of the *Sun*, more than 60,000 Britons paid six figures in telephone bills to listen to that affectionate conversation – illicitly and illegally tape-recorded nearly three years before – in which he called her 'darling' fifty-three times, and she thought aloud, 'Bloody hell, after all I've done for this fucking family . . .'

Few believed the tabloid tale that the bugging was the work of a seventy-year-old retired bank manager, who sat all day in his garden shed idly taping other people's phone calls. Technical experts on both sides of the Atlantic testified that a recording so sophisticated – Gilbey was speaking from a car phone – could only have been an inside job. But who was trying to discredit Diana, and why? With no evidence to support her claim, the princess herself inevitably suspected her husband's office, knowing that Aylard and his staff had returned to their media offensive. 'It was [leaked] to make the public change their attitude towards me,' she said. 'It was, you know, if we are going to divorce, my husband would hold more cards than I would – it was very much a poker game, chess game.'[17]

As the prince retreated to Nottingham for laser surgery on his left knee, and Diana took the chance to be seen visiting hospices and the homeless, September saw widespread publication of a document purporting to be an internal Palace memo criticizing the princess, which was quickly exposed as a fake. But now, for the first time, one tabloid portrayed Diana's relationship with Hewitt as 'physical', while others reported that she had enjoyed six secret rendezvous with Gilbey at a 'safe house' in Norfolk. When Scotland Yard denied the story, apparently at the behest of the Palace, events had reached the point where Britons were surprised to find the Palace defending the princess.

Was the campaign to denigrate Diana being orchestrated by Charles's private office at St James's Palace? The prince still insisted that he had instructed his staff and friends to hold their peace. But the Duchess of York's mother, Mrs Susan Barrantes, was claiming that there was a concerted campaign to discredit her daughter, implying secret service involvement in the topless French photos. Few much cared about the decline and fall of Fergie, who continued to self-destruct with increasingly louche behaviour. For all the assaults on Diana's reputation, by contrast, the relentlessly negative coverage did little to diminish her public popularity. When

During eleven years together the public kisses turned sour.

The birth of William in 1982 and Harry in 1984 offered brief bursts of happiness amid the gathering marital gloom.

Charles played polo to work off his frustrations. But frequent injuries led to depression. He found consolation, he confessed, in talking to his plants.

As the marriage collapsed, Diana sent a forlorn 'postcard home' from the Taj Mahal, while a solitary Charles painted watercolours. But they could not hide their unhappiness on official trips to Canada and Korea (*opposite*) and Australia (*overleaf*).

TO MA[RK]
[CO]MMENCEMENT O[F]
OF THIS [BUIL]
THIS STONE WAS
[O]N SUNDAY 13 FEBR[UARY]
[B]Y
THE HONOURA[BLE]
[SIR] HENRY BOLTE, K.C.[MG]
PREMIER OF VIC[TORIA]

After the marriage broke down, Diana poured out her heart to *Panorama*, while Charles returned to the arms of Camilla Parker Bowles.

As Diana won international awards for her humanitarian work (seen here in Angola, 1997, campaigning against landmines), Charles tried to recover from his unpopularity after the divorce.

Hunting has always
been a joint passion for
Charles and Camilla.
But the prince cannot
marry the 'love of his
life' without the blessing
of his sons.

Balmoral (*right*),
summer 1997.

Charles escorted Diana's coffin home from Paris after her fatal crash in August 1997. On arrival at RAF Northolt, he was joined by the prime minister, Tony Blair, and Diana's sisters Jane and Sarah.

The day before her funeral,
Charles and their sons moved
among the sea of floral tributes
from a nation paralysed by grief.

6 September 1997: Princes Philip and William, Earl Spencer, and Princes Harry and Charles march behind Diana's coffin to her funeral in Westminster Abbey (*opposite*).

Charles paid a touching tribute to his sons' courage at his first public appearance after Diana's death, in Manchester (*above left*). It was back to business as usual by the time he visited Sri Lanka in early 1998 (*above right*). In South Africa, November 1997, he relished a photocall with Nelson Mandela and the Spice Girls.

Canada, March 1998: six months after their mother's death, William and Harry begin to take over the spotlight from their father.

she gave up her state-of-the-art Mercedes sports car that month, at the height of anti-German feeling over the sterling crisis, a caller to a London phone-in suggested that she should have 'kept the car and traded in the husband'.

For the first time, at the beginning of a long process that would climax in the week of Diana's death, a perceptible gap was beginning to open between the self-confidence of the Establishment and the indignation of the British people. However well intentioned, the black propaganda campaign on Charles's behalf was not working. Diana's unshakeable public popularity was seen at its starkest that October, when she escorted him to a service in Westminster Abbey marking the fiftieth anniversary of El Alamein, one of the most significant land battles of the Second World War. The prince must have anticipated what might happen. He knew that Camilla's father, Major Bruce Shand, who had distinguished himself at El Alamein, would be present. As he and his wife processed to their seats, with the press watching minutely, they had to walk straight past Camilla Parker Bowles. Charles gave her a formal little nod and a smile; Diana, of course, looked firmly the other way. The results were all too predictable. MEMORIAL DAY WRECKED BY CAMILLA, proclaimed the next day's *Sun*, anxious to make amends for the Squidgygate tape. PRINCESS SNUBS RIVAL AFTER SHOCK AT MEMORIAL SERVICE.

It was time, Charles decided, to try to get a grip on his press coverage. Within days he had written a lengthy memorandum to Aylard, setting out new policy initiatives on dealing with the media. 'However depressing the thought might be,' Charles wrote, 'I do think we must realise that certain sections of the media have now proved to their own satisfaction that sensationalised royal stories are one of the best ways of selling newspapers in a recession. There is every reason to suppose that they will continue to operate in a thoroughly unpleasant way...'

Insulated from the true values, however lamentable, of the world in which he lived, convinced that his private life was of less consequence than his public work, Charles clung doggedly to his ivory-tower approach to press relations. To him, the relative merits of Diana and Camilla were not a fit subject for public discussion, any more than his respective feelings towards either party. In the absence of any professional media advisers, he still remained locked in the damaging delusion that his marriage was not so much

a constitutional issue as 'sensational' material to newspaper editors
and their circulation managers, who would indeed 'continue to
operate' in ways he himself might well deem 'unpleasant'. In truth,
five years of Palace 'cover-up' was meeting its come-uppance.
Charles's way of acknowledging this was to recommend respond-
ing in a 'positive, self-confident and professional' manner,
emphasizing good news rather than bad, paying special attention
to approaches from film and television companies. To Charles,
the power of television to influence the public was the most
effective way of countering the external 'excesses' of the tabloid
press.[18]

The resultant 'special effort' – a source of some tension between
Buckingham Palace and St James's Palace – began to make itself
felt as October turned to November, and continuing speculation
over the Waleses' marital future overshadowed a gala evening at
Earl's Court, designed to celebrate the Queen's forty years on the
throne. The following evening, when Charles and Diana went to
the Royal Opera House to hear Placido Domingo sing *Otello*, it
was the first time in three years that they had attended the same
function together on two consecutive nights. Knighted newspaper
editors who should have known better were persuaded by St
James's Palace to use this remarkable statistic to run suddenly
optimistic articles about the couple's future. You only had to look
at the princess's smile, ran the captions; all the negative publicity
had been wrong. 'Why Charles and Diana are back together,'
cooed the *Daily Express*. 'Hopes rise', trilled the *Daily Mail*, 'of a
marriage on the mend.'

It took just three days for these fantasies to return to haunt the
Palace strategists, not to mention the editors. Early November saw
the royal press corps off with the Waleses to South Korea. The
princess had tried to pull out of the trip, but Charles had insisted
that she could not let down their hosts. Clumsily billed by his press
office as 'the Togetherness Tour', the visit saw the final death
throes of their marriage finally enacted before a world that
watched slack-jawed.

From the moment they landed in Seoul and emerged from their
aircraft with the aftermath of a row etched on their faces, neither
Charles nor Diana made much effort to hide their misery. So grim
were their looks throughout the five-day trip, so evident their
unwillingness even to speak to each other, that those same papers

who had just proclaimed the 'marriage on the mend' had no alternative but to christen them 'The Glums'. It was, as one of the press corps reported, 'a very public, and very humiliating, end to the love story of the century'.[19]

It was a miserable climax to the worst year of Charles's life. He had married the wrong woman, and was now paying a price he saw as cruelly disproportionate. Even he could not tell what the future might now hold; his destiny seemed to be spinning beyond his control. His sense of duty to the fore, he was prepared to sacrifice any chance of private happiness for public redemption. But now, as so often, emotional problems were accentuating his physical ones, and a recurrence of his back problem even forced him to make the reluctant decision to give up top-flight polo, a prospect that filled him with gloom.[20] Numbed by a sense of sadness, and of failure, he succumbed to another bout of deep, defeatist depression. As he flew from Korea to Hong Kong without his wife, who returned alone to London, the prince poured out his heavy heart in a letter to a friend, concluding, 'I don't know what will happen now, but I *dread* it.'[21]

On her return, with Charles at the other end of the earth, Diana chose to assert herself one last time. Earlier that week she had further established her own distinct identity, thanks to a forty-minute meeting with President Mitterrand of France – the first time in British history that a Princess of Wales had enjoyed any such 'summit' in her own right, with a senior foreign head of state. Now, back in London, she gave the keynote speech of European Drug Prevention Week. Not merely was it one of the longest public speeches she had ever given, another attempt to bulk out her public persona. Given its central theme – lavish physical affection upon your children and they will be less likely to look elsewhere for artificial substitutes such as drugs – the speech was also full of secret messages about her own dilemma, and the apparent inadequacies of her husband.

Herself well known to be a copious hugger of her sons, in contrast to their father, Diana seemed to be offering Charles veiled rebukes, in such phrases as, 'Hugging has no harmful side-effects . . . There are potential huggers in every household . . .' In passing, she also offered some private theories about his personal

shortcomings, given a cold and formal upbringing utterly starved
of physical affection:

> Children are not chores, they are part of us. If we gave them the
> love they deserve, they would not have to try so hard to attract
> our attention . . . Children who have received the affection they
> deserve will usually continue to recognize how good it feels,
> how right it feels and will create that feeling around them.
> We've all seen the families of the skilled survivors. Their
> strength comes from within and was put there by learning how
> to give and receive affection, without restraint, or embarrass-
> ment from their earliest days.

Significantly, in retrospect, she went on, 'If the immediate family
breaks up, the problems created can still be resolved, but only if the
children have been brought up from the very start with the feeling
that they are wanted, loved and valued. Then they are better able
to cope with such crises . . .'

If it was a message about Charles – at the time, before their
formal separation, another cry for help – this heartfelt speech was
also about herself. To the former Diana Spencer, her husband's
friendship with Camilla Parker Bowles was but the latest and most
devastating in the lifelong series of betrayals that had begun
when her mother abandoned her at the age of six. To Aylard,
meanwhile, the speech was nothing less than a betrayal of his
master. Mindful of the prince's memorandum about positive media
coverage, particularly on television, he negotiated special access for
a respected TV journalist, Jonathan Dimbleby, who would spend
the next eighteen months making a film and writing a book about
the prince's public work and private beliefs. Son of the veteran
royal commentator Richard Dimbleby, and himself chairman of
the Council for the Preservation of Rural England, Dimbleby
shared many of Charles's interests and enthusiasms; a great
admirer of the prince, he set out to correct what he saw as gross
public misperceptions of 'an individual of singular distinction and
virtue'.[22]

Amid discussions with his wife about the fine print of their
separation, Charles still found the time and emotional energy to
protest to government ministers about matters close to his heart.
One minute he was writing to the defence secretary protesting

about his 'short-sighted' plans to cut back on regimental bands (which had played 'a crucial role' in the framework of the British army),[23] the next he was arguing with Diana about their plans for the forthcoming weekend. Charles had planned to hold one of his occasional weekend house-parties at Sandringham on the weekend of 20 November 1992, with a dozen or so guests down for three days of shooting, but Diana suddenly announced that she would be taking the children elsewhere. He pleaded with her to relent, or at least to let him have the children, but she proved adamant. The weekend house-party went ahead as planned; but for Charles this was one defeat too many. Five days later he asked Diana for a formal separation.

To Charles, this latest infuriating episode was the climax of a pattern of which the public knew nothing. Time after time Diana had frustrated his plans to spend time with their sons by altering her own plans to sabotage his. Apart from the natural frustration of any devoted parent, he was deeply hurt by the resulting public perception that he was a distant and uncaring father. It was this cruel charge, more than gossip about his triangular marriage, which chewed away at the prince as he steeled himself to the once 'unthinkable' prospect of separation, even divorce.

To him, the coming separation was unwelcome proof of failure in his duty to the Crown, which would have little noticeable impact on his daily way of life. To Diana, by contrast, the sadness was tinged with a sense of liberation, even renewal. In the days that followed, as she busied herself reassuring the children before the news was made public, her friends noticed a dramatic change in the princess. At last she was more cheerful and self-confident than they had seen her in a long time. Two months before, when the 'Squidgygate' episode had sapped her morale, she had seemed to lose the initiative in her long negotiations with her royal in-laws and their lawyers. Her sullen display in Korea, followed by the 'Camillagate' tape, had finally won her the independence she sought – but at what cost to her future credibility?

Then, to her rescue, came the House of Windsor's worst week for sixty years. As it happened, the Sandringham weekend that had proved the last straw for Charles turned out to be a multiple disaster for the prince and his family, as the Friday evening saw

Windsor Castle ravaged by fire. Charles rushed to the scene to console his mother, then returned to his guests at Sandringham. 1992, already the most traumatic year of Elizabeth II's reign, precipitating the House of Windsor's darkest hour since the abdication crisis of 1936, was not over yet. But the Windsor fire was widely taken as some sort of divine judgement, a *Götterdämmerung* reducing the tarnished British Crown to molten metal.

The castle, it transpired to universal astonishment, had not been insured against fire. In the ensuing furore over the cost of repairs, estimated at £60 million, it was pointed out that whereas Balmoral and Sandringham were the Queen's personal property, Windsor Castle was but one among six of her eight residences which belonged to the state. Yes, it was the Queen's favourite place of weekend sojourn, which she regarded as her real home; and yes, technically, it was a state museum; but no, in fact, only some of it was open to the public for some of the year. In other words, as it was succinctly put, 'While the castle stands, it is theirs, but when it burns down, it is ours.'[24] In a series of polls, nine out of ten Britons saw no reason why the taxpayer should foot the bill – as pledged by the government, in the courtly shape of the heritage secretary, Peter Brooke.

The Windsor fire was to prove a double disaster for the monarchy. Not merely did it expose the myth of the government's view of royalty, and indeed royalty's view of itself, as standing at the apex of a blindly loyal society which would rush without question to its aid. It also proved an urgent and irresistible catalyst for change – change of the kind the Queen had so long resisted. Four days later she volunteered the candid confession that 1992 had been an 'annus horribilis', a year on which she would not be able to look back with 'undiluted pleasure'. At what was supposed to be a celebratory lunch in her honour in the City of London's Guildhall, the grim-faced monarch made no specific mention of her children's marital troubles, or the public ill-feeling about her tax-exempt status; nor did she make any offer, as had been widely predicted, to contribute from her huge private wealth to the cost of rebuilding Windsor Castle. Her extraordinary speech was nevertheless the most honest and personal the monarch had ever delivered – a heartfelt confessional made all the more poignant by the throaty weakness of her voice, due to laryngitis inflamed by smoke inhalation at Windsor. Sadly, she croaked:

I sometimes wonder how future generations will judge the events of this tumultuous year. I dare say that history will take a slightly more moderate view than that of some contemporary commentators. Distance is well known to lend enchantment, even to the less attractive views. After all, it has the inestimable advantage of hindsight. But it can also lend an extra dimension of judgement, giving it a leavening of moderation and compassion – even of wisdom – that is sometimes lacking in the reactions of those whose task it is in life to offer instant opinions on all things great and small.

At the end of the Queen's speech, Prime Minister John Major leant conspicuously across their host, the Lord Mayor of London, to offer his sovereign what appeared to be a few words of re-assurance. Forty-eight hours later, Major was on his feet in the House of Commons, announcing that the Queen had indicated her willingness to pay some taxes and to reduce the burden of her family on the taxpayer. Her gesture had the full support of her son Charles, who had himself made the same commitment. Though he convinced no-one, the prime minister went to some pains to stress that the Queen's 'request' to pay tax had been made 'some months ago, before the summer recess', and that the timing of his announcement had nothing to do with public reaction to financing the Windsor repairs. Buckingham Palace, describing the move as 'an appropriate step to take in the 1990s', said it had been mooted by the Queen as early as the previous July.

The prime minister's announcement was a watershed in the modern history of the monarchy's relations with its subjects. In a twentieth-century version of the Peasants' Revolt, the Queen's concession was a clear victory for what was soon to become known as 'people power', forcing further radical change on the monarchy in its quest for survival. Within a month, however, Major was back on his feet in the Commons with an even more momentous announcement.

On 9 December 1992, three days before a summit meeting on which he had staked his political future, the prime minister cancelled a meeting with Jacques Delors, the president of the European Commission, to make a statement to the House. Evidently, Major considered it of more importance to tell Members of Parliament in person that the heir to the throne and his wife had decided, 'with regret', to separate. At 3.30 p.m. he rose to make what his predecessor, Sir Edward Heath, later called 'one of the saddest announcements made by a prime minister in modern times':

> It is announced from Buckingham Palace that, with regret, the Prince and Princess of Wales have decided to separate. Their Royal Highnesses have no plans to divorce and their constitutional positions are unaffected. This decision has been reached amicably, and they will both continue to participate fully in the upbringing of their children.
>
> Their Royal Highnesses will continue to carry out full and separate programmes of public engagements and will, from time to time, attend family occasions and national events together.
>
> The Queen and the Duke of Edinburgh, though saddened, understand and sympathize with the difficulties that have led to this decision. Her Majesty and His Royal Highness particularly hope that the intrusions into the privacy of the prince and princess may now cease. They believe that a degree of privacy and understanding is essential if their Royal Highnesses are to provide a happy and secure upbringing for their children, while continuing to give a whole-hearted commitment to their public duties.

On an engagement in the north of England, Diana heard the announcement on the radio with 'deep, deep, profound sadness . . . The fairy tale had come to an end, and our marriage had taken a different turn'.[25] But Major did not seem content with merely ending the fairy tale. Two weeks after announcing the Queen's tax concession, the prime minister strove to secure the prospects of the heir to the throne by taking personal charge of the separation announcement, yet somehow managed to achieve the opposite. Not content with calling the immediate future of the Crown into some doubt, he contrived to talk his way into a deeper constitutional crisis. There was an audible gasp in the chamber as Major continued:

> The House will wish to know that the decision to separate has no constitutional implications. The succession to the Throne is unaffected by it; the children of the Prince and Princess retain

their position in the line of succession; and there is no reason
why the Princess of Wales should not be crowned Queen in due
course. The Prince of Wales's succession as head of the Church
of England is also unaffected.[26]

Major's addenda to the Palace's unadorned statement quite
avoidably opened a whole new can of royal worms. The prime
minister had chosen to make public, with the full authority of
his office, remarks confined by the Palace press office to off-
the-record, background 'Guidance Notes' distributed to newspapers and broadcasting stations. Was he really suggesting, for
instance, that the Supreme Governor of the Church of England,
whose canon is firmly fixed against divorce, could be crowned
alongside a queen long since estranged from her husband?
Could the Church, come to that, comfortably crown an adulterous
king?

Already in a state of schism, since its recent vote in favour of the
ordination of women, the Church of England was made to look
more hypocritical and less relevant than ever. Thanks to Major it,
too, was now enmeshed in the unenviable problems of the Crown.
In questioning the future of two major national institutions, the
prime minister raised issues that elbowed aside more humane
expressions of sympathy for the royal couple. What should have
been a poignant moment, whose implications could well have un-
folded with a gradual dignity, turned instead into a constitutional
spasm.

The details of Major's statement were based on talks he had held
some months earlier, when it was clear that the marriage was heading towards separation, with the Lord Chancellor, Lord Mackay,
and the Archbishop of Canterbury, Dr George Carey. It was
Carey's view that a formal separation within marriage 'would be
likely to win widespread understanding . . . By putting [the institution of marriage] above their emotions as individuals, the royal
couple would be widely admired for their dedication to serving the
public interest.' But the Archbishop added an important proviso:
that extra-marital affairs that might reach the newspapers would
'need to be avoided'.[27]

That evening, for the first and only time in her life, Mrs Camilla
Parker Bowles felt obliged to issue a statement to the press.
Speaking as a 'close friend' of the prince, she said, 'If something has

gone wrong, I'm obviously very sorry for them. But I know nothing more than the average person in the street. I only know what I see on television.'[28]

CHAPTER FIFTEEN

'THEY WILL FORGIVE ME'

TWO DAYS AFTER THE PRIME MINISTER HAD ANNOUNCED THE WALESES' formal separation, the Queen hosted a formal dinner aboard *Britannia* for European leaders attending the Edinburgh summit. It was a measure of Diana's continuing importance to the monarchy's future that the seating plan placed her with the Queen at the top table, between President Mitterrand of France and the British foreign secretary, Douglas Hurd.

Charles was relegated, along with Prime Minister Major, to table three. It was a rare moment of sharp public relations on the Palace's part, reluctantly reflecting public support for the princess as the wronged party in the marital breakdown. A poll that week showed 50 per cent saying that Diana had 'done most to improve the standing of the royal family over the last two years', compared with 29 per cent for the Queen and just 14 per cent for Charles. Asked who was responsible for the collapse of the Waleses' marriage, Charles was held to blame by twice as many respondents as Diana – 57 per cent 'sympathized most' with her, a mere 12 per cent with him.[1]

'God knows what the future will hold,'[2] Charles wrote that day to his friend Nicholas Soames, before travelling north to attend his sister Anne's remarriage at Crathie Kirk, beside the Balmoral estate, to Captain Tim Laurence, a self-effacing soldier formerly seconded to the Windsors as a royal equerry. Even that was marred by the need for a clandestine, almost conspiratorial ceremony, screened from press and public by a phalanx of royal Range-Rovers.*

Although the traditional family gathering at Sandringham that Christmas welcomed a new family member in the shape of Anne's new husband, more accustomed to eating downstairs with the staff, several more familiar royal faces were conspicuous by their absence. While the Princesses Beatrice and Eugenie joined their father, Prince Andrew, at the Queen's Christmas lunch table, their mother was exiled two miles away to Wood Farm, a cottage on the Sandringham estate, where King George V had once pored over the royal stamp collection.

For the first time in more than a decade, the Princess of Wales was also absent. Although invited to lunch by the Queen, Diana opted for the company of her brother and his family at Althorp. So Diana's Christmas was marred not merely by the unwonted absence of her father, but also of her children, who were at Sandringham at their grandmother's bidding. Every chance was seized for the Prince of Wales to be photographed out walking with his sons, teaching them to shoot (or, as their mother used to put it, to 'kill things'). Diana's absence was used by her foes to criticize her hitherto unimpeachable qualities as a mother; like it or not, the argument went, she should have put up with an uncomfortable Yuletide amid the royals for the sake of her sons. The consensus, however, was that the Palace had again miscalculated. So brutal a demonstration that the young princes were regarded as the monarch's grandchildren first, and Diana's sons second, smacked of all that was wrong with the House of Windsor. To The Times, it was 'the unacceptable face of monarchy'.

Within days William and Harry were back where the nation evidently believed they belonged: at their mother's side. After an unprecedented six days apart from her sons, Diana swept them off for a New Year vacation on the Caribbean island of Nevis. On the nine-hour journey on a scheduled British Airways flight, the princess travelled in an economy seat while her royal sons sat up front in first class. It was another typically shrewd piece of public relations – as was the deal she made with the paparazzi who besieged her holiday hotel: in exchange for a brief, relaxed photo session each morning, they would leave her in peace for the rest of

* In February 1997 Princess Anne's first husband, Captain Mark Phillips, married an American heiress, Sandy Pflueger, in an exotic ceremony at her family's estate in Hawaii.

the day. In the resulting deluge of public 'postcards home', the future King William and his brother looked much happier at play beneath the West Indian sun than they had amid the freezing formality of royal Norfolk.

So Charles's sons were away, mercifully, when his worst fears were realized on 12 January 1993. For some time Charles had been aware of rumours that a transcript of one of his late-night phone calls with Camilla had fallen into the wrong hands. Like Diana the previous summer, he too wondered who had chosen this moment to leak it, and why. British Intelligence could be assumed to have monitored many of his calls, as they do those of elected public figures as much as appointed or hereditary ones. But the royal family, of all figures at the apex of public life, could tradition-ally assume that the hidden forces at work in British society were loyal to their cause, working to protect them from embarrassments such as this. Was this another assumption he would now have to discard? The question of betrayal soon paled into insignificance beside his utter mortification at the contents of the transcript itself.

At first in Australia, then in America, then in newspapers and magazines all over Europe, the transcript of the 'Camillagate' tape was published in full.

'I want to feel my way along you, all over you and up and down you and in and out,' the future head of the Church of England told the wife of one of his oldest friends. 'I fill up your tank! I need you several times a week,' said the heir to the throne to Mrs Silver Stick-in-Waiting.

Most of the mainstream British press at first funked publication in full, not least because that very week they were fighting off the threat of legislation to curb press freedom. But photocopiers and fax machines whirred samizdat copies from Fleet Street to the City of London, from Whitehall to Downing Street, from Land's End to John o'Groats. The wonders of modern technology thus averted a repeat of the establishment conspiracy of 1936, when the rest of the world knew all about King Edward and his Mrs Simpson while the British were kept in ignorance. By the weekend, two British Sunday papers summoned the nerve to follow their Australian col-leagues in publishing the text in full.

'Oh, God,' moaned Fred to his Gladys, 'I'll just live inside your trousers or something. It would be so much easier.'

'What are you going to turn into?' she giggled. 'A pair of knickers or something?' Both giggled. 'Oh, you're going to come back as a pair of knickers!'

'Or, God forbid, a Tampax,' he ventured. 'Just my luck to be chucked down a lavatory and go on and on forever swirling round on the top, never going down.'

Even more damaging than the sex-talk, for the man aspiring to the nation's moral leadership, was the open, unashamed deception of his friend, the hapless Andrew Parker Bowles. 'Not Tuesday,' said Camilla. 'A's coming home.' Arrangements were then discussed for clandestine meetings at the homes of friends. Amid profuse declarations of love, the couple finally displayed a winsome teenage inability to hang up.

'Press the button,' said Camilla.

'Going to press the tit,' said Charles.

'All right, darling, I wish you were pressing mine.'

'God, I wish I was. Harder and harder.'

That weekend Charles was summoned to a summit with his parents at Sandringham. Never had the reputation of her son and heir, or indeed that of the monarchy, sunk so low. Although she had long known of Charles's friendship with Mrs Parker Bowles, and had even upset the Church by endorsing it, with her public embrace of Camilla, the Queen had never raised its precise nature with her son. Even with her family, she has a habit of avoiding personal conversations, preferring to stick to safer subjects such as the weather. On this occasion, however, Charles's behaviour amounted to family business. The future of what Prince Philip called 'the firm' was at stake. Upon Charles's arrival, Elizabeth II made it very clear to her son that she was distinctly unamused.

Previous Princes of Wales had, of course, kept mistresses, while also keeping the golden Establishment rule of not getting caught. This was one aspect of royal history that the historian in Charles had overlooked when he said to his wife one day, in a moment of exasperation, 'Do you seriously expect me to be the first Prince of Wales in history not to have a mistress?'[3] There was thus a certain retrospective romance to Edward VII's dalliance with Lillie Langtry, and a generous grace in his wife's invitation to his favourite mistress, Camilla's great-grandmother, to visit the King on his deathbed. But neither he nor his adulterous grandson,

Edward VIII, had been caught in public with their trousers down. Charles's love of his mobile phone was to prove far more damaging than his love of a homely Gloucestershire housewife, devoted enough to beg for sneak previews of his speeches.

Close to despair, the prince stage-managed a panicky newspaper campaign of damage containment via his ever-talkative staff and friends. THEY WILL FORGIVE ME proclaimed the front page of the *Daily Mail* on the heir to the throne's behalf, after an 'emotional' chat with 'a member of his circle'. Although twenty-seven more such tapes of Charles–Camilla sex-talk were rumoured to be in circulation, the prince apparently believed the worst was over. 'Things', he was quoted as saying, 'can only get better.' By 'distance and silence', his private secretary told *The Times*, he hoped to 'douse the fires of a nine-day wonder'. Time, his advisers believed, was on his side: 'He still has many years in which to prove his worth as the next monarch.'[4]

It was a claim that rang hollow in certain quarters, notably the habitually loyal Tory press, where a major recently drummed out of the Army for provoking 'unwelcome publicity' was permitted to wonder whether the same should not apply to his brother officer, the Prince of Wales.[5] Annex C of chapter sixty-two of the Army's General Administrative Instructions specifically forbade affairs with the wives of fellow officers; among eight statutes under which officers can be called upon to resign or retire for misconduct, rule D cited adultery with 'a spouse of a serving member of the armed forces'. The prince, as the nation was reminded, was colonel in chief of no fewer than seven regiments. 'You cannot have one rule for the serving army officer, and another for the honorary colonel in chief,' said a senior military man who preferred, for obvious reasons, to remain anonymous. 'The Army has got to lead by example, and Prince Charles is clearly not doing so.'[6]

At the time, the prince was still in hiding at Sandringham, considering his future tactics with his coterie of friends and advisers. On the same day that he and Mrs Parker Bowles both declined an invitation from the Press Complaints Commission to lodge a formal protest over the transcript's publication, he also remained silent on demands for his resignation from the Army. Not that he had become newspaper-shy. The previous day, his office had telephoned the *Observer* to deny a front-page story by its political editor suggesting that Charles had abandoned hope of becoming king. The same day's *Sunday Telegraph* led with a similarly sourced assertion that Charles's affair with Camilla was over, and that he would become celibate for the rest of his life. The prince would meanwhile be carrying on with his schedule 'as normal'; the very next day, as planned, he would be meeting local worthies in King's Lynn.

Alas, the meeting never took place, as he was struck down overnight by a convenient bout of gastroenteritis. Lest anyone wonder just how convenient, the Palace was quick to stress that numerous other Sandringham residents had caught the bug, including the Queen herself. After two days Charles was said to have made a full recovery. But still he cancelled his engagements, unlike his mother, also fully recovered, who accompanied her own mother to the local Women's Institute.

Charles did not dare show his face in public again until ten days later, when he visited a north London housing development. Buckingham Palace sent advance orders to the hosts that he did not want to meet 'too many people'. Children, especially, were to be kept away from the Prince of Wales 'because they tend to ask awkward questions'. They duly were. The following day, however, as Charles left a health centre in Whitechapel, east London, a Cockney pensioner shouted, 'Have you no shame?' Looking shaken, the prince climbed into his limousine and sped away. 'What right has he got to come to the East End after what he's been up to?' demanded the feisty old man, who refused to give his name to reporters. 'He's a disgrace.'

The damage was inestimable. At the beginning of February 1993, a Gallup poll in the *Daily Telegraph* showed that Charles's support was haemorrhaging in the propaganda war with his estranged wife. Where Diana remained the royal family's most popular member, on exactly the same figure as eighteen months before, Charles's approval rating had slumped from 15 per cent to just 4 per cent.[7] That weekend another poll for the *Sunday Times* showed that four out of five respondents thought that 'too many members of the royal family lead an idle, jet-set kind of existence'. Bookmakers cut the odds against the monarchy's abolition by the year 2000 from 100–1 to 8–1.[8]

Any doubts about the public significance of Charles's adultery had now been dispelled by the Church of England's second most senior clergyman, the Archbishop of York. Speaking while the Archbishop of Canterbury was abroad, and thus with the authority of the Church's 'day-to-day leader', Dr John Habgood said he certainly considered it a matter of public concern. 'Looking back over history, the nation has been extraordinarily tolerant of all sorts of behaviour among its monarchs, but all tolerance has its limits and I would not want myself now to say where those limits might lie.' A week later, from South Africa, the Archbishop of Canterbury signalled his agreement: 'We expect our leaders at every level to embody Christian values.'[9]

Although neither archbishop said as much, it was beginning to look as if Charles might have some difficulty finding a prelate prepared to crown him. There was much discussion of a 'revision' of the Coronation Oath. Said the Archdeacon of York, the Venerable George Austin: 'I've been a monarchist all my life, but I must say my support is not what it was. If Prince Charles divorces and remarries, I would have very great difficulties.' The prince's adultery would seem to 'disqualify' him from heading the Church of England, added the Revd David Streater, head of the Church Society.

Charles's 'nine-day wonder' did not look as if it was going to disappear quite as fast as he had hoped. Amid his constitutional woes, the prince had become the butt of humour as cruel as it was crude. When the American film of Morton's book was shown on British cable TV, to an estimated audience of 2 million, Tampax was the leading product advertised between segments. On American TV's *Saturday Night Live*, Mick Jagger dressed up as a bewigged butler to present 'Camilla' with a present from the Prince of Wales on a silver tray – a gift box of tampons. Thanks to Charles, Jagger told the BBC, the royal family were in 'a right old mess . . . They've shot themselves in the foot. There's not a lot you can say in their support.'[10] When a brief trip to the United States took Charles to Williamsburg, Virginia, the local radio rebroadcast the 'Camillagate' tape, dubbing him 'the phone-sex prince', and students at the College of William and Mary celebrated its tercentenary with 'Charles and Camilla slumber parties' – somewhat overshadowing their honorary fellow's sombre call for a return to 'traditional values'.

Among young British women, a 'Charlie' was now a synonym for a Tampax. One British tabloid carried a cartoon showing

Charles entering his greenhouse to find his plants begging, 'Talk dirty to us.'[11] As if this were not enough, the Privy Council reportedly endorsed arrangements whereby Princess Anne would become Regent if the Queen died before Prince William reached eighteen, the age at which he could accede to the throne. The plan had apparently been initiated by Prince Philip, 'who has accepted for some time now that his eldest son is not king material'.[12]

The look on Philip's face signified as much when he accompanied Charles to the scene of an oil-spill in the Shetland Islands. If Charles was putting a brave face on things, Philip found it conspicuously difficult to muster much more than a furious scowl.

As the prince gritted his teeth for a visit to Mexico, polls now showed that almost half his mother's subjects, 42 per cent, thought he should 'never become king'. Asked if he should take over the throne 'within the next couple of years', a resounding 81 per cent said no.[13]

On the fourth and last day of his visit to Mexico, at the invitation of some local farmers, the prince hooked up two oxen to an ancient wooden plough and determinedly steered it through two hard-wrought furrows. Another dream photo opportunity, duly relayed home by an unusually large posse of travelling press, though not, perhaps, with quite the effect intended. Blazoned in colour across the front pages, the pictures bespoke an uncomfortably apt metaphor for the prince's life at that moment. His marriage over, his reputation in tatters, Charles had many more long, hard furrows to plough before any reassessment could be made of his standing in Britain and around the world.

In the meantime, though drained by a combination of jet lag, polo and pollution, he chose the end of his visit to Mexico to clarify his immediate aspirations. The tour had included a meeting with 100 business leaders, from whom he had wrung promises of a wide range of environmental and social projects. It was the fourteenth such gathering under the auspices of his Business Leaders Forum, set up in 1990 primarily to offer assistance to the fledgling democracies of Eastern Europe.

Positively publicized back home, the Mexican tour had proved quite a contrast with that in South Korea three months before, where Charles's attempts to set up a waste-recycling programme had been obscured by saturation coverage of his failing marriage.

Given an unusually strong media escort on his Mexican tour, thanks to the 'Camillagate' embarrassments, even the tabloids were reporting his speeches, hammering home a call, as *The Times* distilled it, for 'sustainable development, quality of life and the need for a spiritual dimension in a technological age'. Charles left Mexico, according to briefings from his staff, convinced that 'his future lies as a leading player on the world environmental stage'.[14]

The prince had apparently taken a conscious decision to 'bury himself in his work' and 'rededicate himself to his perceived messianic role as an ecological prophet of the new world order'. A chastened new Prince of Wales would be re-presented for public approval in July 1994, on the twenty-fifth anniversary of his investiture as Prince of Wales – the peg for the book and film by Jonathan Dimbleby. On the ski slopes, at his various homes, even on the overnight sleeper from Scotland, a film crew was already at work shaping a mature, purposeful prince-with-a-heart to be presented for public re-evaluation, in the hope of winning back the affection and trust of the British people.

In the meantime, Charles's problem was that everywhere he went, even in Mexico, people tended to ask where his wife was. British children were told by the Palace advance party not to mention Diana's name; but the inevitable happened when an eleven-year-old Mexican girl tried to take his photograph. Charles asked her not to, bizarrely explaining that he did not photograph well. 'Diana does,' replied innocent little Maria, like a child in an H. M. Bateman cartoon, mentioning the unmentionable.

Would reed-bed sewage-disposal systems and Third-World waste-recycling plants prove enough to bring the British flocking back to their prince's banner, forgiving him his trespasses against their favourite princess? Diana was doing her best to prove otherwise. On 16 February 1993, while Charles was communing with rural farmers in Mexico, his estranged wife was effortlessly up-staging him again back home. As he, across the world, bemoaned 'a cynical disbelief in the relevance of the past to the present, in the value of what is traditional and timeless', she was talking in London about what was seen as a rather more urgent contemporary concern: 'Too many people have used AIDS as an issue to which they could add their own prejudices. If their views were voiced to help fight the disease, that would be fine. However, too often their attitudes reveal only a narrowness of mind and a sad lack of common humanity.'[15]

Was this another coded reference to Charles? If so, Diana had good reason. When the Princess of Wales arrived in Kathmandu a few days later, escorted by the overseas aid minister, Baroness (Lynda) Chalker, the Nepalese welcoming band owned up to some disappointment at 'instructions from London' not to play the national anthem. Travelling journalists were briefed to write that Diana had been 'snubbed' by the Nepalese royal family, who would not be hosting an official dinner in her honour.

Charles consistently denied that he had any knowledge of it, but visitors to St James's Palace were becoming increasingly aware of a 'dirty tricks' campaign by his staff to rehabilitate the prince by discrediting Diana.[16] 'I was now the separated wife of the Prince of Wales,' she said. 'I was a problem. I was a liability . . . This hadn't happened before.' Now she found that 'overseas visits were being blocked and letters going astray'. Diana's 'enemies' – the people 'on my husband's side' – were making her life 'very difficult'.[17] When the princess attempted to arrange a visit to British troops and refugees in Bosnia, under the auspices of the Red Cross, she was told that Charles's own plans to go there took precedence.

It was not like Charles to stoop to vindictiveness, but it was like a few of his friends, and some members of his staff, to do so on his behalf. It was another 'remarkable coincidence', as Diana herself put it, that a missing extract from the 'Squidgygate' tape surfaced just as she was making her own bid for solo glory on the world stage. Charles, at the time, was offering upbeat photo opportunities on the ski slopes of Klosters, 'getting up smiling' each time he fell down – to quote but one set of mid-market picture captions – and 'looking like a man again enjoying life'.[18]

The only way to proceed, as Charles saw it, was to get on with his new life and hope for the best. At his request, Camilla was getting on with the redecoration of Highgrove, expunging all trace of Diana. In London, meanwhile, the prince fulfilled a longstanding ambition by establishing his own press office in St James's Palace, independent of the Buckingham Palace machine. The busy public prince was thus more effectively contrasted with the softer, private side of Charles. That flying visit to British troops in Bosnia, for instance, and a dash to the bedsides of IRA bomb victims, were followed on Easter Sunday by a winsome appearance as a would-be Pied Piper in *The Legend of Lochnagar*, an animated television version of his story for children.

The previous Sunday, his mother had been persuaded to leave the parish church at Sandringham via the back door, so as not to crowd the photographers' view of Charles and his sons exiting by the front. Cynical though the Palace's tactics might appear, the prince's camp believed that they were beginning to work, and that Operation 'Caring Prince' was forcing Diana on to the defensive. Then, with the crudest of public gestures, Buckingham Palace contrived to give the game away.

Mid-April saw a memorial service in Warrington, Lancashire, for Tim Parry and Johnathan Ball, teenagers killed by an IRA bomb in the town's shopping centre two weeks before. In a grave misjudgement, the Palace overruled Diana's expressed wish to attend, announcing that it would instead be sending Prince Philip. Pressed for its reasons – and a response to the suggestion that Philip, not noted for his concern for children, was widely perceived as the royal family's least compassionate member – the Palace explained that this was a job for 'the most senior royal available'. In the absence of the Queen, 'who never attends memorial services, except those of very close friends', her husband was next in line.

This had not been its policy in the past; in 1988, for instance, pre-fall Fergie had been the official choice to attend a service for the victims of the Clapham train disaster. The Warrington ceremony, as one paper pointed out, was 'precisely the kind of delicate royal duty that the princess handles so well . . . Diana's presence in Warrington would have been the best possible advertisement for a united royal family desperately in need of some positive publicity. It would also have given the lie to the persistent rumours that staff of the "born" royals are out to reduce the princess's public work to an ineffective side-show'.[19]

Charles was not directly involved in the furore, but it did not reflect well on him or his family. The service went ahead without Diana, and with Philip in her stead. The night before, it became public knowledge that the princess had telephoned the parents of the two dead boys to offer her sympathy, and to express regret that she would not be able to join them for the service. 'She was ever so nice. It gave me a big boost to talk to her,' said Mrs Wendy Parry, who revealed that Diana, as 'one mother to another', had said she would like to have given her a hug. 'It is a great comfort that some-one in her position should take the time to think of us,' said Maria Ball.

The wide airing given the bereaved parents' delight at Diana's phone calls did not deter friends of the Palace, such as Lord Wyatt, from trying to turn the episode against her. Careful to call her condolences 'genuine', to avoid losing his audience, Wyatt declared that they were 'mixed up with her vanity'. The princess was 'addicted to the limelight her marriage brought. It's like a drug. To feed her craving she'd do anything, even if it meant destroying the throne she solemnly swore to uphold.' With a disingenuous plea that he was 'far from anti-homosexual', Wyatt also took the chance for a passing sideswipe at the princess's work for AIDS victims: 'This elevates them to heroes to be copied by the young. It's well known that AIDS stems mainly from sodomy.'[20] Much more in keeping with popular opinion was the outspoken columnist Julie Burchill: '[Diana's] phone calls were utterly in character; Prince Philip's attendance was not . . . Day by day, despite their pathetic PR efforts, the [royal] family seems more and more to be the most unnatural, destructive and loathsome family since Charles Manson's homicidal gang of the same name.'[21]

The town of Warrington itself chose to settle the issue by inviting the princess to a charity concert for the bereaved families' appeal fund the following weekend. She was unable to go, but sent a message of condolence, offered a 'substantial donation' to the appeal fund, and promised to meet the families privately as soon as possible.

The Palace, by general consensus, had shot itself in the foot, undoing all its work to promote the newly 'caring' prince by a clumsy attempt not just to tarnish his wife, but to shut her out of her natural public habitat. It was a tactic which never looked like working with the British people, who had long since recognized Diana's genuine sense of compassion and her rare gift for expressing it. In an action 'quite typical of her', as Burchill wrote, the princess was 'yet again displaying the warmth and spontaneity which comes harder than speaking Swahili to the Windsors'.

A survey by the *Daily Mail*, which had mounted a huge operation to 'monitor' the royal couple 'in minute detail' throughout the four months since their separation, showed that Diana had attracted more than 9,000 spectators to her sixteen public appearances, while Charles had attracted barely 4,000 to his thirty-one. Diana, concluded the paper, had 'got the better' of Charles; the Palace's tactics were 'clearly not working' for the heir to the throne.

Where, meanwhile, had Charles been while his father attended the Warrington memorial service? In Spain, at the funeral of King Juan Carlos's father. Although Diana was spending the day alone at home – as by now, thanks to the Palace, the entire nation knew – the prince chose not to send their sons back to their mother during his absence, instead sticking rigidly to the schedule, by which they were with him until the following day.

Over the Easter weekend, the television début of his *Legend of Lochnagar* cartoon was marginalized by a current affairs programme that broadcast, for the first time in Britain, the 'Camillagate' tape. Indeed, the royal Easter at Windsor was further marred by a distinct absence of royals. Princes William and Harry were with their mother in London; Prince Edward was away skiing; Prince Andrew made a hurried exit to spend the day at home with his estranged wife and their children. Apart from Charles, only Princess Anne and her new husband, Tim Laurence, lined up alongside the Queen, Prince Philip and the Queen Mother for the traditional family photos – for which only one of the royal grandchildren, Zara Phillips, was on hand. On Easter Monday, the Queen was spotted wandering Windsor Great Park on her own, deep in thought. She may well have been wondering if the 'Diana problem' was being handled in quite the right way.

That February, a despondent Charles had contemplated his future on a lone Caribbean cruise aboard *Britannia*. In his absence, the Princess of Wales took their sons to the Trocadero Centre in London's Piccadilly Circus. For several hours, amid crowds as astonished as they were delighted, the junior Waleses had fun under their mother's careful watch, enjoying the video games of 'Funland' alongside equally excited children their own age. Like the previous week's go-karting near Windsor, or their annual trip to the water slides of Thorpe Park, it was a great day out – of a kind they had never shared with their father.

Charles has never been known to take his sons with him to any public place frequented *en masse* by his future subjects, apart, of course, from polo fields. Thanks to his upbringing, and premature middle age, it would not even occur to him. The princess's Trocadero expedition was not merely a sign of the 'natural touch' that so endeared her to a vast and unshakeable band of followers, it was a deliberate display of the way royalty can behave if it chooses. Since her formal separation from Charles, Diana had consciously been pioneering a royal style then quite alien to her in-laws – an anathema to the House of Windsor, but a breath of welcome and long-overdue fresh air to its subjects.

Charles's three-day sunshine break that weekend cost the British taxpayer more than a million pounds. When Diana herself had been to the Caribbean the previous month, she had sat in the crowded economy cabin of a scheduled British Airways flight beside the lavatory, which made for even longer queues than usual. She had since used scheduled flights for her official visit to Nepal and a skiing holiday in Austria, just after Charles had travelled to and from Klosters by private jet. It would seem 'profligate', she told a friend, to use aircraft of the Queen's Flight.[22]

In February 1993, when the princess travelled to Cardiff Arms Park for the England–Wales rugby international – an official royal engagement, announced in the Court Circular – she passed up the chance to use the royal train, opting instead for a regular seat aboard British Rail's InterCity service. That weekend, she took her girlfriends Kate Menzies and Lulu Blacker, plus escorts and detectives, to the Royal Ballet at Covent Garden. Far from arriving in a chauffeur-driven royal Rolls, the party climbed happily out of a British-made Ford minibus, which soon became the norm for such visits. At Easter, when Diana took her sons to watch motor racing at Donnington Park, she was herself at the wheel of the family's Ford station wagon.

Instinctively, Diana was pioneering a British version of the Scandinavian-style monarchy, which was supposedly under discussion by the royal family's 'Way Ahead' group as one of a reformed House of Windsor's few hopes of salvation. As a tactic in the guerrilla war forced upon her by Buckingham Palace, it was a typically adroit piece of public relations. The minibus trip to Covent Garden, for instance, came within twenty-four hours of the prime minister's Commons statement detailing the Queen's proposed tax payments. Still dazzled by figures, Britain's twenty-five million recession-hit taxpayers had yet to wake up to the true extent of their monarch's future contribution to the Exchequer. Once they realized that it would come down to a mere 1 or 2 million pounds per annum, they began to feel much the same about building the Queen a new £80 million yacht as they had about footing the £60 million bill for the Windsor fire.

After more than forty years' service, the royal yacht *Britannia* was beyond yet another multi-million-pound overhaul. On the eve of the 1997 general election, however, a Tory promise to build a new royal yacht did not prove the vote-winner the party had hoped; on the contrary, Tony Blair made Labour's refusal to do so a campaign pledge, and *Britannia* was duly decommissioned within six months of his landslide victory. The royal family watched in tears.

To many observers, the Windsors showed more emotion over the loss of *Britannia* than they had over that of Diana only weeks before. It was a reminder of the savagery with which, five years earlier, the corporate might of the British Establishment had rounded on the Princess of Wales, within a month of her formal separation from the heir to the throne. As publication of the 'Camillagate' tapes threatened to damage Prince Charles's reputation beyond repair, leaders of every major British institution were urged to close ranks round the prince and set out to sideline his wife.

To Parliament and Church, the legislature and the armed forces, all of whom would one day swear oaths of allegiance to him, the prince's relationship with Mrs Parker Bowles was not the issue. It was Diana's failure to put up with it. 'The public are deceived in the princess,' declared John Casey, a historian at Caius College, Cambridge (whose chancellor is Charles's father). 'They will see that her friends are everything that is shallow and third-rate – a ghastly milieu where she fits in very happily. She will be diminished, especially when she loses her youthful looks.' Charles, to Casey, had 'long-term qualities', whereas the princess did not 'stand for anything'. The 'great question' about Diana and her friends was whether they had plotted to displace the rightful prince. 'If the public thinks that, it will very much turn against her.'

The conspiracy theme was taken up, without any visible sign of evidence, by Lord McAlpine, former treasurer of the Tory Party, then a big wheel in government circles. Accusing Diana of a prop-aganda campaign against the royal family, McAlpine proclaimed that she should not be 'allowed to enjoy the spoils of that victory'. Lord St John of Fawsley, master of Emmanuel College at Cambridge University, was sure she would not. 'I am reasonably optimistic that, having been through a difficult period, we are mov-ing out of the shadows and into the sunlight . . . All the feeling of loyalty will constellate around the Prince of Wales as heir to the throne.'[23]

Charles kept his head down, communing with Camilla in the 'safe houses' of friends, as the forces of the Establishment went to war on his behalf. At times of crisis, when threatened with change or disruption on any significant scale, the senior echelons of British society can always be relied upon to rally round the status quo. Soon even Diana's own step-grandmother, the romantic novelist Barbara Cartland, disowned the princess for the crime of 'outshining' her husband. From the world of knighted media folk, Sir Peregrine Worsthorne rashly predicted that the 'electric charge' between Diana and the public would dissipate once she was perceived as Princess of Wales in name only: 'I don't see her carrying on as a star in her own right, as if she's got some momentous glamour of her own.'

At least Sir Perry had some cautionary words for the prince. Predicting 'a rather austere and unworldly' period of transition for the heir to the throne, he recalled the atonement paid by King Henry II for the murder of Thomas à Becket: 'The King ostentatiously had himself lashed on the steps of Canterbury Cathedral. Charles has got to find some equivalent.' But the Church of England was not bothered about penance. To the Bishop of Peterborough, the Rt Revd William Westwood, it was Diana's position that was 'perilous'. Unless she was careful, she would find herself greatly reduced: 'If you live by the media you should die by the media.' Charles had the continuity of his family's lineage and the necessary time to indulge in a period of reflection. 'My honest view is that Prince Charles should really move a bit out of the public eye. Doing ordinary things – openings and visits, that sort of stuff – wins people's hearts.' The former Lord Chancellor, Lord Hailsham, agreed : 'I think it best for the prince to be left alone. Let it simmer for a bit.'[24]

Charles continued to do just that, while now it was Diana's turn to suffer more grief, this time at the hands of her own brother Charles, who, amid the national debate, changed his mind about offering her the use of a cottage on the Althorp estate. The princess had looked forward to quiet weekends at the 'cosy nest' she would make out of the Garden House at Althorp. But Charles Spencer withdrew his offer because of the 'unacceptable levels of intrusion' that would inevitably result from the 'extra police presence, the inevitable cameras and other surveillance equipment'.[25] For several months the princess's relationship with her brother cooled.

At the time, she was anyway dealing with the much more pressing problems of any recently separated parent: reassuring the children. After one of their first weekends visiting their downbeat father, morose in the wake of the 'Camillagate' transcript, William and Harry returned to their mother full of questions about why he was so unhappy. Like any devoted mother, Diana herself was putting on an especially cheerful front to her sons, who could not fail to notice the contrast. She seemed all right, so why was Daddy so miserable? Was it all her fault? Diana reassured them that it was no-one's fault, least of all theirs. Their father can be expected to have told them much the same.

'The one thing we never fought over', she later confided, 'was the boys. It was an unspoken agreement between us. During the worst days of the marriage, when I threw a wobbly over something, Charles would just walk away, calmly turn his back and shut the door, leaving me hysterical, worse than ever. We tried to hide it all from the children, but I don't really know how much we succeeded. They were always sweet to both of us, but I suppose they knew things were bad. Children always do, don't they?

'I know I'm accused of smothering them in too much love, but I don't think a mother – especially a separated mother – *can* smother her children in too much love. Like Charles, who handles it all rather differently, I am just desperately concerned to minimize the effect on them. I want to make sure they feel secure. I'm terrified of their being damaged by all this. I suppose, in the end, it's impossible to avoid, but I pray they don't turn out as dysfunctional as our families. Yes, both our families . . .'[26]

Like all children of divorce, William and Harry will have felt reluctant to take sides. In most other imaginable ways, their feelings about their parents' separation will have been as desolate as those of any other children their age. Most such children are aware, however remotely, of problems between their parents, and can even feel relief when they are openly resolved in separation. Few such children, however, have to watch their parents' marital spats conducted in terms of public warfare. And the worst was yet to come.

CHAPTER SIXTEEN

'TIME AND SPACE'

FOR A QUARTER OF THE EARTH'S POPULATION, THE MONTH OF JUNE 1953 symbolized the dawn of a post-war age of unimagined promise. On the morning of Elizabeth II's coronation, her subjects awoke to the inspirational news that Mount Everest had been conquered by a British expedition – as if endorsing a poll showing that one-third of them believed the monarch to have been chosen by God. The editors of *Time* magazine, casting around for a figure to symbolize the hopeful spirit of the Fifties, nominated the twenty-six-year-old British monarch to 'represent, express and affect the aspirations of the collective sub-conscious' of the entire free world.

Forty years on, in June 1993, most of those aspirations seemed to have been cheated. After the false boom of the Eighties, the United Kingdom languished beneath the worst recession since the 1930s. Amid record numbers of homeless and unemployed, bankrupt and redundant, the monarchy too slumped into a seemingly symbolic decline. With the failure of the marriage of the heir to the throne, and all the public hope reposed in it betrayed by an ugly spate of mutual recriminations, the fortieth anniversary of the Queen's accession to the throne was marked less by retrospective rejoicing than a sudden and unexpected struggle for survival.

The Crown, like the country, had its back to the wall. Throughout the 1980s a festive succession of royal marriages and births had rendered the institution of monarchy as popular as at any time in its thousand-year history. Now that all those marriages had collapsed, and with them the royal ratings, Elizabeth II found herself ambushed by woes, and the stability of the Crown threatened as at no time since the abdication of her uncle, Edward VIII, in 1936. The royal melodrama had taken on Shakespearean proportions, as civil war between the future king and queen divided the nation, more in sorrow than in anger, into fiercely feuding camps.

At centre-stage was the world's most popular princess – cruelly wronged by her husband, to the majority, and schemed against by his coterie of cronies. A vandalized icon, a betrayed innocent, a manipulative hysteric: Diana, Princess of Wales, was many things to many people. But for the editors of *Time*, as for the vast majority, there was no doubt who had now come to 'represent, express and affect the aspirations of the collective sub-conscious'. Diana was 'another Joan of Arc . . . a feminist heroine'.[1]

At the beginning of June 1993, the fortieth anniversary of her mother-in-law's coronation, *Time*'s feminist heroine chose to draw up her will. Six months after her separation from her husband, Diana was advised that, though barely into her thirties, she should make arrangements for her children's future. The will she signed on 1 June 1993 was later described as a document drawn up by someone who 'did not expect to die in the near future'; it was a formulaic affair, with little serious thought given to the division of assets, goods and chattels. But it did have one distinguishing feature: a clause insisting that, in the event of her death, her husband should 'consult with my mother with regard to the up-bring, education and welfare of our children'.[2]

To be echoed in her brother's belligerent speech at her funeral four years later, Diana's 'express wish' was an overt rebuff to Charles, implicitly portraying him as an inadequate father. The truth at the time was that Charles was seeing less of his sons than he would have wished; when he did see them he tried to be as attentive and caring as any other father. The prince, according to Diana's camp, was an absentee parent more interested in spending time with his mistress, which precluded the presence of his children. Diana, according to the prince's camp, was still constantly up-ending their prearranged schedules, often at the last minute, to prevent him seeing them. It was a mutual stand-off about which the detailed truth will never now be known. What is known is that Charles, in the wake of his formal separation, was seeing more of Camilla than ever.

At first, in the immediate wake of the drama, the prince was super-careful. Fearful of calls being bugged, and aware of the public's hostility to Camilla, he cancelled their usual spring tryst at Birkhall, the Queen Mother's home on the Scottish estate. She and her husband, meanwhile, made several deliberate public appearances together, as much for the sake of their own children as the Prince of Wales's sagging reputation. That May, for instance, Andrew and Camilla arrived arm in arm at the Wiltshire wedding of Sarah Ward, daughter of Gerald Ward – one of the group at Annabel's back in 1972, when Charles and the premarital Camilla had danced the night away before returning to her flat.

By midsummer, however, as Diana signed the document that would eventually reveal her deep mistrust of her husband, Charles was under greater public pressure than ever, and thus in greater need of Camilla. A relentless spate of polls showed that an increasing majority of the British people now considered him 'unfit to be King', and wished the throne to pass straight to his son William. Although this was constitutionally impossible, without the (highly unlikely) agreement of the Queen and the prince himself, it was immensely damaging to his public standing, and a huge psychological strain on the man himself. So St James's Palace's disinformation machine, personified by those ubiquitous 'friends of Prince Charles' went back to work on the prince's behalf.

CHARLES GAVE UP CAMILLA TWO YEARS AGO ran the headline in the *Daily Express*, the one paper whose knighted editor could then be relied upon to print anything the Palace slipped its way, regardless of the hollow laughter on its own editorial benches. 'The prince', read the story, was 'beginning to grow in confidence as he puts the controversy of his marriage behind him'. Falsehood number one. 'There is nothing more that can come out about the prince's relationship with Camilla,' said a source 'close to' Charles. 'As far as we are concerned it's old hat.' Falsehood number two. 'The prince's relationship with Camilla has been over for more than two years, a full twelve months before Andrew Morton's book was published.' Falsehood number three. Paving the way for falsehood number four, the most shameless yet, implying it was all really Diana's fault. 'It was all so unnecessary,' said a 'high-ranking' source. 'All the humiliation, pain and heartache that followed could have been avoided. The prince ended his relationship with Camilla two years ago in the spring of 1991. He knew he had to give her up, and he did.'

But the 'dirty tricks department' wasn't finished yet. Referring to the so-called 'Togetherness Tour' of Korea, which had gone so badly wrong, Charles's 'friend' continued, 'After that trip he knew his marriage was finished, but suggestions that he again turned to Camilla are just not true. The prince feared that if he was ever seen with Camilla again, it would finally wreck his chances of becoming king. The people would not accept him.' So Charles had apparently held 'an emotional meeting' with Camilla, at which he had 'broken off their relationship'.

Now it became clear that Charles's 'friend' was making this up as he went along, and was heading towards another bright idea, even more despicable than pinning the blame on Diana. In the previous paragraph Charles 'knew his marriage was finished'; yet this post-Korea summit with Camilla now became a 'final effort to save his troubled marriage', since when he had 'stuck to his word' and avoided Camilla. There followed the paragraph showing that Charles's anonymous champion was prepared to stoop to anything – even, heaven forfend, a lie that also offended courtly chivalry – in the effort to save the prince's neck.

> In fact, it was 45-year-old Camilla, now beginning to lose her looks, who could not cope with being dumped by the man she cherished. She pursued him. In January, after the Camillagate scandal hit the monarchy even further, the prince made a gentleman's agreement with Brigadier Parker Bowles never to see his wife again.[3]

This was one of the lowest points in the lengthening catalogue of black propaganda on Charles's behalf: that the prince's 'friends' felt able to advance Camilla's 'failing looks' as proof positive that the prince had no alternative but to abandon her. With friends like these, the prince had no further need to be his own worst enemy. They even felt free to impugn his own honour with the lie about that gentleman's agreement with his fellow officer, the long-suffering brigadier.

So it was not entirely helpful that the brigadier's sister-in-law Carolyn now chose to confirm, in an interview with an Australian magazine, the widely known suspicions that the Parker Bowleses' marriage itself had long been one of convenience. 'Everyone knows Camilla and Andrew have an arranged marriage,' said Carolyn.

'Ever since they married they have had a fairly free life together . . . What they do suits them both very well.' Since the publication of the 'Camillagate' tapes, said her sister-in-law, Camilla 'just doesn't go out, except to private parties. Can you blame her? Imagine going out to the supermarket after you have had those tapes quoted at you in all the newspapers and magazines'.

Small wonder that Camilla's friends described her that summer as 'showing the strain'. Alarmed at the state of her health, just as Diana's friends had been twelve months earlier, they talked anonymously to the press of the 'intolerable strain' she was under. 'I am genuinely worried about her,' said one. 'The spark has gone out of her life, and she looks haunted and hunted.' Adding to the pressure on Camilla, who was looking older than her forty-five years, was the strain of maintaining the fiction that she had not seen Charles for six months – slightly out of synch with the Palace's fictional 'two years' – while in truth she was 'in touch' with him the whole time.[4]

When Camilla disappeared to India that autumn with two girl-friends, Emilie van Cutsem and Gerald Ward's wife, Amanda, her husband felt obliged to deny rumours that she had suffered a nervous breakdown: 'She is perfectly all right. She has gone away on holiday with a couple of other girls, that's all.' Soon after her return, she and Diana were both present at a memorial service for the Earl of Westmorland, the former Master of the Queen's Horse. This time, unlike the El Alamein service a year earlier, the two women managed to avoid each other. But the contrast between them could not have been more marked. Diana, newly liberated by life without Charles, looked stunningly beautiful and self-assured; Camilla, bowed down by the complexities of Charles's continuing presence in her life, looked to one observer 'shattered – almost old enough to be Diana's mother'.

As the great British public attempted to sift fact from fiction, opinion polls suggested that its instincts were sound. People did not believe the Palace's crude propaganda machine, assuming that Charles and Camilla were still very much an item – the very item, indeed, which had broken the heart and the marriage of the increasingly sainted Diana, the martyr-turned-comforter of the afflicted.

Winning the occasional battle, but losing the war, Charles spent most of 1993 maintaining a judicious silence. As Diana seized the chance for the kind of photo opportunities that were fast becoming her trademark – ladling food, for example, for suffering children in Zimbabwe – Charles was little seen or heard. He scored one private coup, which caused him some quiet, if cruel, satisfaction; Diana was visibly annoyed, on returning early from a holiday with her friends Lucia Flecha da Lima and Rosa Monckton, to find that Charles was using a junior member of his staff, Alexandra 'Tiggy' Legge-Bourke, as a surrogate stepmother to their sons. Harry's mother was especially upset by a front-page photo of her smiling son sitting on Tiggy's knee in a royal Range-Rover. In Diana's mind, Charles was using Tiggy to keep the boys happy while he blithely continued his normal routine, leaving them behind at Balmoral or Highgrove while he went shooting or hunting. But the boys seemed to like Tiggy, and Diana was forced, for now, to bite her tongue. Charles, meanwhile, continued to keep a very low public profile.

Or so it seemed. In 1993, according to official records, Charles undertook eighteen state functions, fifty charity events, twelve environmental and sixteen architectural engagements; attended eight occasions promoting healing and complementary medicine, twenty meetings involving the Duchy of Cornwall; visited Cambridge, Derby, Birmingham, Stoke-on-Trent, Yorkshire and Kent, as well as Mexico, Poland, Czechoslovakia, Turkey and four Gulf states. He founded the Prague Heritage Fund, took the chair of the Royal Collection Trust and also fitted in thirty-five miscellaneous functions 'promoting a range of good causes'.[5]

From his point of view, in other words, it was business as usual, worthy but dull stuff, unreported by a press still obsessed with his wife and mistress. Even to those around him, however, Charles's *faux-naïf* act was wearing a bit thin, as was his insistence on pursuing lost causes. On issues like architecture he had been so publicly discredited that there was little point in his spin doctors trying to draw attention to his speeches and engagements; much the same applied to holistic medicine and organic farming, princely obsessions of little or no interest to a public more concerned about his apparent betrayal of the world's most popular woman. A party to launch the Prague Heritage Fund was marred by his failure to appear in person, and his over-eager aides' hijacking of the occasion to discredit Diana; and his visit to Czechoslovakia was obscured by the use of that gas-guzzling Bentley. Even the chair-manship of the Royal Collections Trust, scarcely the most onerous of tasks, earned him little more than criticism about the Windsor wealth, its exploitation of visitors to Buckingham Palace to pay for the Windsor fire, and its failure to share the national art collection with the nation.

All occasions seemed to inform against Charles, or win him precious little of the positive publicity his press office craved. Too busy dealing with his private life, Aylard's propaganda machine was getting nowhere. While Jonathan Dimbleby and his film crew soldiered on – 'For a whole year,' said a senior figure at the Prince's Trust, 'it felt more like we were working for Dimbleby than for Charles'[6] – the results were still a year away, as was his twenty-fifth anniversary as Prince of Wales. While his aides ran out of ideas, Charles chose to pour his heart out to the prime minister.

In October 1993, out of the blue, a puzzled John Major suddenly received a letter bemoaning the public's loss of faith in people in public life. The Prince deplored as 'incredibly sad' the growing tendency to snipe at public servants as people with 'jobs for life' who waste the taxpayers' money. It is doubtful that Major, his mind more on the backbench revolt of his party's Eurosceptics, recognized this as a *cri de cœur* from a man who regarded himself as a much-maligned public servant, constantly accused of wasting tax-payers' money. But the PM's reply was suitably emollient, welcoming the prince's unexceptional remarks and blandly agreeing with him about 'the importance of the public services'.[7]

Major, in truth, was understandably playing a double game. Prompted by his foreign secretary, Douglas Hurd, who had been charmed by the princess and her quest to become an unofficial ambassador for Britain, Major held several sympathetic meetings with Diana and promised her his help. The prime minister suggested to Buckingham Palace that the princess might, with government support, prove a valuable asset to Britain on the world stage, using her global popularity to promote the country's image abroad and win valuable export deals for Britain. The Palace replied with an emphatic negative. That role, it firmly told Downing Street, was reserved for the heir to the throne.

So Charles now decided the time was right to break cover. On the eve of a trip to the Gulf states, on which he had invited along a *Financial Times* correspondent to report his work for British exports, he made a speech in Oxford 'praying' that the West could overcome its 'unthinking prejudices' against the Muslim religion and 'join forces with Islam' against Saddam Hussein's assaults on Iraq's Marsh Arabs.

Any attack on Saddam was likely to earn Charles favourable headlines, at the price of upsetting the Foreign Office, who accused him of jeopardizing the lives of three Britons then held in Iraq. But the speech went much further in its praise of Islam – 'part of our past and present, in all fields of human endeavour', which had 'helped to create modern Europe' and was 'part of our inheritance, not a thing apart'.

> More than this, Islam can teach us today a way of understanding and living in the world which Christianity itself is poorer for having lost. At the heart of Islam is its preservation of an integral view of the Universe. Islam – like Buddhism and Hinduism – refuses to separate man and nature, religion and science, mind and matter, and has preserved a metaphysical and unified view of ourselves and the world around us.[8]

Widely reported the next day, Charles's speech naturally had the Church of England muttering in its collective beard. Its future Supreme Governor seemed more intoxicated by Islam than by Anglicanism, on which, according to the Archbishop of Canterbury, he had 'given up'.[9] Charles's description of the 'unmentionable horrors' perpetuated by Saddam's regime, and the 'obscene lies' used to justify them, were meanwhile condemned by the FO as 'ill-judged', 'mistimed' and 'delivered without proper consultation'. Mrs Julie Ride, wife of one of the three Britons jailed for ten years for 'illegally entering' Iraq, said the prince's speech was 'not very helpful . . . His comments were pretty out of hand.'[10]

The prince's infatuation with Islam would soon lead him to form an advisory committee on Islamic matters, housed in his Institute of Architecture, thus blessing it with a much-needed financial boost from Middle Eastern potentates. Patron of the Oxford Centre for Islamic Studies, he first took an interest in the religion when the publication of Salman Rushdie's novel *The Satanic Verses* brought down a potentially fatal fatwa on the British writer in 1987. Perversely, perhaps, Charles came down on the side of the Ayatollah Khomeini, as he revealed in 1992 over dinner in Paris with the French philosopher Bernard-Henri Levy. The prince, according to Levy, launched into an attack on Rushdie, then approaching his fifth year in hiding, insisting that he was 'a bad writer'. Politely disagreeing, Levy conceded that Charles was entitled to his view. When the prince went on to protest that Rushdie was costing the British taxpayer too much, however, it struck the French philosopher as 'a bit steep'.*

'And the Crown of England?' Levy replied. 'Have you never asked yourself how much the Crown of England costs the British taxpayer?' Charles did not, apparently, come up with an answer.[11]

The membership of the prince's Islamic committee comprises a Roman Catholic and six Anglicans, including two bishops, as well as five Muslims. All are anxious to assert that the Prince of Wales is not, as is sometimes wondered, drifting towards conversion to Islam. 'People come up and ask me if he has become a Muslim,' says one of them, Dr Zaki Badawi, Egyptian-born principal of the Muslim College in London. 'I assure them that he is a very committed Christian, and there is no conflict at all between his Christianity and an appreciation of Islam.'[12]

But there are those in high clerical places who wish the prince was a more committed Christian than he appears. 'It would help if he loved the Church of England a bit more,' said the former Archbishop of Canterbury, Lord Runcie. The prince's views were 'so inconsistent . . . He would go in with the *Spectator* gang on "the lovely language of the Prayer Book", but then he would say, "Instead of interfering with politics, the Church should be creating centres of healing in the inner cities – ought to be bringing together the spiritual, the intellectual and the architectural" . . . I think he'd given up on the Church of England before I arrived [in 1980].' Although 'quite pious', Charles was 'deeply into Laurens van der Post spirituality . . . I don't think he took the Church of England very seriously.' The Archbishop's relationship with the prince was 'friendly', but 'I couldn't get much depth out of it. He is a mass of contradictions . . . so that the public don't really know where they are.'[14]

---

* France seems to bring out the worst in the prince. Also in 1992, the gourmet in him overcame the diplomat as he made an impassioned speech in favour of French cheese. Within months, back in France, the agronomist in Charles was mounting a defence of protectionist French farmers, thus compromising Britain's position in the already embattled GATT talks, and alienating the UK farming community, of which he considers himself an enlightened leading member. 'It was', to one observer, 'a characteristic contribution: well-meaning but, in political terms, breathtakingly ill-judged.'[13]

*

The night after his Oxford speech, Charles organized a 'Shakespeare evening' in the ballroom of Buckingham Palace, at which his own handwritten letters had secured the services of such titled luminaries as Sir John Gielgud, Sir Derek Jacobi and Dame Judi Dench. A celebration of his Shakespeare summer school for young would-be actors at Stratford, it took place before an invited audience of 'the great and the good', without one youngster, including his own sons, in sight. Diana, of course, would have stuffed the place with youth at the expense of those ageing grandees, and invited the cameras in to record the results.

It was a measure of the state of play, as the war of the Waleses moved towards its climax, that such an idea never even crossed the mind of the prince or his advisers. Not merely did they lack the princess's natural instinct for public relations; Charles's sense of royal propriety is such that it would not occur to him to invite schoolchildren to an event at the Palace that was portrayed as being laid on in their interests. As he sat down to dinner that night with theatrical knights and corporate fat cats, only too ready to give money to the Royal Shakespeare Company for the privilege of dining at the Palace, the prince was far more at home among the great and the good. To his authorized biographer, indeed, this was an evening quite out of character with the 'starchy formalities' normally associated with Buckingham Palace. The prince brought to the evening 'an élan ... redolent of the age of Prince Albert'.[15]

But this neo-Albert lacked the common touch. Everything he came into contact with seemed to be turning to base metal. Now Charles's plans for his 'model village' at Poundbury faltered seriously, to the point where he had to convene a weekend 'crisis' summit, while Diana regained the initiative in the battle for public attention. Although she had always benefited from the attentions of photographers, she was now complaining that they would not leave her alone. 'You make my life hell!' she had recently shouted at paparazzi who jostled her and the young princes as they left a London cinema. But the final indignity came that November, when she beheld the front page of the Sunday Mirror, adorned by a series of photographs of herself working out at her London health club. Dressed only in a revealing leotard, the princess was shown with her legs apart as she pushed up a shoulder press. The most voyeuristic photos of her yet published, they were also the least flattering; her emergent cellulite was but one detail of her naked thighs over which the nation pored that weekend. 'It was', in the judgement of one magazine editor, 'a crotch shot, plain and simple.'

She had, of course, been completely unaware that the pictures were being taken. The culprit turned out to be the gymnasium's manager, a New Zealander named Bryce Taylor, who had bored holes in the walls of his office to secure a scoop worth a six-figure sum. Against Palace advice Diana sued the *Mirror*, securing an injunction to prevent the paper or its daily sibling publishing more of Taylor's pictures. Amid the ensuing controversy, the princess won the support of Parliament, press and people against an editor who admitted he was a 'scumbag' and a photographer who was unrepentant. 'What I did was sneaky, surreptitious and pre-planned,' admitted Taylor. 'I don't make excuses. It was underhand. But if I told you I had an absolutely legal scam, which didn't hurt anyone and would make you a million pounds, wouldn't you say yes?'

On the eve of a court case in which Diana would have been grilled by one of Britain's most forceful barristers, Geoffrey Robertson, an Australian with republican sympathies, a settlement was reached in which Taylor was effectively paid off to disappear and keep his mouth shut. For Diana, accused by Charles's camp of courting the publicity, even co-operating with the photographer, it was more than she could take.

'Those pictures', she said, 'were horrid, simply horrid.' In early December, at a charity function at the Park Lane Hilton, the princess announced that she was withdrawing from public life. In a voice charged with emotion, she pleaded for some 'time and space' after more than a decade of incessant attention, both on- and offstage.

> When I started my public life twelve years ago, I understood that the media might be interested in what I did. I realized then that their attention would inevitably focus on both our public and private lives. But I was not aware of how overwhelming that attention would become, nor the extent to which it would affect both my public duties and my personal life, in a manner that has been hard to bear.

Over the next few months, she continued, 'I will be seeking a more suitable way of combining a meaningful public role with, hopefully, a more private life.' She could not be making this sort of statement without 'the heartfelt support' of the British public, whose 'kindness and affection have carried me through some of the most difficult periods' and whose 'love and care have eased the journey'.[16]

As the public bemoaned the apparent loss of its beloved princess, there were those who saw Charles's hand behind his troublesome wife's departure, albeit temporarily, from the public stage. In her speech Diana had referred to the support offered her throughout her ordeal by the Queen and the Duke of Edinburgh, but conspicuously failed to mention her husband. 'Did She Go or Was She Pushed?' was the question asked even by the magisterial *Times* newspaper.

In fact Charles had been forewarned of the speech by his mother, to whom Diana, as a matter of courtesy, had given advance notice of her intentions, and he had tried to talk her out of making it. Far better, surely, to phase out her public engagements, if she so wished, without 'grandstanding' in public like this. But Diana was adamant: she owed her public some explanation of her decision. 'The pressure was intolerable then,' she explained, 'and my work was being affected. I wanted to give one hundred and ten per cent to my work, and I could only give fifty. I was constantly tired, exhausted, because the pressure was so cruel . . . It was my decision to make that speech because I owed it to the public to say, "Thank you. I'm disappearing for a bit, but I'll come back." '

Besides, she added, it was always a good idea to 'confuse the enemy'. So who was the enemy? 'The enemy was my husband's department, because I always got more publicity, my work was more . . . was discussed much more than his. And, you know, from that point of view I understand it. But I was doing good things, and I wanted to do good things. I was never going to hurt anyone, I was never going to let anyone down.' They wanted to 'undermine' her, she said, 'out of fear', because 'here was a strong woman doing her bit, and where was she getting her strength from to continue?'[17]

All that remained, after his wife had left her adoring fan club in a state of shocked dismay, was for 'the enemy' to wonder publicly 'why someone so anxious for seclusion should have chosen to stage such a melodramatic exit'.[18]

*

Charles spent that weekend with Camilla at Highgrove. Their relationship remained so clandestine that few could know this, least of all the Venerable George Austin, Archdeacon of York, who nonetheless chose this moment to declare the prince unfit to be King. 'He made solemn vows before God about his marriage, and it seems – if the rumours about Camilla are true – that he began to break them almost immediately.'[19]

As the media floodgates opened again, with Austin's assault coming so hard on the heels of Diana's 'time and space' speech, the Palace could think of nothing to say. In due course, Austin would be crudely abused on Charles's behalf as 'a minor cleric of Pickwickian demeanour and modest accomplishments well-known for his eagerness to animadvert on public issues'.[20] At the time, the equally Pickwickian figure of Nicholas Soames again chose to fill the void left by the Palace, now preoccupied with the need for denials that Prince Andrew had AIDS or Prince Edward was gay.

Mustering all his new authority as a junior government minister ('a triumph', to one senior parliamentarian, 'of birth over ability'[21]), Soames dismissed the renewed calls for Charles to step aside in favour of William. Always ready to go out on a limb for his future king, as indeed when taunting female MPs in the chamber with sexist remarks, the portly son of the late Lord Soames – redolent, like his party at the time, of a bygone age – declared that 'being heir to the throne is not an ambition but a duty, and one which will befall him on a sad moment later in his life'. Charles would 'inherit the throne and that is the end of the matter', declared Soames, adding for good measure that Austin's 'hugely unrepresentative vapourings' had filled him with 'outrage and disgust'.[22]

Soames's own vapourings soon looked like a rather hasty rush to judgement. Among leading churchmen who boldly spoke out in Austin's support was the Revd Tony Higton, a member of the Synod of the Church of England, who had also 'reached the conclusion', albeit 'with great sadness', 'that Prince Charles is not fit to be the next King of England'. Higton spoke for many more reticent rank-and-file churchmen, mindful of the Scriptures, when he declared that Charles could become king only 'if he totally denies adultery with Camilla Parker Bowles'. If that were not possible, he should 'make a public expression of remorse and

penitence', confirming that 'the romance was over'. Failing either
of these options, 'I have to say that I think he is unfit to be king,
and it would be better if the Crown passed straight to Prince
William – provided he maintained the highest standards in his own
private life.'

Higton conceded that both Church and people 'require higher
standards from people in public places today than we did in the
past', adding that he felt it his duty to take 'a firm stand' on adultery. 'I think it is very unfortunate if people in such high places as
Prince Charles cannot behave morally.'[23]

Charges of hypocrisy were levelled, quite reasonably, at public
figures who chose to pass judgement on the prince's morality in an
age when more than a third of British marriages end in divorce,
and most major institutions of British life, from Parliament to the
Church itself, were constantly beset by sex scandals. Charles's
problem was his putative role as Supreme Governor of the Church
of England. History bore witness to countless adulterous princes
and kings; but senior members of the Anglican Church, itself in a
state of some disarray, felt the need to take a stand on the morality
of the man next in line to become its titular head.

Yet again, Charles was caught in a timewarp fraught with irony;
in previous centuries, whose values he cherished more than those
of his own, his private life would have been far less likely to
become the subject of public debate. As it was, Charles faced not
merely the hostility of a Church struggling to justify its continuing
existence, but a public whose natural loyalty to the monarchy, as a
symbol, above all, of moral values, was severely stretched by his
conduct.

On the day that Soames leapt to his defence, Charles made an
official visit to Southwark, south London, to meet 'Gateway
Project' volunteers providing job training and accommodation for
unemployed and homeless people. The headcount of those waiting
to see him was thirteen photographers, ten reporters and two
members of the public. On the same day Diana was in Belfast, on
a visit not announced in advance for security reasons. The count
there was 30 photographers, 10 reporters and 160 members of the
public. An opinion poll that month showed that now a negligible
number of Britons, merely 3 per cent, blamed Diana for the break-
up of the marriage. Only Fergie, the topless, toe-sucking,
adulterous Duchess of York, commanded a lower public approval

rating than the heir to the throne. A leading Labour MP, Frank
Field, was calling for a committee of privy counsellors, chaired by
the prime minister, to supervise the upbringing of Princes William
and Harry.

It was a bleak midwinter indeed at Sandringham, with Diana
spending Christmas Eve there with her sons but departing on
Christmas morning after the family's annual parade to church.
Back at Kensington Palace, she ate Christmas lunch alone off a
tray, brooding about the beloved boys she had left behind with the
alien Windsors. Next day she flew to Washington, to spend a few
days with her friend Lucia Flecha da Lima, whose husband had
been transferred there from London. 'I cried all the way out and all
the way back,' said Diana, 'I felt so sorry for myself.'

It was the first time in her life she had ever travelled anywhere
alone – 'a very strange sensation, liberating but rather frightening.'
On the way home, Diana spent a night at the Carlyle Hotel, New
York – the first time she had ever stayed alone in a hotel suite. 'No-
one telling me what not to do. It was wonderful.' She discovered
the joy of room service, cable TV, 'even' (giggling) 'blue movies'.
Then the phone rang, and she realized there was no-one but her to
answer it.

'Hello,' said the hotel switchboard, 'is that Lady Di?'

'No,' replied Diana.

'Sorry, ma'am, is that the Princess of Wales?'

'Yes.'

'Well, there's a man on the phone says he's your husband. Says
his name is Charles Windsor and he's calling from a payphone
down the block.' At this point, when telling her story, Diana would
pause to insert a few footnotes: 'First of all, my husband' – the
word was spat out venomously – 'never rings me. Second, he
wouldn't know what a payphone is. And third, even if someone
explained it to him, he wouldn't have any money in his pocket to
put in the slot . . . So I took the call.'

Diana had worked out that some enterprising passerby had
glimpsed her furtive flit from limo to lobby, done a double-take,
and tried his luck from a local call box. In recognition of his
enterprise she chatted to him for forty minutes, preserving his
privacy by refusing to reveal what they talked about. What she
loved about the story was the thought of this stranger subsequently
doing the rounds of Manhattan bars, telling anyone who would

listen: 'You'll never guess who I just talked to . . .'

'Yeah,' she would drawl the inevitable reply, 'and I'm the Queen of Sheba!'[24]

Charles might have been pleased to leave this dismal landscape, were it not for the lack of enthusiasm with which he contemplated another visit to Australia, reluctant to be drawn into its developing debate about abandoning the monarchy. On 26 January – Australia Day, celebrated as the anniversary of the arrival of the first British settlers in 1788 – the prince was standing at a microphone before a convivial throng in Tumbalong Park, in Darling Harbour, Sydney, waiting to present prizes to schoolchildren, when a young man suddenly ran towards the platform, apparently firing shots, and Charles's protection officer dramatically barged the prince out of his line of fire.

This 'demented' person – the prince's own word[25] – turned out to be one David Kang, a twenty-three-year-old student of Cambodian extraction, protesting about the plight of the 'boat people' in Australia; his 'gun' was in fact a starting pistol, and the 'shots' he was firing were blanks. But the prince was not to know that, nor indeed were the horrified spectators, one of whom thought, 'Oh my God, it's Kennedy all over again.'[26] Charles, testified another, 'had a bewildered look, but showed no sign of fear or panic'.[27]

'It's all right for you,' Charles told the audience, 'you've had a drink.' Later that day he duly delivered the keynote speech of his visit, arguing that it was the sign of 'a mature and self-confident country' to reconsider its constitutional arrangements. Back home in England, the Prince of Wales's grace under pressure generated the first positive headlines in as long as he could remember.

CHAPTER SEVENTEEN

'THE SADDEST DAY OF MY LIFE'

ON 4 APRIL 1900, WHEN A YOUNG ANARCHIST TOOK A POT-SHOT AT the Prince of Wales in Brussels, the future King Edward VII promptly telegraphed his mistress, Mrs Alice Keppel, to assure her that he was unharmed.[1] In Sydney almost a century later, his great-great-grandson telephoned her great-grand-daughter to say much the same.

It was proof positive, if proof were needed, that the Charles–Camilla relationship was on again, if indeed it had ever been off. During the prince's reluctant tour of Australasia, it emerged from his own staff that he had been 'in touch' with Camilla throughout, which rather gave the lie to a story that appeared while he was still there, the very weekend after the 'blanks' attack. Anxious to capitalize on the sudden spate of positive headlines, those tireless 'friends of Prince Charles' had been back in action. MY DUTY BEFORE LOVE, yelled the front page of the *Mail on Sunday*. PRINCE CHARLES SEVERS ALL LINKS WITH CAMILLA PARKER BOWLES.

Under the byline of Nigel Dempster, the recipient of those counter-productive leaks about Diana's thirtieth-birthday party, Charles was said to have 'renounced' his friendship with Camilla. 'He has decided to sacrifice his close friendship with the mother-of-two for the sake of his duty to the country,' wrote Dempster. 'The prince has resolved, after months of heart-searching, to remove any obstacle to his succession by finally severing their twenty-four-year relationship.' According to 'a royal confidant', the prince had made 'an irrevocable decision' on the matter. Charles recognized that, if he wanted to be king, which he did, 'there is no room in his life for Mrs Parker Bowles'. The prince had decided they must henceforth 'lead separate lives, which cannot cross at any point'. Camilla herself was said to be 'frantic'. She was 'very unhappy' about the fact that the prince was 'no longer taking her calls'.[2]

In fact, of course, the prince took her call in Australia that very day, to discuss that very story, about which he was furious. Charles was angry less about its inaccuracy than about the fact that his name was being mentioned at all in connection with Camilla's. There were those in his circle who were counselling him to abandon his mistress, as his only hope of public rehabilitation; the prince believed, quite rightly, that he could detect their hand behind the story. And they were defying his orders. Before leaving England, on a tour designed to restore some of his tarnished reputation at home, he had left strict instructions with both staff and friends to desist from leaking stories, however well intended, about himself and Mrs Parker Bowles. The disappearance of her name from the newspapers, especially in the context of his, was the prince's only chance to rise above the legacy of 'Camillagate'.

So the following month, when an Italian tourist burgled Charles's apartment in St James's Palace, his office sternly denied that those famous cufflinks with the intertwined 'C's were among his haul of jewellery. Those cufflinks, said the Palace, had never existed. Nor, it seemed to imply, had Mrs Parker Bowles.*

Camilla was being whited out of the public photos of the prince's entourage, while occupying pride of place at his side in private. They would ride with the Beaufort Hunt on alternate days, to avoid the least chance of being photographed together; she pottered about her garden while he played polo; unselfishly, she stayed away from her usual haunts, from social gatherings to race meetings, if he planned to attend. By night, however, or during those weekends when Charles's sons were with their mother in London, Camilla was still the mistress of Highgrove, the prince's openly acknowledged hostess at house-parties with their intimate circle.

In March he had a chance to make amends for the previous year's débâcle over the Warrington memorial service, as he

---

*In May 1998, when the stolen booty was finally returned to Charles by this latter-day 'Raffles', police listed the haul as including love letters from Camilla, five brooches, six gold buttons, a gold watch, two jewellery boxes, a clock – and five pairs of cufflinks.

happened to be on Tyneside when a deranged gunman invaded Hall Garth School near Middlesbrough, stabbing a twelve-year-old pupil to death and injuring two others. Charles altered his schedule to divert to the school, where he arrived with a lavish wreath. For ten minutes he spoke to the children and staff involved in the attack, telling them how he had coped with the loss of Mountbatten, and urging them not to bottle up their feelings. 'We were very touched by his visit,' said the headmaster, Peter Smith, 'and the trouble he obviously took to make it right.' The next day's headlines duly suggested that Diana had no monopoly on the caring, compassionate face of royalty.

But Charles's respite was brief. The launch that month of his architecture magazine, *Perspectives*, served only to draw attention to the failure of Poundbury, just as its closure four years later (with losses approaching £2 million as its circulation slumped from a launch figure of 20,000 to barely 5,000) would highlight the continuing problems of his Institute of Architecture.

A speech that May denouncing the fad for 'political correctness', in which he urged his future subjects to resist the forces of 'intellectual fanaticism', attracted much less attention than the loss at Balmoral of his beloved Jack Russell terrier, Pooh. When Pooh's sister turned out to belong to Camilla, who was said to be consoling the prince in his loss, it signalled the demise of the six-month campaign to conceal her continuing role in his life. Again he began to sink in the public esteem. This was a man who had now tried to sell the nation two lies: the first about a happy marriage, the second about a non-existent mistress. As so often in his life, Charles was proving his own worst enemy.

And the following month, as if to dispel all doubt about his capacity for misjudgement, he made the biggest mistake of his life – volunteering for the role of prime prosecution witness, against himself.

For eighteen months Jonathan Dimbleby and his team had been toiling on a 600-page book and a 150-minute television film about the prince. They had been granted almost unlimited access to every department of his life, private and public, even his letters and diaries. Officially, this unprecedented media event was designed to mark the twenty-fifth anniversary of Charles's investiture as Prince of Wales; unofficially, it was part of a long-term game plan, masterminded by Richard Aylard, not merely to enhance the prince's tattered public image but to win acceptance for Camilla as his consort. It was also, of course, Charles's personal riposte to Diana's assault on him via Andrew Morton.

Both book and film covered the prince's public work to the point of tedium – an attempt to demonstrate, in Dimbleby's own words, that the prince was 'thoughtful, sensitive and intelligent', with a 'quick wit and a warm way', a 'daunting' range of commitments – a 'diligent' man, driven by 'a powerful sense of duty and destiny'.[3] But both broadcaster and prince had made a fatal miscalculation. Only ten seconds of those 150 minutes remained in the minds of the 14 million Britons who watched *Charles: The Private Man, The Public Role* on the ITV network on 29 June: the agonized moment in which the heir to the throne, would-be Supreme Governor of the Church of England, admitted that, yes, he had committed adultery with Mrs Camilla Parker Bowles. Camilla was the mainstay of his life – 'a great friend of mine . . . she has been a friend for a very long time, and will continue to be a friend for a very long time'.[4]

Thinking honesty the best policy, Charles was hoping to win the best of both worlds: respect for himself as a dutiful future king, devoting his time to the plight of the less fortunate, and thus indulgence of his private life, as a separated husband in love with another man's wife. Between them, Aylard and Dimbleby had persuaded him that the one could well lead to the other, if not at once, then in the longer term. It was a fatal misjudgement.

At the time, of course, Charles was still married to Diana, and Camilla to Andrew Parker Bowles. That in itself was enough to alienate most of his audience, the millions sufficiently loyal to the monarchy to expect him to set the nation some sort of moral example. Those who could not care less about his relationship with Camilla – people of their age, with less stringent moral standards – were also those indifferent to the monarchy, and interested in Charles merely as a celebrity in distress, an interesting case study in the art of the sales pitch. The vast majority, however, were fans of his wife, who could not forgive him the betrayal to which he now confessed, and could not believe he was rash enough to do so. The underlying irony, of course, is that honesty was to prove an effective policy for his wife, endearing her to the nation; in Charles's case, it had entirely the opposite effect.

The prince's version was that he had enjoyed three affairs with Mrs Parker Bowles: the first before her marriage in 1973, the second after she had her children, the third since 1986. This last, he insisted, had not happened until his own marriage had 'irretrievably broken down'. But it had happened. So that caveat, too, was soon forgotten as the prince himself caused a collective gasp around the nation, gave journalists licence to delete the dread word 'alleged' before the much more satisfying word 'mistress', outraged the most devout monarchists as much as the most rabid republicans, and launched a damaging debate in the Church of England which lasts to this day.

Whatever Everyman's view of Charles's public confession of adultery, it was the final indignity for Andrew Parker Bowles, the loyal courtier whose discretion had been stretched to extremes, but who was now publicly branded a cuckold. For two years Charles had asked him to postpone any thoughts of divorcing Camilla; the prince, as always, was anxious to preserve the status quo. The gallant brigadier, who also held the honorific post of Silver Stick-in-Waiting to the monarch, had endured public and private taunts; his heartier friends had taken to addressing him as 'Ernest Simpson'.

Some in his circle even thought he rather relished the notoriety. 'Having your wife bonked by the future King of England', as one put it, 'lends cachet.' But now his patience snapped. Whatever the prince's wishes, Parker Bowles had always intended to postpone his divorce until he left the army – an institution he loved, and to which he wished to cause minimal embarrassment. But his military career had now peaked; from commanding the Household Cavalry, he had been transferred to the rather unlikely command of the Royal Army Veterinary Corps.

The first non-veterinarian to be given the job in the corps' 200-year history, Parker Bowles found himself beset by more controversy when his appointment precipitated the resignation of its colonel commandant, Brigadier Robert Clifford, after more than thirty years' service with the RAVC. 'I have just been notified by the director that his successor is Colonel A. H. Parker Bowles OBE, late Blues and Royals,' wrote Clifford to the Ministry of Defence. 'As Officer Commanding Household Cavalry, Silver Stick-in-Waiting to HM The Queen and Steward of the Jockey Club, he is no doubt eminently qualified for the promotion, but he is not a veterinary surgeon.' The clear implication was that the husband of Prince Charles's paramour had been found a role which had 'less to do with his want of professional qualifications and more to do with his extra-mural activities and friendships'.[5]

Now Parker Bowles was accused of 'ducking' foreign postings, preferring, for reasons no-one could quite bring themselves to spell out, to stay in London. As the Royal College of Veterinary Surgeons joined in the dispute, forcing the Ministry of Defence to limit his remit to 'management' rather than 'clinical' matters, the brigadier felt understandably hard done by. His distinguished service career was ending on a sour note, in a less than glamorous posting, fraught with unseemly politics. Due to leave the army, anyway, at the end of 1994, he now set in train legal proceedings that would formalize his divorce from Camilla as soon as possible thereafter.

Diana, meanwhile, chose to be seen out and about on the evening of Charles's televised confessions, looking happy and self-assured as she attended a glitzy fundraising dinner at the Serpentine Gallery in Hyde Park. In a short, slinky black evening dress, she greeted her friend Lord Palumbo with a kiss on the cheek, then bubbled her way through a receiving line arranged by the American magazine *Vanity Fair*. The princess, who had declined Dimbleby's invitation to take part in the film, had also turned down his offer of an advance screening. 'My first concern was for the children,' she said. 'I wanted to protect them.' When eventually she did see it, she added, 'I was pretty devastated myself. But then I admired the honesty.'[6]

The logical consequence of Charles's adultery was their own divorce – a subject on which he declined to be drawn. It was 'not a consideration in my mind', he said; it lay 'very much in the future'. Diana, too, would brook no mention of what she called 'the D-word'. She did not want a divorce, she argued, and she would certainly not be the one to start proceedings. 'I'm not going anywhere. I'm staying put,' she insisted, arguing that it was Charles who had asked her to marry him, so it was he who must make the first moves towards 'unmarrying'.

Again Diana cast herself in the role of victim. It sat awkwardly with her new-found self-confidence, but it worked with her adoring public, to the point where Charles found himself obliged to return to the counter-attack. His irritation with Diana's huge weekly bill for clothes and beauty treatments, which he was, of course, still paying, somehow found its way into the tabloid press. Diana's worst fears were being vindicated: the 'men in grey', alias 'the enemy', were back at work to discredit her.

That summer, the tabloids somehow got hold of the fact that she had apparently been making anonymous phone calls to the art dealer Oliver Hoare, an old friend of both the prince and princess. A mystery caller had been dialling Hoare's number, then hanging up if his wife answered the phone. Sometimes the caller stayed on the line without speaking, which alarmed Hoare and spooked his wife Diane. An expert in Islamic art – he had been on some of Charles and Camilla's trips to Turkey – Hoare at first feared the possibility of a terrorist assault on his family. So he called in the police, who tapped his phone and traced the calls back to Diana's private line at Kensington Palace, to her mobile number, even to her sister's home on weekends when the princess was staying there.

Diana steadfastly maintained her innocence, blaming the anonymous calls on a delinquent schoolchild, but only the most devout loyalists failed to accept her guilt. The clear inference was that she had been having an affair with Hoare, who had declined to press charges. When his ex-chauffeur spoke to the press of a 'love nest' in Pimlico, where the couple had enjoyed 'secret assignations over a four-year period', both denied it emphatically. 'What have I done to deserve this?' said Diana via the only journalist she felt she could trust, Richard Kay of the *Daily Mail*. 'I feel I am being destroyed.'[7] For a while the Hoare marriage collapsed under the pressure, but the couple were later reconciled. Charles looked on in dismay, worried at the effect on the children. 'They are the ones who will suffer from all this,' he was quoted as saying. 'It will all be played back to them when they return to school.' His once close friendship with Hoare was broken off, and has never been resumed.

Otherwise, Charles seemed to have found unwonted peace of mind since his separation from Diana. Friends spoke of him as happier, more relaxed, more confident and far less prone to bouts of depression. They had seen his sense of humour return, and with it a *joie de vivre* that had for several years been 'stifled by melancholy'.[8] His main problem that autumn was the book through which this approved self-analysis was communicated to the outside world, published, with singular ill-timing, just as the Queen left on an official visit to Russia, the first by a sitting British monarch since the 1917 revolution.

Back home, his mother's historic handshakes in the Kremlin were upstaged by Charles's portrayal of her via Jonathan Dimbleby as a cold, distant parent with whom he had never been able to share his troubles. He was 'emotionally estranged' from both his parents, craving affection that they were 'unable or unwilling to offer'. His father was a bullying tyrant who had pushed him into marriage with Diana against his own better judgement. Passages excised from the author's manuscript on the Palace's insistence contained even harsher judgements of Philip from his beleaguered son.

As for Diana, Charles's portrayal of her via Dimbleby is distilled simply by a few highlights from the book's index: 'volatile behaviour ... jealousy of Camilla Parker Bowles ... alleged suicide attempts ... resentment of the prince's interests ... attempts to control the prince's life ... self-absorption ... psychiatric help ... outshines the prince ... persuades the prince to drop some of his friends ... disagreements about the children ...'[9] The text described Diana as 'hysterical ... obsessive' and prone to 'violent mood swings ...' Through Dimbleby, to one observer, Charles made it clear that Diana was 'nothing more than a hired womb'.[10]

The prince's indiscretions hurt and enraged his parents, 'shocked and horrified and disappointed'[11] his wife, offended his siblings, agonized courtiers and bemused his future subjects. Their effect on his children can only be imagined. In the process he even managed to upset such dropped names as Barbra Streisand, once his 'only pin-up', who had recently raised hundreds of thousands for the Prince's Trust by breaking a twenty-eight-year absence from the stage to serenade him with 'Someday My Prince Will Come' at the Wembley Arena. He confided that, while Streisand no doubt still had great sex appeal to the masses, for him her charms had faded.[12] After permitting Dimbleby to share this with the world, Charles felt obliged to make amends by inviting Streisand to Highgrove for a weekend. Even his staff were amazed by the singer's advance demands: white flowers only in her bedroom, an omelette of egg whites for breakfast. But they talked philosophy deep into the night, and apparently made their peace.[13]

Five years on, both book and film are now referred to by Charles's staff simply as 'the Dimbleby débâcle'. Rarely one to take responsibility for his own mistakes, the prince would eventually pin the blame on the man who had talked him into it, Richard Aylard, whose own marriage had by then broken up amid the pressures of royal service. The same was true of his protection officer, Colin Trimming. Diana was not the only one to talk of a 'marital jinx' surrounding the Prince of Wales.

The beginning of 1995 saw the formal end of the Parker Bowles marriage; by the year's end, the brigadier was already remarried to an 'old friend', Rosemary Pitman. Another marriage which broke up that year was that of the England rugby captain, Will Carling, whose name had been romantically linked with the Princess of Wales. There was more to Carling's friendship with Diana, believed his wife, Julia, than the rugby coaching he gave her sons.

The princess panicked, and mounted a rearguard action via sympathetic journalists like Richard Kay, insisting that her relationship with Carling was innocent. 'I don't need a lover,' she said. 'I am happy on my own. I've got my children to keep me company, and my work to keep me going.'[14] Diana feared that such publicity would be used against her in the event of a formal end to her marriage; above all she feared losing custody of her children, like her mother before her. Still the princess insisted that she did not want a divorce, and still Charles maintained that nothing was further from his thoughts.

But the warfare was continuing, in a scrappy, spasmodic way, and few could see how divorce could be postponed much longer. Whatever damage it might cause the Crown was as nothing to the gradual corrosion currently taking place. There was no modern precedent for a divorce settlement between the heir to the throne and his potential queen, and the power of the Palace was never to be underestimated. Feeling that she was losing ground in the public-relations war, Diana secretly hatched the most daring coup of her young life.

One Sunday in early November 1995 the princess gave all her staff an unexpected day off. Against the advice of her closest friends, and behind the backs of her senior staff, she had decided to give a major interview to the BBC's flagship current affairs programme, *Panorama*. For some months a *Panorama* reporter named

Martin Bashir had been researching one of the programme's occasional specials on the monarchy; now, with the same lucky timing as Andrew Morton, he found himself with a major scoop on his hands.

Bashir and a minimal crew, equipped with specially lightweight compact cameras, slipped into Kensington Palace undetected that Sunday morning. Diana was alone apart from one trusted adviser and friend, the psychotherapist Susie Orbach. The princess had told no-one at the Palace of her plans, and the *Panorama* team had also maintained conditions of the utmost secrecy. Even after the filming, while the programme was being edited, its existence was kept from the BBC's governors, some of whom had close contacts with the Palace. Whether or not Diana was well advised to give the interview, the conditions in which it was made were proof positive of her fear of the power of those 'men in suits' whom she now dubbed her 'enemies'.

Diana did not inform the Queen that she had given the interview until a week before its transmission on Monday, 20 November. The BBC chose Charles's forty-seventh birthday, 14 November, to reveal its forthcoming scoop. Diana had deceived the two most senior members of her staff: her press secretary, Geoff Crawford, who felt obliged to resign at once (to return to Buckingham Palace, where he soon became the Queen's press secretary); and her private secretary, Patrick Jephson, who also departed within weeks, quitting the royal employ to enter public relations. The Queen's revenge was to terminate the BBC's sixty-year monopoly on the monarch's annual Christmas message, which would henceforth be shared with ITV, the commercial network.

Britain's electricity generating board quite rightly catered for a huge surge at 9.40 p.m., after the BBC news, that Monday evening in November. Made up with heavy eyeliner, to look browbeaten and defensive, Diana spoke with astonishing candour of her depressions, her eating disorders and her suicide attempts. Chronicling the slow collapse of her marriage, she said that Charles had made her feel 'no good at anything . . . useless and hopeless and a failure in every direction – with a husband who loved someone else'. He had taken a mistress, Camilla Parker Bowles, and then blamed her for getting upset about it. 'There were three of us in this marriage,' as she put it, 'so it was a bit crowded.' Charles had told her she was 'an embarrassment' to the royal family, and unstable enough to be committed to an institution.

The princess went on to admit her own adultery with James Hewitt, conceding that she was 'absolutely devastated' when his collaboration on a lurid book betrayed their secret. In one phrase she subsequently came to regret, she said she no longer harboured any hope or desire of becoming queen, but would rather be 'a queen in people's hearts'. Someone, she said, 'has to go out there and love people and show it'. The phrase stuck, becoming the butt of much satire before her death, and one of the epitaphs most favoured by the millions who mourned her. At the time, she felt it drowned out another message she took the chance to convey: that she wanted to be an 'unofficial ambassador' for Britain: 'I've been in a privileged position for fifteen years. I've got tremendous knowledge about people, and I know how to communicate, and I want to use it.'

She had allowed her friends to co-operate with Morton's book, she admitted – failing to reveal the truth that she herself had made secret tape-recordings – because 'I was so fed up with being seen as a basket-case. I am a very strong person and I know that causes complications in the system that I live in.' Questioned about the prince's attitude towards her within their marriage, she went on: 'I think that I've always been the eighteen-year-old girl he got engaged to, so I don't think I've been given any credit for growth. And, my goodness, I've had to grow.' Still maintaining that she did not want a divorce, Diana implied that her 'enemies' in the Palace were cornering her into one. They were trying to push her out of public life. But this was one princess who would not 'go quietly'. She would 'fight to the end, because I believe that I have a role to fulfil, and I've got two children to bring up.'

And did she think her husband would ever be king? 'I don't think any of us knows the answer to that. Who knows what fate will produce, who knows what circumstances will provoke?' It was a devastating rejection, couched in the most calculated terms. 'I would think that the top job, as I call it, would bring enormous limitations to him. I don't know whether he could adapt . . . My wish is that my husband finds peace of mind, and from that follows other things.' Yes, she suggested, because of this 'conflict', Charles might well be happier if he allowed the throne to pass directly to their son William.[15]

On the BBC's *Newsnight* programme, immediately after the

interview, Charles's friend Nicholas Soames denounced Diana's performance as 'toe-curlingly dreadful', suggesting that she was 'in the advance stages of paranoia'. But the popular response was overwhelmingly supportive. Twenty-three million Britons watched the interview – twice as many as had watched Dimbleby's film on Charles the previous year – which was later seen by more than 200 million viewers in around a hundred countries. Polls showed public support for Diana running at 85 per cent.

Among senior commentators, even the most devout monarchists were sufficiently impressed to take her side. In contrast to the princess, 'an exceptionally able woman in a group of not particularly able people', wrote Lord Rees-Mogg, its former editor, in *The Times*, Soames had appeared 'a blustering fool, a grotesque confirmation of everything she had been implying about the inadequacy and malice of the royal establishment'. Diana's performance had been 'one of the most formidably skilful political performances by a woman since Margaret Thatcher'. The public would sympathize with her position as 'a badly supported royal bride, with her postnatal depression which the royal family did not at all understand, with her distress at finding her husband was in love with another woman'. So wronged was Diana that, unlike Charles, she could even get away with adultery. As a 'neglected' wife, predicted Rees-Mogg, she would even be 'forgiven for having fallen for the dubious charms of the miserable Hewitt'.[16]

The historian Paul Johnson also called Diana a 'heroine', whose sexual indiscretions he too forgave because 'she was chaste when the prince began the adultery game'. Johnson went on to quote Jane Austen on Queen Caroline, the estranged wife of the unpopular George IV. 'She was bad, but she would not have become as bad as she was if he had not been infinitely worse.'[17]

Charles simply could not believe what Diana had done. It was billed, of course, as her reply to Dimbleby, which had in turn been his reply to Morton. The tit-for-tat went all the way back to his piqued leak about her thirtieth-birthday party, now more than four long years earlier. But this was an interview too far. The prince saw it as a gratuitous attack by the princess on himself and his family, even on the institution of monarchy, the princess as an urgently needed ploy to strengthen her bargaining position in the divorce negotiations. Whichever one of them was nearer the truth, it worked on both counts.

Elizabeth II had now had enough. It took less than a month for the Queen to write formal letters to both her son and daughter-in-law, on 17 December, arguing that it was now time to settle their differences 'amicably and with civility' by agreeing to a divorce 'sooner rather than later'. Leading clerics were dismayed by the spectacle of the Anglican Church's Supreme Governor not merely sanctioning, but actively encouraging divorce; yet the Queen had been advised by her prime minister, John Major, with the knowledge and support of the Archbishop of Canterbury, that the monarchy could not withstand much more of the Waleses' civil warfare.

Taken aback by the Queen's letter, Diana consulted her lawyers, who urged caution. Cancelling her plans to spend Christmas with the royal family at Sandringham, she wrote no immediate reply. Charles responded to his mother at once, and positively. If he had been pushed by his father into marrying Diana, he now appeared to have been pushed by his mother into divorcing her.

At stake, as the lawyers settled into months of bargaining, was Charles's bank balance as much as Diana's dignity and lifestyle. By now, the prince was ready to concede almost anything to rid himself of his turbulent spouse. What he most definitely did not want was more than the minimum contact with her necessary to stay in touch with his children. So Diana's request to share the facilities of his office in St James's Palace, where he would also make his home after the divorce, was high on his hit-list. She could stay in their marital apartment at Kensington Palace, which would also provide valuable continuity for William and Harry, but she should also establish her own office there. He, of course, would finance it.

Whatever 'lump sum' was finally agreed for the global settlement, he insisted that it must be paid in instalments. The Prince of Wales, according to public statements from his office, was not as well-off as people might imagine. In truth, his insistence on a 'drip-drip' financial settlement was his way of regulating Diana's public behaviour. If she broke the discretion clauses written into their agreement – if, God forbid, she wrote or authorized another book – he could cut her off without a penny.

The matter of her 'HRH' – those three magic letters signifying seniority in the royal pecking order, then meriting a statutory bow or curtsey – was one of supreme indifference to him. But it wasn't to Diana, who was told by friends that she had been careless to offer them as a bargaining chip for other more practical aspects of the settlement, especially a lump-sum pay-off rather than the humiliation of instalments. When the details leaked, even as the lawyers were still negotiating, there was a public hue and cry about the insult to their princess: the appalling potential prospect, for instance, of her having to curtsey to Fergie, ex-Duchess of York, whose divorce settlement was itself still under negotiation.*

The talks dragged on through Christmas, when Diana's impetuous nature got her into potentially deeper legal trouble. She was tired from an overnight trip to New York, where she had collected a Humanitarian of the Year award from Henry Kissinger, when she arrived at London's Lanesborough Hotel for what, this year, was something of a charade: the Prince and Princess of Wales's annual Christmas party for their staff.

Entering separately from Charles, Diana strode straight over to 'Tiggy' Legge-Bourke, whom she now resented sufficiently to believe that she, too, was having an affair with her husband. The room was naturally agog to see Diana head straight across the room towards her *bête noire*, and whisper in her ear. Whatever it was that she said – 'seven words' was all the newspaper-reading public were told – was enough to send Tiggy reeling from the room in tears. By the weekend, the prince's right-hand woman was publicly threatening to sue his wife.

With Charles's encouragement, Tiggy consulted one of Britain's leading libel lawyers, Peter Carter-Ruck, who promptly issued a statement deploring 'a series of false rumours which are a gross reflection on our client's moral character'. They were, of course, 'utterly without the very slightest foundation'. Charles was even prepared to countenance Tiggy mounting a lawsuit against his wife; but again it took wiser heads to counsel caution. Diana, they told him, would relish her day in court; there was no telling what soiled private linen she might choose to wash in public before the

---

*One of the reasons Diana's divorce proceeded so slowly was the determination of her lawyer, Anthony Julius of Mishcon de Reya, to use the Duchess as a 'canary'. When the princess asked him what this meant, Julius explained that miners used to dispatch canaries into the pits as a precaution against lethal gases; on the same principle, they would use Fergie as their legal 'stalking-horse'.

divorce settlement gagged her for life. Quietly, Tiggy was persuaded to let the matter drop.

In a gross breach of protocol, meanwhile, breaking a lifetime's habit of dealing promptly with all correspondence, Diana never replied to the Queen's letter of December. Three times she was nudged to do so by Her Majesty's private secretary, who also happened to be her own brother-in-law, but ten weeks elapsed without any response. All this time the lawyers' meters kept ticking, to the point where Charles himself intervened with a desperate letter to Diana, pleading for a meeting. Finally she agreed, but set strict terms. She would come to his office at St James's Palace, at 4.30 p.m. the following Wednesday, 28 February 1996, on condition they could meet alone. No lawyers, no aides, no flunkies. To the dismay of his staff, Charles agreed.

'They'll probably bug us, anyway,' snorted Diana as the last of her husband's staff backed reluctantly out of the room, where she and Charles then talked alone for forty-five minutes. By her own account, filtered to the world via Richard Kay, she told him, 'I loved you, and I will always love you because you are the father of my children.' The prince was horrified when this appeared in print the next morning. By his own account of the meeting, Diana's attitude was a more graphic version of her public threats on *Panorama* three months earlier: 'You will never be king. I will destroy you.'[18]

Later that afternoon, without warning Charles or the Queen, Diana issued a statement revealing that they had agreed to an uncontested divorce. It was, she said, 'the saddest day of my life'. Unilaterally, and thus most provocatively, she offered the world her own version of the conclusions negotiated with Charles:

> The Princess of Wales has agreed to Prince Charles's request for a divorce. The Princess will continue to be involved in all decisions relating to the children, and will remain at Kensington Palace, with offices at St. James's Palace. The Princess of Wales will retain the title and be known as Diana, Princess of Wales.

So furious was the Queen about Diana's pre-emption of Palace protocol that she gave aides rare authorization to leak her displeasure. The Queen was 'most interested', mused her spokesman, to hear that the Princess of Wales had agreed to divorce her son.

Her Majesty was even more interested, it seemed, in Diana's version of the details of the settlement, especially concerning the little matter of her title, which would naturally 'take time' to resolve.

In the event, it took four more months. Diana's lawyers began by asking for a lump-sum settlement of £50 million. But the complex legal negotiations went way past mere money and titles to jewellery, office space, even freedom of movement. The one matter about which there was never any argument, for all Diana's fears, was custody of the children – to be shared equally.

'The one thing I was terrified of', she constantly told friends, 'was losing the children. Once I knew they were safe, that the royal machine was not going to steal them from me, I didn't really care about anything else.' If a mite disingenuous, the remark was made with an almost scary passion. 'Not Charles,' she would say when she had calmed down. 'Not Charles, but his people. And his family – some of them.

'Not Margaret, who was always very nice to me, even defended me against the occasional tirades of my father-in-law. Nor Anne, who could be surprisingly supportive at times. Her relations with Charles have always been pretty strained, anyway. Nor, of course, the Queen, who behaved pretty impeccably throughout, would have me to tea from time to time to see how I was doing. I got the impression – though she never, of course, said so in so many words – that she knew her son was not an easy man to be married to. I think she thought I had been pretty hard done by. Okay, by now I'd done things that had upset her, like *Panorama*, but I always had the feeling she disapproved of his relations with you-know-who. Not the woman herself – the Queen, for some reason, rather likes her – but the way he handled the affair. She was devastated when it became so public. Still is, I think. I don't know that she would ever approve of Charles marrying her. And he wouldn't without her blessing.'

By now, Diana herself was past caring. Among her ever-changing circle of friends, she was famous for saying different things to different people, playing them off against each other for her own, often devious, ends. On this occasion, however, she chose to say, 'Oh, what the hell, let him go ahead and marry her. Why not? It might bother a lot of people – and I would watch all the fuss with some enjoyment – but it wouldn't bother me any more. I'm past caring.'[19]

Diana's post-marital title proved one of the most contentious issues. Though Charles still professed not to care, his father certainly did. Philip felt that Diana had unforgivably let down the 'family firm', and must be punished. He was outraged by her apparent demand that any future children by another man should bear hereditary titles. Nor could he forgive her for suggesting that Clarence House become her official residence on the death of the Queen Mother. Philip wanted Diana to be downgraded to Duchess of Cornwall, minus her HRH.

For a while, those three magic letters became a sticking point in the negotiations. As Diana reconsidered her previous offer to drop them – with widespread public support, as the mother of the future king – Charles's lawyers even made the absurd suggestion of HFRH, Her Former Royal Highness. Then one day, according to Diana, her son William said to her, 'I don't care what you're called. You're Mummy.' That settled it. She agreed to surrender her royal status, in return for a title very similar to her current one: Diana, Princess of Wales.

When the final terms were made public, Diana received a lump-sum settlement of £17 million (most of which Charles had to borrow from his mother), plus £400,000 a year for an office and staff separate from his. She was stripped of her HRH, formally expelled from the royal family, and her name deleted from the prayers said for them each Sunday in churches throughout Christendom. Letters patent to that effect were rather brutally published, on the Queen's personal instructions, in the 'noticeboard of the Establishment', the *London Gazette*.

The Prince of Wales was granted a decree nisi on 15 July, which became absolute on 28 August. The fifteen-year ordeal was finally over for both of them – if not for their children. Yelled the front page of the *Sun*, on Diana's behalf: BYE BYE, BIG EARS.[20]

PART FIVE

After Diana

CHAPTER EIGHTEEN

'I WILL NEVER REMARRY'

BACK IN 1993, AS CHARLES MOVED OUT OF THE KENSINGTON PALACE apartment they had shared for twelve years, the first thing Diana did was to change the locks – a purely symbolic gesture, as neither ever carried keys. At Highgrove, meanwhile, Charles himself lit an equally symbolic bonfire, on which he threw everything that reminded him of Diana, including many of their wedding presents. Staff were dismayed to see the prince sipping champagne as he watched objects not merely of some value, but of potential use to others, going up in smoke. Then he got Camilla to take charge of a complete refurbishment of the house, blotting out all memory of his former wife.[1]

That was at the apex of their mutual antipathy, when neither knew how the story of their 'fairy-tale' marriage would end. Now that they did, some three and a half years later, Charles went in for a further act of symbolism. At the end of August 1996, the weekend before his divorce became absolute, the prince took another step down the long road of trying to win his mistress public acceptance as his consort. After a telephone tip-off from 'a well-spoken woman', giving 'precise instructions' on how to find their 'remote Welsh love-nest', long-distance lensmen snatched the first photographs of Charles and Camilla together for twenty years.

The 'remote Welsh love-nest' was in fact a retreat in the hills of Powys, which the couple had been using undetected for some time: Glyn Celyn House near Brecon, the home of Camilla's former brother-in-law Nic Paravacini, a millionaire banker, and his second